Agile Web Application Development with Yii 1.1 and PHP5

Fast-track your web application development by harnessing the power of the Yii PHP Framework

Jeffery Winesett

PUBLISHINGopen source
community experience distilled

BIRMINGHAM - MUMBAI

Agile Web Application Development with Yii 1.1 and PHP5

First published: August 2010

Production Reference: 1030810

Published by Packt Publishing Ltd.
32 Lincoln Road
Olton
Birmingham, B27 6PA, UK.

ISBN 978-1-847199-58-4

www.packtpub.com

Cover Image by Vinayak Chittar (vinayak.chittar@gmail.com)

Credits

Author

Jeffery Winesett

Reviewers

Imre Mehesz

Jonah Turnquist

Kyle Ferreira

Acquisition Editor

Usha Iyer

Development Editors

Dhwani Devater

Reshma Sundaresan

Technical Editors

Aditya Belpathak

Hyacintha D'Souza

Indexer

Hemangini Bari

Editorial Team Leader

Aanchal Kumar

Project Team Leader

Priya Mukherji

Project Coordinator

Prasad Rai

Proofreader

Lesley Harrison

Graphics

Geetanjali Sawant

Production Coordinator

Melwyn D'sa

Cover Work

Melwyn D'sa

About the Author

Jeffery Winesett is the director of software engineering and application development at Control Group Inc., a New York based consulting firm specializing in delivering technology for big ideas. He has spent the last five of his twelve years of software development focused on delivering large-scale PHP-based applications. Jeffery also writes articles on the topics of PHP, web application frameworks, and software development. He has enjoyed being a Yii evangelist since its early alpha version.

I'd like to thank all of the technical reviewers, editors, and staff at Packt for their fantastic contributions, suggestions, and improvements. I'd like to thank Qiang Xue and the entire Yii Framework developer team for creating and maintaining this brilliant framework. Ryan Trammel at Scissortail design for his attention to detail and CSS assistance. My lovely wife Tiffany, for her endless patience throughout this project and Lemmy and Lucie for providing me with an endless supply of sunshine.

About the Reviewers

Imre Mehesz is a long-time open source and PHP enthusiast. He started with the classic LAMP stack around 2000 and grew into the MVC world with CakePHP, ZendFramework, and now Yii. He brought Yii into his professional life and runs the Yii Radio podcast.

> I would like to thank Qiang for creating this framework, and my wife who puts up with my craziness for open source development.

Jonah Turnquist is a self-taught web developer and a college student. He is a part of the developer team for the Yii Framework, mainly contributing to the official extension library, Zii. Meanwhile, he is attending a junior college in California, and he is on his way to being transferred to a four year degree in college in the Fall of 2010. He is studying Electrical Engineering and Computer Sciences.

Kyle Ferreira is a student at the University of Ontario, Institute of Technology taking a four year degree in IT (BIT) under Network Security. As a student, he has spent a lot of time researching IT security-related topics, and has valued experience working with various computer languages and equipment. He's currently running his own business in web design and development, using the Yii Framework as the basis for a lot of large projects.

> I would like to thank Packt Publishing and its staff for this opportunity to contribute to this production. I'd also like to thank Qiang Xue for his exceptional devotion to a well designed and functioning framework, and for his guidance in helping me learn and contribute to the framework.

Table of Contents

Preface

Yii is a high-performance, component-based application development framework written in PHP. It helps ease the complexity of building large-scale applications. It enables maximum reusability in web programming, and can significantly accelerate the development process. It does so by allowing the developer to build on top of already well-written, well-tested, and production-ready code. It prevents you from having to rewrite core functionality that is common across many of today's web-based applications, allowing you to concentrate on the business rules and logic specific to the unique application being built.

This book takes a very pragmatic approach to learning the Yii Framework. Throughout the chapters we introduce the reader to many of the core features of Yii by taking a test-first approach to building a real-world task tracking and issue management application called TrackStar. All of the code is provided. The reader should be able to borrow from all of the examples provided to get up and running quickly, but will also be exposed to deeper discussion and explanation to fully understand what is happening behind the scenes.

What this book cover

Chapter 1—Meet Yii introduces Yii at a high level. We learn the importance and utility of using application development frameworks, and the characteristics of Yii that make it incredibly powerful and useful.

Chapter 2—Getting Started walks through a simple Hello, World! style application using the Yii Framework.

Chapter 3—The TrackStar Application provides an introduction to the task management and issue tracking application, TrackStar, that will be built throughout the remainder of the chapters. It also introduces the Test Driven Development (TDD) approach.

Chapter 4 — Iteration 1:Creating The Initial TrackStar Application demonstrates the creation of a new database-driven, Yii web application.

Chapter 5 — Iteration 2: Project CRUD introduces the automated code generation features of Yii, as we work to build out the "C"reate, "R"ead, "U"pdate and "D"elete functionality for the project entity in our TrackStar application.

Chapter 6 — Iteration 3: Adding Tasks introduces us to relational active record and controller class filters in Yii, as we add in the management issues into TrackStar.

Chapter 7 — Iteration 4: User Management and Authentication covers the first part of Yii's user authentication and authorization framework, Authentication.

Chapter 8 — Iteration 5: User Access Control covers the second part of the user authentication and authentication framework, Authorization. Both Yii's simple access control and role-based access control are covered.

*Chapter 9 — Iteration 6: Adding User Comment*s takes a deeper dive into writing relational Active Record queries in Yii as well as introduce a basic portlet architecture for reusing content across multiple pages.

Chapter 10 — Iteration 7: Adding an RSS Web Feed demonstrates how easy it is to integrate other third-party frameworks into a Yii application by integrating the Zend Framework's Web Feed library to create simple RSS feed within our application.

Chapter 11 — Iteration 8: Making It Pretty: Design, Layout, Themes and Iternationalization (i18n) delves deeper into the presentation tier of Yii, introducing layout views, themes as well as internationalization and localization in Yii.

Chapter 12 — Iteration 9: Modules – Adding Administration introduces the concept of a module in Yii by using one to add administrative functionality to the application.

Chapter 13 — Iteration 10: Production Readiness covers error handling, logging, caching and, security as we prepare our TrackStar application for production.

What you need for this book

To follow along in building the TrackStar application, you will need PHP 5, a web server capable of servicing PHP 5 pages, and a database server. The code has been tested using the Apache 2 web server and a MySQL 5 database. It is certainly possible to use a different PHP5-compatible web server and /or different database server product. While we have attempted to make the examples work independent of the specific web server or database server, we cannot guarantee 100% accuracy if you are using something different. Slight adjustments may be required.

Who this book is for

If you are a PHP programmer with knowledge of object-oriented programming and want to rapidly develop modern, sophisticated web applications, then this book is for you. No prior knowledge of Yii is required to follow this book

Conventions

In this book, you will find a number of styles of text that distinguish between different kinds of information. Here are some examples of these styles, and an explanation of their meaning.

Code words in text are shown as follows: "You can type in `help` to see a list of commands available to you within his shell."

A block of code is set as follows:

```
<h1>Hello, World!</h1>
<h3><?php echo $time; ?></h3>
<p><?php echo CHtml::link("Goodbye",array('message/goodbye'));
?></p>
```

When we wish to draw your attention to a particular part of a code block, the relevant lines or items are set in bold:

```
<h1>Hello, World!</h1>
<h3><?php echo $time; ?></h3>
<p><?php echo CHtml::link("Goodbye",array('message/goodbye'));
?></p>
```

Any command-line input or output is written as follows:

```
%cd /WebRoot/demo/protected/tests
```

```
%phpunit unit/MessageTest.php
```

New terms and **important words** are shown in bold. Words that you see on the screen, in menus or dialog boxes for example, appear in the text like this: "Clicking on the **About** link provides a simple example of a static page."

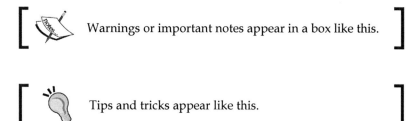

Warnings or important notes appear in a box like this.

Tips and tricks appear like this.

Reader feedback

Feedback from our readers is always welcome. Let us know what you think about this book—what you liked or may have disliked. Reader feedback is important for us to develop titles that you really get the most out of.

To send us general feedback, simply send an email to feedback@packtpub.com, and mention the book title via the subject of your message.

If there is a book that you need and would like to see us publish, please send us a note in the **SUGGEST A TITLE** form on www.packtpub.com or email suggest@packtpub.com.

If there is a topic that you have expertise in and you are interested in either writing or contributing to a book, see our author guide on www.packtpub.com/authors.

Customer support

Now that you are the proud owner of a Packt book, we have a number of things to help you to get the most from your purchase.

Downloading the example code for the book
Visit http://www.packtpub.com/files/code/9584_Code.zip to directly download the example code.
The downloadable files contain instructions on how to use them.

Errata

Although we have taken every care to ensure the accuracy of our content, mistakes do happen. If you find a mistake in one of our books—maybe a mistake in the text or the code—we would be grateful if you would report this to us. By doing so, you can save other readers from frustration, and help us to improve subsequent versions of this book. If you find any errata, please report them by visiting http://www.packtpub. com/support, selecting your book, clicking on the **let us know** link, and entering the details of your errata. Once your errata are verified, your submission will be accepted and the errata added to any list of existing errata. Any existing errata can be viewed by selecting your title from http://www.packtpub.com/support.

Piracy

Piracy of copyright material on the Internet is an ongoing problem across all media. At Packt, we take the protection of our copyright and licenses very seriously. If you come across any illegal copies of our works, in any form, on the Internet, please provide us with the location address or web site name immediately so that we can pursue a remedy.

Please contact us at `copyright@packtpub.com` with a link to the suspected pirated material.

We appreciate your help in protecting our authors, and our ability to bring you valuable content.

Questions

You can contact us at `questions@packtpub.com` if you are having a problem with any aspect of the book, and we will do our best to address it.

1
Meet Yii

The past several years have marked a significant 'framework boom', and almost everyone involved in web application development these days is a part of a new generation of 'framework boomers'. Web development frameworks help jumpstart your application by immediately delivering the core foundation and plumbing needed to quickly turn your ideas scribbled on the whiteboard into a functional and production-ready code. With all of the common features expected from web applications today and available framework options that meet these expectations, there is little reason to code your next web application from scratch. A modern, flexible, and extensible framework is almost as essential a tool as the programming language itself to today's web developer. Moreover, when the two are particularly complementary, the results are an extremely powerful toolkit: *Java* and *Spring*, *Ruby* and *Rails*, C# and *.NET*, and *PHP* and *Yii*.

Yii is the brainchild of its founder Qiang Xue who started the development of this open source framework on January 1st, 2008. Prior to this, Qiang had previously developed and maintained the PRADO framework for many years. The years of experience and user feedback cultivated from the PRADO project solidified the need for a much easier, more extensible and more efficient PHP5-based framework to meet the ever-growing needs of application developers. The initial alpha version of Yii was officially released to meet these needs in October of 2008. Its extremely impressive performance metrics when compared to other PHP-based frameworks immediately drew very positive attention. On December 3rd, 2008, Yii 1.0 was officially released and as of March 14th, 2010, the latest production-ready version is 1.1.2. It has a growing development team and continues to gain popularity among PHP developers everyday. We feel that with just a little help from the information contained in this book, you will soon understand why.

The name **Yii** (an acronym for *Yes, it is*, pronounced as *Yee* or *[ji:]*) stands for easy, efficient, and extensible. Yii is a high-performance, component-based, web application framework written in PHP 5. Yii makes it easier to create and maintain large-scale web applications. It also makes them more efficient and extensible. Let's take a quick look at each of these characteristics of Yii in turn.

Yii is easy

To run a Yii-powered web application, all you need is the core framework files and a web server supporting PHP 5.1.0 or higher. To develop with Yii, you only need to know PHP and **object-oriented programming(OOP)**. You are not required to learn any new configuration or templating language. Building a Yii application mainly involves writing and maintaining your own custom PHP classes, some of which will extend from the core Yii Framework component classes.

Yii incorporates many of the great ideas and work from other well-known web programming frameworks and applications. So, if you are coming to Yii after using other web development frameworks, it is likely you will find it familiar and easy to navigate.

Yii also embraces a *convention over configuration* philosophy, which contributes to its ease of use. This means that Yii has sensible defaults for almost all aspects of wiring your application. If you follow the prescribed conventions, you will write less code and spend less time developing your application. If desired, Yii allows you to customize and easily override all of these conventions. We will be covering some of these defaults and conventions later in this chapter and throughout the book.

Yii is efficient

Yii is a high-performance component-based framework for developing web applications on any scale. It encourages maximum code reuse in web programming, and can significantly accelerate the development process. As mentioned previously, if you stick with Yii's built-in conventions, you can get your application up and running with little to no manual configuration.

Yii is also designed to help you with DRY development. **DRY (Don't Repeat Yourself)** is a key concept of agile application development. All Yii applications are built using the **Model-View-Controller (MVC)** architecture. Yii enforces this development pattern by providing a place to keep each piece of your MVC code. This minimizes duplication and helps promote code reuse and ease of maintainability. The less code you need to write, the less time it takes to get your application to market. Similarly, the easier it is to maintain your application, the longer it will stay on the market.

Of course, the framework is not just efficient to use, it is also remarkably fast and performance is optimized. Yii has been developed with performance optimization in mind from the very beginning, and the result is that it is one of the most efficient PHP frameworks around. The Yii development team has performed performance comparison tests with many other PHP frameworks, and Yii outperformed them all. This means that the additional overhead Yii adds to applications written on top of it is negligible.

Yii is extensible

Yii has been carefully designed to allow nearly every piece of its code to be extended and customized to meet almost any need or requirement. In fact, it is difficult not to take advantage of Yii's ease of extensibility as a primary activity when developing a Yii-driven application, which is extending the core framework classes. If you want to turn your extended code into useful tools for other developers to use, Yii provides easy-to-follow steps and guidelines to help you create such third-party extensions. This allows you to contribute to Yii's ever-growing list of features and actively participate in extending Yii itself.

What is also remarkable about Yii is its ease of use, superior performance, and its depth of extensibility which does not come at the cost of sacrificing features. Yii is packed with features to help you meet those high demands placed on today's web applications. AJAX-enabled widgets, web service integration, enforcement of an MVC architecture, DAO and relational Active Record database layer, sophisticated caching, hierarchical role-based access control, theming, internationalization (I18N), and localization (L10N), are just the tip of the Yii iceberg. As of version 1.1, the core framework is now packaged with an official extension library called Zii. These extensions are developed and maintained by the core framework team members who continue to extend Yii's core feature set. With a deep community of users who are also contributing by writing Yii extensions, the overall feature set available to a Yii powered application is growing daily. For a complete list of all available user contributed extensions, see `http://www.yiiframework.com/extensions/`.

MVC architecture

As mentioned previously, Yii is an MVC framework and it provides an explicit folder structure for each piece of model, view, and controller code. Before we start building our first Yii application, we need to define a few key terms, and look at how Yii implements and enforces this MVC architecture.

The model

Typically in an MVC architecture, the **model** is responsible for maintaining state. Thus, it should encapsulate the business rules that apply to the data that defines this state. A model in Yii is any instance of the framework class CModel or its child class. A model class typically comprises data attributes that can have separate labels (something user-friendly for the purpose of display), and can be validated against a set of rules defined in the model. The data that makes up the attributes in the model class could come from a row of a database table or from the fields in a user input form.

Yii implements two kinds of models: The form model (CFormModel class) and the active record model (CActiveRecord class). They both extend from the same base class CModel. CFormModel represents a data model that collects inputs in HTML form. It encapsulates all the logic for form field validation and any other business logic that may need to be applied to the form field data. It can then store this data in memory, or with the help of an active record model, store data in a database.

Active Record (AR) is a design pattern used to abstract database access in an object-oriented fashion. Each AR object in Yii is an instance of CActiveRecord or its child class that wraps a single row in a database table or view, encapsulates all the logic and details around database access, and houses much of the business logic that is required to be applied to that data. The data field values for each column in the table row are represented as properties of the AR object. AR is described in more detail a little later.

The view

Typically, the **view** is responsible for rendering the user interface, based on the data in the model. A view in Yii is a PHP script that contains user interface related elements, often built using HTML, but can also contain PHP statements. Usually any PHP statements within the view are very simple conditional or looping statements, or refer to other Yii UI-related elements such as HTML helper class methods or prebuilt widgets. More sophisticated logic should be separated from the view and placed appropriately in either the model (if dealing directly with the data), or in the controller for a more general business logic.

The controller

The **controller** is our main director of a routed request and is responsible for taking user input, interacting with the model, and instructing the view to update and display appropriately. A controller in Yii is an instance of CController or its child. When a controller runs, it performs the requested action, which then interacts with needed models and renders an appropriate view. An action, in its simplest form, is a controller class method whose name starts with the word *action*.

Stitching these together: Yii request routing

In most MVC implementations, a web request typically has the following lifecycle:

1. The browser sends the request to the server hosting the MVC application.
2. A controller is invoked to handle the request.
3. The controller interacts with the model.
4. The controller invokes the view.
5. The view renders the data (often as HTML) and returns it to the browser for display.

Yii's MVC implementation is no exception. In a Yii application, incoming requests from the browser are first received by a router. The router analyzes the request to decide where in the application it should be sent for further processing. In most cases, the router identifies a specific action method within a controller class to which the request is passed. This action method will look at the incoming request data, possibly interact with the model, and perform other needed business logic. Eventually, this action class will prepare the response data and send it to the view class. The view will then massage this data to conform to the desired layout and design, and return it for the browser to display.

Blog posting example

To help all of this make more sense, let's look at a fictitious example. Pretend we have used Yii to build ourselves a new blog site, `yourblog.com`. This site is similar to most typical blog sites out there. The home page displays a list of recently posted blog posts. The names of each of these blog postings are hyperlinks that take the user to the page that displays the full article. The next diagram illustrates how Yii handles an incoming request sent from clicking on one of these hypothetical blog post links.

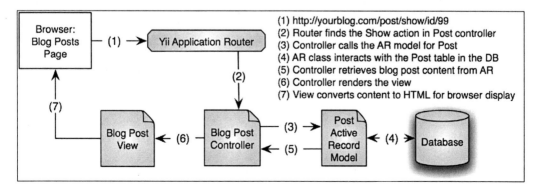

The figure traces the request made from a user clicking on the following link:

```
http://yourblog.com/post/show/id/99
```

First, the request is sent to the router. The router parses the request to decide where to send it. The structure of the URL is key to the decision the router will make. By default, Yii recognizes URLs with the following format:

```
http://hostname/index.php?r=ControllerID/ActionID
```

The `r` querystring variable refers to the route that is analyzed by the Yii router. It will parse this route to determine the appropriate controller and action method to further handle the request. Now, you may have immediately noticed that the URL mentioned in the previous example does not follow this default format. It is a simple matter to configure the application to recognize the more search engine friendly format:

```
http://hostname/ControllerID/ActionID
```

We will continue to use this simplified format for the purposes of this example. The `ControllerID` in the URL refers to the name of the controller. By default this is the first part of the controller class name, up to the word `Controller`. For example, if your controller class name is `TestController`, the `ControllerID` would be `Test`. Similarly, `ActionID` refers to the name of the action that is defined by the controller. If the action is a simple method defined within the controller, this will be whatever follows the word `Action` in the method name. For example, if your action method is named `actionCreate()`, the `ActionID` is `Create`.

 If the `ActionID` is omitted, the controller will take the default action, which is a method in the controller called `actionIndex()`. If the `ControllerID` is also omitted, the application will use the default controller. The Yii default controller is called `SiteController`.

Turning back to the example, the router will analyze the following URL, `http://yourblog.com/post/show/id/99`, and will take the first part of the URL path, `post` to be the `ControllerID` and the second part, `show` to be the `ActionID`. This will translate to routing the request to the `actionShow()` method within the `PostController` class. The last part of the URL (`id/99`) is a name/value `querystring` parameter that will be available to the method during processing. In this example, `99` represents the unique internal `id` for the selected blog post.

The `actionShow()` method handles requests for specific blog post entries. In this case, it uses the `querystring` variable, `id` to determine which specific post is being requested. It asks the model to retrieve information about blog post entry number `99`.

The model AR class interacts with the database to retrieve the requested data. After retrieving the data from the model, the controller class further prepares it for display by making it available to the view. The view then renders the needed HTML in a response back to the user's browser.

This MVC architecture allows us to separate the presentation from the model, and the controller from the view. This makes it easy for developers to change aspects of the application without affecting the **User Interface (UI)** and for UI designers to freely make changes without affecting the model or business logic. This separation also makes it very easy to provide multiple presentations of the same model code. For example, you could use the same model code that drives the HTML layout of yourblog.com to drive a Flash/Flex RIA presentation or a mobile application or web services, or a command-line interface. In the end, following this set conventions and separating the functionality will result in an application that is much easier to extend and maintain.

Yii does a lot more to help you enforce this separation than simply providing some naming conventions and suggestions for where your code should be placed in a folder structure. It helps to take care of all the lower-level *glue* code needed to stitch all the pieces together. This allows you to reap the benefits of a strict MVC designed application without having to spend all the time coding the details yourself. Let's take a look at some of these lower-level details.

Object-relational mapping and Active Record

For the most part, the web applications we build house their data in a relational database. The blog posting application we used in the previous example holds blog post content in database tables. However, web applications need the data that is held in the persistent database storage mapped to in-memory class properties that define the domain objects. **Object-relational mapping (ORM)** libraries provide this mapping of database tables to domain object classes.

Much of the code that deals with ORM is about describing how fields in the database correspond to fields in our objects, which is tedious and repetitive to write. Luckily, Yii comes to our rescue to save us from this repetition and tedium by providing the ORM layer in the form of the AR pattern.

Active Record

As was previously mentioned, AR is a design pattern used to abstract database access in an object-oriented fashion. It maps tables to classes, rows to objects and columns to object attributes. In other words, each instance of an active record class represents a single row in a database table. However an AR class is more than just a set of attributes that map to columns in a database table; it also houses the needed business logic behavior to be applied to that data. The end result is a class that defines everything about how it should be written to and read from the database.

By relying on convention and sticking with reasonable defaults, Yii's implementation of AR will save the developer a ton of time normally spent in configuration or in writing tedious and repetitive SQL statements required to create, read, update and delete data. It also allows the developer to access data stored in the database in a much more object-oriented way. To illustrate this, here is some example code that uses AR to operate on a specific blog posting whose internal id, which is also used as the table's Primary Key, is 99. It first retrieves the posting by Primary Key, it then changes the title, and then updates the database to save the changes:

```
$post=Post::model()->findByPk(99);
$post->title='Some new title';
$post->save();
```

Active Record completely relieves us of the tedium of having to write any SQL or otherwise deal with the underlying database.

Active Record does even more than this. It integrates seamlessly with many other aspects of the Yii Framework. There are myriad *active* html helper input form fields that tie directly to their respective AR class attributes. This way, Active Record extracts the input form field values directly into the model. It also supports sophisticated, automated data validation, and if the validation fails, the Yii view classes easily display the validation errors to the end user. We will be revisiting AR and providing many concrete examples throughout this book.

The view and controller

The view and the controller are very close cousins. The controller makes the data available for display to the view and the view generates the pages that trigger events, which sends data to the controller.

In Yii, a view file belongs to the controller class that rendered it. This way, inside a view script, we can access the controller instance by simply referring to $this. This implementation makes the view and controller very intimate. Thankfully, all of these details are handled for us by Yii, so we can focus on coding the specific application.

There is also a lot more to Yii controllers than just calling the model and rendering views. Controllers can manage services to provide sophisticated pre- and post-processing on requests, implement basic access control rules to limit access to certain actions, manage application-wide layout and nested layout file rendering, manage pagination of data, and many other behind-the-scenes services. Again, we have Yii to thank for not needing to get our hands dirty with these messy details.

There is a lot to Yii. The best way to explore all its beauty is to start using it. Now that we have some of the basic ideas and terminology under our belt, we are in a great position to do just that. In the next chapter, we will go through the simple Yii installation process, and then build a working application to better illustrate these ideas.

Summary

In this chapter, we were introduced at a very high level to the Yii PHP web application framework. We also covered a number of software design concepts embraced by Yii. Don't worry if the abstract nature of this initial discussion was a tad lost on you. It will all make sense once we dive into specific examples. But, to recap, we specifically covered:

1. The importance and utility of application development frameworks.
2. What Yii is and the characteristics of Yii that make it incredibly powerful and useful.
3. The MVC application architecture and the implementation of this architecture in Yii.
4. A typical Yii web request lifecycle and URL structures.
5. Object-relational mapping and Active Record in Yii.

2
Getting Started

The real pleasures and benefits of Yii are quickly revealed by simply using it. In this chapter, we will see how the concepts introduced in the previous chapter, *Meet Yii*, are manifested in an example Yii application. In the spirit of Yii's philosophy to follow conventions, we will write a `Hello, World!` program to try out this new framework.

In this chapter, we will cover:

- Yii Framework installation
- Creating a new application
- Creating controllers and views
- Adding dynamic content to view files
- Yii request routing and linking pages together

Before we can use it we need to first install the framework. Let's do that now.

Installing Yii

Prior to installing Yii, you must configure your application development environment as a web server capable of supporting PHP 5.1.0 or higher. Yii has been thoroughly tested with Apache HTTP server on Windows and Linux operating systems. It may also run on other web servers and platforms, provided PHP 5 is supported. There are myriad free resources available on the Internet to assist you in getting your environment configured with a PHP 5 compatible web server. We assume the reader has previously engaged in PHP development and has access to such an environment. We will leave the installation of a web server and PHP itself as an exercise to the reader.

The basic Yii installation is almost trivial. There are really only two necessary steps:

1. Download the Yii Framework from http://www.yiiframework.com/download/.

2. Unpack the downloaded file to a web-accessible folder.

 There are several versions of Yii from which to choose when downloading the framework. We will be using version 1.1.2 for the purposes of this book, which is the latest stable version as of the time of writing. Though most of the sample code should work with any 1.1.x version of Yii, there may be some subtle differences if you are using a different version. Please use 1.1.2 if you are following along with the examples.

After installation, it is advised that you verify that your server satisfies all of the requirements for using Yii and to ensure the installation was a success. Luckily, doing so is easy. Yii comes with a simple requirement checking tool. To invoke the tool and have it verify the requirements for your installation, simply point your browser to:

`http://yourhostname/path/to/yii/requirements/index.php`

The following screenshot shows the results we see for our configuration:

Yii Requirement Checker

Description

This script checks if your server configuration meets the requirements for running Yii Web applications. It checks if the server is running the right version of PHP, if appropriate PHP extensions have been loaded, and if php.ini file settings are correct.

Conclusion

Your server configuration satisfies the minimum requirements by Yii. Please pay attention to the warnings listed below if your application will use the corresponding features.

Details

Name	Result	Required By	Memo
PHP version	Passed	Yii Framework	PHP 5.1.0 or higher is required.
$_SERVER variable	Passed	Yii Framework	
Reflection extension	Passed	Yii Framework	
PCRE extension	Passed	Yii Framework	
SPL extension	Passed	Yii Framework	
DOM extension	Passed	CWsdlGenerator	
PDO extension	Passed	All DB-related classes	
PDO SQLite extension	Warning	All DB-related classes	This is required if you are using SQLite database.
PDO MySQL extension	Passed	All DB-related classes	This is required if you are using MySQL database.
PDO PostgreSQL extension	Warning	All DB-related classes	This is required if you are using PostgreSQL database.
Memcache extension	Warning	CMemCache	
APC extension	Passed	CApcCache	
Mcrypt extension	Passed	CSecurityManager	This is required by encrypt and decrypt methods.
SOAP extension	Passed	CWebService, CWebServiceAction	
GD extension	Passed	CCaptchaAction	

passed failed warning

Using the **Requirement Checker** is not itself a requirement for installation, but it is certainly recommended to ensure proper installation. As you can see, not all of our results under the **Details** section received a **Passed** status, as some display a **Warning**. Of course, your configuration will most likely be slightly different from ours and consequently, your results may slightly differ as well. That is okay. It is not necessary that all of the checks under the **Details** section pass, but it is necessary to receive the following message under the **Conclusion** section:

> **Your server configuration satisfies the minimum requirements by Yii.**

Installing a database

Throughout this book, we will be using a database to support many of our examples and the applications that we will be writing. In order to properly follow along with this book, it is recommended you install a database server. Though you can use any database that is supported by PHP with Yii, if you want to use some of built-in database abstraction layers and tools within Yii, you will need to use one that is supported by the framework. As of version 1.1, those are:

- MySQL 4.1 or later
- PostgresSQL 7.3 or later
- SQLite 2 and 3
- Microsoft SQL Server 2000 or later
- Oracle

Now that we have installed the framework, and we have verified that we have met the minimum requirements, let's create a brand new Yii web application.

Creating a new application

To create a new application, we are going to use a little powerhouse of a tool known as `yiic` that comes packaged with the framework. This is a command-line tool that one can use to quickly jumpstart a brand new Yii application. It is not mandatory to use this tool, but it saves a lot of time and guarantees that the proper folder and file structure is in place.

To use this tool to create your first Yii application, open up a shell window, and navigate to a place in your filesystem where you will want to create your application's folder structure. For the purpose of this demo application, we will assume the following:

- `YiiRoot` is the folder where you have installed Yii

- `WebRoot` is configured as the document root of your web server

- From your command line, change to your `WebRoot` folder and execute the following:

```
% cd WebRoot
% YiiRoot/framework/yiic webapp demo
Create a Web application under '/Webroot/demo'? [Yes|No]
Yes
    mkdir /WebRoot/demo
    mkdir /WebRoot/demo/assets
    mkdir /WebRoot/demo/css
    generate css/bg.gif
    generate css/form.css
    generate css/main.css
```

Your application has been created successfully under /Webroot/demo. The webapp command is used to create a brand new Yii web application. It takes just a single argument to specify either the absolute or relative path to the folder in which the application should be created. The result is the generation of all the needed folders and files to provide a default Yii web application skeleton.

Now we can change into the newly created demo folder and look at what was created for us:

```
% cd demo
% ls -p
assets/     images/     index.php   themes/
css/    index-test.php  protected/
```

A description of the high-level items that were automatically created is shown as follows:

```
demo/
index.php      Web application entry script file
index-test.php  entry script file for the functional tests
assets/     containing published resource files
```

```
css/        containing CSS files
images/     containing image files
themes/     containing application themes
protected/     containing protected application files
```

With the execution of one simple command from the command line, we have created all the folder structure and files needed to immediately take advantage of Yii's sensible default configuration. All of these folders and the files, along with the subfolders and files they contain, can look a little daunting at first glance. However, we can ignore most of them as we are getting started. All these folders and files are actually a working web application. The `yiic` command has populated the application with enough code to establish a simple home page, a typical **Contact Us** page to provide an example of a web form, and a login page with enough autogenerated code to demonstrate basic authorization and authentication in Yii. If your web server supports the GD2 graphics library extension, you will also see a CAPTCHA widget on the **Contact Us** form, and the application will have the corresponding validation for this form item.

As long as your web server is running, you should be able to open up your browser and navigate to `http://localhost/demo/index.php`. Here you will be presented with a **My Web Application** home page along with the friendly greeting **Welcome to My Web Application**, followed by some helpful information on the steps to be taken next. The next screenshot shows this example home page:

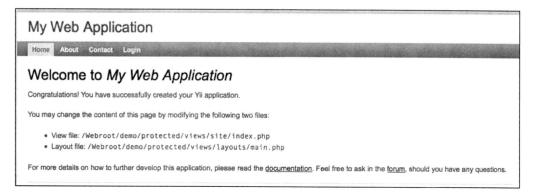

You'll notice that there is a working application navigation bar along the top of the page. From left to right there is: **Home, About, Contact,** and **Login**. Let's explore by clicking around. Clicking on the **About link** provides a simple example of a static page. The **Contact** link will take you to the **Contact Us** form that was mentioned before, along with the CAPTCHA input field in the form (again, you will only see the CAPTCHA field if you have the GD graphics extension as part of your PHP configuration).

The **Login** link will take you to a page displaying a login form. This is actually working code with form validations, as well as username and password credential validation and authentication. Using either **demo/demo** or **admin/admin** as the username/password combination will get you logged into the site. Try it out. You can try a login that will fail (any combination other than **demo/demo** or **admin/ admin**), and see the error validation messages display. After successfully logging in, the **Login** link in the header changes to a **Logout(username)** where username is either **demo** or **admin**, depending on which username you used to login. It is amazing that so much has been accomplished without having to do any coding.

Hello, World!

All of this autogenerated code will start to make more sense once we walk through a simple example. To try out this new system, let's build that Hello, World! program we promised at the start of this chapter. A Hello, World! program in Yii will be a simple web page application that sends this very important message to our browser.

We have already discussed about Yii being a Model-View-Controller framework in *Chapter 1, Meet Yii,*. A typical Yii web application takes in an incoming request from a browser, parses information in that request to find a controller, and then calls an action within that controller. The controller can then invoke a particular view to render and return content to the user. If dealing with data, the controller may also interact with a model to handle all the **Create, Read, Update,** and **Delete (CRUD)** operations on that data. In our simple Hello, World! application, all we will require is the code for a controller and a view. We are not dealing with any data, so a model will not be needed. Let's begin our example by creating our controller.

Creating the controller

As we did when we created the initial application, we will again call on the yiic command to help us create our controller. In this case, we are going to use the yiic shell command to start the application within an interactive shell in which we can invoke other commands. To start the shell, navigate to the root of your demo application by running the following command:

```
%cd /Webroot/demo
```

Then execute `yiic` with the following `shell` command:

```
%YiiRoot/framework/yiic shell
Yii Interactive Tool v1.1
Please type 'help' for help. Type 'exit' to quit.
>>
```

 If you have navigated into your web application folder, you can also envoke the `yiic` command-line tool by referencing the relative path `protected/yiic` rather than the fully qualified path to where Yii is installed. So, the equivalent way to start the shell from within the folder would be:

```
% protected/yiic shell
```

You are now at the prompt within the interactive shell. You can type `help` to see a list of commands available to you within this shell:

```
>> help
At the prompt, you may enter a PHP statement or one of the following
commands:
 - controller
 - crud
 - form
 - help
 - model
 - module
Type 'help <command-name>' for details about a command.
```

We see there are several command options available. The `controller` command looks like the one we want, as we want to create a controller for our application. We can find out more about this command by typing `help controller` from the shell prompt. Go ahead and type that in. It provides usage, a general description, parameter descriptions, and some examples.

```
>> help controller
USAGE
  controller <controller-ID> [action-ID] ...

DESCRIPTION
  This command generates a controller and views associated with
  the specified actions.
```

PARAMETERS

* controller-ID: required, controller ID, e.g., 'post'.
  If the controller should be located under a subdirectory,
  please specify the controller ID as 'path/to/ControllerID',
  e.g., 'admin/user'.

  If the controller belongs to a module, please specify
  the controller ID as 'ModuleID/ControllerID' or
  'ModuleID/path/to/Controller' (assuming the controller is
  under a subdirectory of that module).

* action-ID: optional, action ID. You may supply one or several
  action IDs. A default 'index' action will always be generated.

EXAMPLES

* Generates the 'post' controller:
        controller post

* Generates the 'post' controller with additional actions 'contact'
  and 'about':
        controller post contact about

* Generates the 'post' controller which should be located under
  the 'admin' subdirectory of the base controller path:
        controller admin/post

* Generates the 'post' controller which should belong to
  the 'admin' module:
        controller admin/post

NOTE:
In the last two examples, the commands are the same, but the generated
controller file is located under different folders. Yii is able to detect
whether admin refers to a module or a subfolder.

So, from reading the `help`, it is clear that the `controller` command will generate the controller, actions, and the views associated with the specified actions. As our application's primary function is to display a message, let's call our controller, `message`, and let's name our action method after the simple message we want to display:

```
>> controller message helloWorld
generate MessageController.php
      mkdir /Webroot/demo/protected/views/message
   generate helloworld.php
   generate index.php


Controller 'message' has been created in the following file:
    /Webroot/demo/protected/controllers/MessageController.php


You may access it in the browser using the following URL:
    http://hostname/path/to/index.php?r=message
>>
```

It should respond by indicating the successful creation of the `MessageController` in the default `protected/controllers/` folder.

This is great. With one simple command, we have generated a new controller PHP file, called `MessageController.php`, and it was placed properly under the default controllers folder, `protected/controllers/`. The generated `MessageController` class extends an application base class, `Controller`, located at `protected/components/Controller.php`. This class in turn extends the `base framework class`, `CController`, so it automatically gets all of the default controller behavior. Since we specified an `actionID` parameter, `helloWorld`, a simple action was also created within `MessageController` called `actionHelloWorld()`. The `yiic` tool also assumed that this action, like most actions defined by a controller, will need to render a view. So, it added the code to this method to render a `view` file by the same name, `helloworld.php`, and placed it in the default folder for view files associated with this controller, `protected/views/message/`. Here is the code that was generated for the `MessageController` class:

```php
<?php

class MessageController extends Controller
{
  public function actionHelloWorld()
```

```
{
  $this->render('helloWorld');
}

public function actionIndex()
{
  $this->render('index');
}

}
```

We see that it also added an `actionIndex()` method that simply renders a `view` file that was also auto-created for us at `protected/views/message/index.php`. As was discussed in *Chapter 1, Meet Yii* by convention, a request that specifies `message` as the `controllerID`, but does not specify an action, will be routed to the `actionIndex()` method for further processing. The `yiic` tool was smart to know to create a default action for us.

Try it out by navigating to `http://localhost/demo/index.php?r=message/helloWorld`. You should see something similar to the following screenshot:

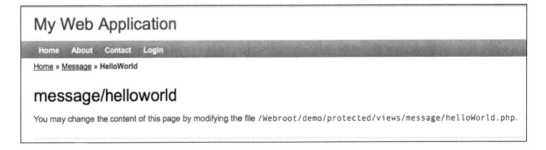

One final step

To turn this into a Hello, World! application, all we need to do is customize our `helloWorld.php` view to display `Hello, World!`. It is easy to do this. Edit the file `protected/views/message/helloWorld.php` so that it contains just the following code:

```
<?php
$this->breadcrumbs=array(
```

```
    'Message'=>array('message/index'),
    'HelloWorld',
);?>
<h1>Hello, World!</h1>
```

Save your code, and view the page again in your browser: `http://yourhostname/index.php?r=message/helloWorld`

It now displays our introductory greeting in place of the autogenerated copy, as displayed in the following screenshot:

We have our simple application working with stunningly minimal code. All we have added is one line of HTML to our `helloWorld` view file.

Reviewing our request routing

Let's review how Yii is analyzing our request in the context of this example application:

1. You navigate to the Hello, World! page by pointing your browser at the following URL: `http://yourhostname/demo/index.php?r=message/helloWorld`.

2. Yii analyzes the URL. The route `querystring` variable indicates that the `controllerID` is *message*. This tells Yii to route the request to the `MessageController` class, which it finds in `protected/controllers/MessageController.php`.

3. Yii also discovers that the `actionID` specified is `helloWorld`. So, the action method `actionHelloWorld()` is invoked within the `MessageController`.

4. The `actionHelloWorld()` method renders the `helloWorld.php` view file located at `protected/views/message/helloWorld.php`. And we altered this view file to simply display our introductory greeting, which is then returned to the browser.

5. This all came together without having to make any configuration changes. By following Yii's default conventions, the entire application request routing has been seamlessly stitched together for us. Of course, Yii gives us every opportunity to override this default workflow if needed, but the more you stick with the conventions, the less time you will spend in tweaking configuration code.

Adding dynamic content

The simplest way to add dynamic content to our view template is to embed PHP code into the template itself. View files are rendered by our simple application to result in HTML, and any basic text in these files is passed through without being changed. However, any content between the `<?php` and `?>` tags is interpreted and executed as PHP code. This is a typical way PHP code is embedded within HTML files and is probably familiar to you.

Adding the date and time

To spice up our page with dynamic content, let's display the date and time. Open up the `helloWorld` view again and add the following line below the greeting text:

```
<h3><?php echo date("D M j G:i:s T Y"); ?></h3>
```

Save, and view it at the following URL: `http://yourhostname/demo/index.php?r=message/helloWorld`

Presto! We have added dynamic content to our application. With each page refresh, we see the displayed content changing.

Admittedly, this is not terribly exciting, but it does show how to embed simple PHP code into our view templates.

Adding the date and time, a better approach

Although this approach of embedding PHP code directly into the view file does allow for any PHP code of any amount or complexity, it is strongly recommended that these statements do not alter data models and that they remain simple, display-oriented statements. This will help keep our business logic separate from our presentation code, which is part of the agenda of an MVC architecture.

Moving the data creation to the controller

Let's move the logic that creates the time back to the controller and have the view do nothing more than display the time. We'll move the determination of the time into our `actionHelloWorld()` method within the controller and set the value in an instance variable called `$time`.

1. First, let's alter the controller action. Currently our action in our `MessageController`, `actionHelloworld()`, simply makes a call to render our `helloWorld` view by executing the following code:

   ```
   $this->render('helloWorld');
   ```

   Before we render the view, let's add the call to determine the time, and then store it in a local variable called `$theTime`. Let's then alter our call to `render()` by adding a second parameter which includes this variable:

   ```
   $theTime = date("D M j G:i:s T Y");
   $this->render('helloWorld',array('time'=>$theTime));
   ```

   When calling `render()` with a second parameter containing array data, it will extract the values of the array into PHP variables and make those variables available to the view script. The keys in the array will be the names of the variables made available to our view file. In this example, our array key `time` whose value is `$theTime`, will be extracted into a variable named `$time`, which will be made available in the view. This is one way to pass data from the controller to the view.

2. Now let's alter the view to use this instance variable, rather than calling the date function itself. Open up the `helloWorld` view file again, and replace the line we previously added to echo the time with the following:

   ```
   <h3><?php echo $time; ?></h3>
   ```

3. Save and view the results again at: `http://yourhostname/demo/index.php?r=message/helloWorld`

The next screenshot shows the end result of our **Hello, World!** application thus far (of course, your date and time will differ).

We have demonstrated two approaches to adding PHP generated content to the view template files. The first approach puts the data creation logic directly into the view file itself. The second approach housed this logic in the controller class, and fed the information to the view file by using variables. The end result is the same, the time is displayed in our rendered HTML file, but the second approach takes a small step forward in keeping the data acquisition and manipulation, that is business logic, separate from our presentation code. This separation is exactly what a Model-View-Controller architecture strives to provide, and Yii's explicit folder structure and sensible defaults make this a snap to implement.

Have you been paying attention?

It was mentioned in *Chapter 1, Meet Yii* that the view and controller are close cousins. So much so that $this within a view file refers to the controller class that rendered the view.

In the preceding example, we explicitly fed the time to the view file from the controller by using the second argument in the render method. This second argument explicitly sets variables that are immediately available to the view file, but there is another approach we encourage you to try out for yourself.

Alter the previous example by defining a public class property on MessageController, rather than a locally scoped variable, whose value is the current date and time. Then display the time in the view file by accessing this class property through $this.

Linking pages together

Typical web applications have more than one page within them for users to experience, and our simple application should be no exception. Let's add another page that displays a response from the World, 'Goodbye, Yii developer!', and link to this page from our `Hello, World!` page, and vice-versa.

Normally, each rendered HTML page within a Yii web application will correspond to a separate view (though this does not always have to be the case). So, we will create a new view and will use a separate action method to render this view. When adding a new page like this, we also need to consider whether or not to use a separate controller. As our **Hello** and **Goodbye** pages are related and very similar, there is no compelling reason to delegate the application logic to a separate controller class at the moment.

Linking to a new page

Let's have the URL for our new page be of the following form:
`http://yourhostname/demo/index.php?r=message/goodbye`

1. Sticking with Yii conventions, this decision defines the name of our action method we need in the controller as well as the name of our view. So, open up `MessageController` and add an `actionGoodbye()` method just below our `actionHelloworld()` action:

```
class MessageController extends CController
{
  ...

  public function actionGoodbye()
  {
    $this->render('goodbye');
  }

  ...
}
```

2. Next we have to create our view file in the `/protected/views/message/` folder. This should be called `goodbye.php` as it should be the same as the `actionID` we chose.

 Please do keep in mind that this is just a recommended convention. The view does not have to have the same name as the action by any means. The view filename just has to match the first argument of `render()`.

3. Create an empty file in that folder, and add the single line:

```
<h1>Goodbye, Yii developer!</h1>
```

4. Saving and viewing again: `http://yourhostname/demo/index.php?r=message/goodbye` should display the goodbye message.

5. Now we need to add the links to connect the two pages. To add a link on the Hello screen to the Goodbye page, we could add an `<a>` tag directly to the `helloWorld` view template, and hardcode the URL structure like:

```
<a href="/demo/index.php?r=message/goodbye">Goodbye!</a>
```

This does work, but it tightly couples the view code implementation to a specific URL structure, which might change at some point. If the URL structure were to change, these links would become invalid.

Remember in *Chapter 1, Meet Yii* when we went through the blog posting application example? We used URLs that were of a different, more SEO friendly format than the Yii default format, namely:

```
http://yourhostname/ControllerID/ActionID
```

It is a simple matter to configure a Yii web application to use this path format as opposed to the querystring format we are using in this example. Being able to easily change the URL format can be important to web applications. As long as we avoid hardcoding them throughout our application, changing them will remain a simple matter of altering the application configuration file.

Getting a little help from Yii CHtml

Luckily, Yii comes to the rescue here. It comes with myriad helper methods that can be used in view templates. These methods exist in the static HTML helper framework class, `CHtml`. In this case, we want to employ the helper method link which takes in a `controllerID/actionID` pair, and creates the appropriate hyperlink for you based on how the URL structure is configured for the application. As all these helper methods are static, we can call them directly without the need to create an explicit instance of the `CHtml` class.

1. Using this link helper, our `helloWorld` view becomes:

```
<h1>Hello, World!</h1>
<h3><?php echo $time; ?></h3>
<p><?php echo CHtml::link("Goodbye",array('message/goodbye'));
?></p>
```

2. Save your changes, and view the **Hello, World!** page at:

`http://yourhostname/demo/index.php?r=message/helloWorld`

You should see the hyperlink, and clicking it should take you to the Goodbye page. The first parameter in the call to the link method is the text that will be displayed in the hyperlink. The second parameter is an array that holds the value for our `controllerID/actionID` pair. The results are displayed in the following figure:

3. We can follow the same approach to place a reciprocal link in our goodbye view:

```
<h1>Goodbye, Yii developer!</h1>
<p><?php echo CHtml::link("Hello",array('message/helloWorld'));
?></p>
```

4. Save and view the **Goodbye** page at the following link:

`http://yourhostname/demo/index.php?r=message/goodbye`

You should now see an active link back to the Hello, World! page from the **Goodbye** page, as shown in the following screenshot:

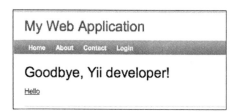

Summary

In this chapter, we constructed an extremely simple application to demonstrate:

- How to install the Yii Framework
- How to use the `yiic` command to bootstrap the creation of a new Yii application
- How to use the `yiic` command to create a new controller within the application
- How Yii turns incoming requests into calls to your code
- How to create dynamic content within a controller and have it accessible to the view files for display to the browser
- How to link internal application pages together

We have demonstrated ways to link web pages together in our simple application. One approach added an HTML `<a>` tag directly to the view file and hardcoded the URL structure. The other (preferred approach) made use of Yii's `CHtml` helper class to help construct the URLs based on `controllerID`/`actionID` pairs, so that the resulting format will always conform to the application configuration. This way, we can easily alter the URL format throughout the application without having to go back and change every view file that happens to have internal links.

Our simple `Hello, World!` application really reaps the benefits of Yii's convention over configuration philosophy. By applying certain default behavior and following the recommended conventions, the building of this simple application, (and our entire request routing process) just fell together in an easy and convenient way.

While this incredibly simple application has provided concrete examples to help us better understand using the Yii Framework, it is far too simplistic to demonstrate Yii's ability to ease the building of our real-world applications. In order to demonstrate this, we need to build a real-world web application (and we will do just that). In the next chapter, we will introduce you to the project task and issue tracking application that we will be building throughout the remainder of this book.

The TrackStar Application

3

We could continue to keep adding to our simple demo application to provide examples of Yii's features, but that won't really help us to understand the framework in the context of a real-world application. In order to do that, we need to build something that will more closely resemble the types of applications web developers actually have to build. That is exactly what we are going to be doing throughout the rest of this book.

In this chapter, we introduce the project task tracking application called TrackStar. There are many other project management and issue tracking applications out there in the world, and the basic functionality of ours will not be any different from many of these. So why build it, you ask? It turns out that this type of user-based application has many features that are common to a great many web applications out there. This will allow us to achieve two primary goals:

- Showcase Yii's incredible utility and feature set as we build useful functionality and conquer real-world web application challenges
- Provide real-world examples and approaches that will be immediately applicable to your next web application project

Introducing TrackStar

TrackStar is a **Software Development Life Cycle (SDLC)** issue management application. Its main goal is to help keep track of all the many issues that arise throughout the course of building software applications. It is a user-based application that allows the creation of user accounts and grants access to the application features, once a user has been authenticated and authorized. It allows a user to add and manage projects.

Projects can have users associated with them (typically the team members working on the project) as well as issues. The project issues will be things such as development tasks and application bugs. The issues can be assigned to members of the project and will have a status such as *not yet started*, *started*, and *finished*. This way, the tracking tool can give an accurate depiction of projects with regard to what has been accomplished, what is currently in progress, and what is yet to be started.

Creating user stories

Simple user stories are a great way to identify the required features of your application. User stories, in their simplest form, state what a user can do with a piece of software. They should start simple, and grow in complexity as you dive into more and more of the details around each feature. Our goal here is to begin with just enough complexity to allow us to get stared. If needed, we'll add more detail and complexity later.

We briefly touched on the three main entities that play a large role in this application: *users*, *projects*, and issues. These are our primary domain objects, and are extremely important items in this application. So, let's start with them.

Users

TrackStar is a user-based web application. There will be two high-level user types:

- Anonymous
- Authenticated

An anonymous user is any user of the application that has not been authenticated through the login process. Anonymous users will only have access to register for a new account or to log in. All other functionality will be restricted to authenticated users.

An authenticated user is any user that has provided valid authentication credentials through the login process. In other words, authenticated users are logged-in users. They will have access to the main features of the application such as creating and managing projects, and project issues.

Projects

Managing the project is the primary purpose of the TrackStar application. A project represents a general, high-level goal to be achieved by one or more users of the application. The project is typically broken down into more granular tasks (or *issues*) that represent the smaller steps that need to be taken to achieve the overall goal.

As an example, let's take what we are going to be doing throughout this book, that is, building a project and issue tracking management application. Unfortunately, we can't use our yet-to-be-created application as a tool to help us track its own development. However, if we were using a similar tool to help track what we are building, we might create a project called *Build The TrackStar Project/Issue Management Tool*. This project would be broken down into more granular project issues such as 'Create the login screen' or 'Design database schema for issues', and so on.

Authenticated users can create new projects. The creator of the project within an account has a special role within that project, called the *project owner*. Project owners have the ability to edit and delete these projects as well as add new members to the project. Other users associated with the project—besides the project owner—are referred to simply as *project members*. They have the ability to add new issues, as well as edit existing ones.

Issues

Project issues can be classified into one of the following three categories:

- **Features**: Items that represent real features to be added to the application. For example, 'Implement the login functionality'
- **Tasks**: Items that represent work that needs to be done, but is not an actual feature of the software. For example, 'Set up the build and integration server'
- **Bugs**: Items that represent application behaviors that are not working as expected. For example, 'The account registration form does not validate the format of input e-mail addresses'

Issues can have one of the following three statuses:

- **Not yet started**
- **Started**
- **Finished**

Project members can add new issues to a project, as well as edit and delete them. They can assign issues to themselves or other project members.

For now, this is enough information on these three main entities. We could go into a lot more detail about what exactly account registration entails' and how exactly one adds a new task to a project', but we have outlined enough specifications to begin on these basic features. We'll nail down the more granular details as we proceed with the implementation.

However, before we start, we should jot down some basic navigation and application workflow. This will help everyone to better understand the general layout and flow of the application we are building.

Navigation and page flow

It is always good to outline the main pages within an application, and how they fit together. This will help us quickly identify some needed Yii controllers, actions and views as well as help to set everyone's expectations as to what we'll be building towards at the onset of our development.

The figure below shows the basic idea of the application flow from logging in, through the project details listing:

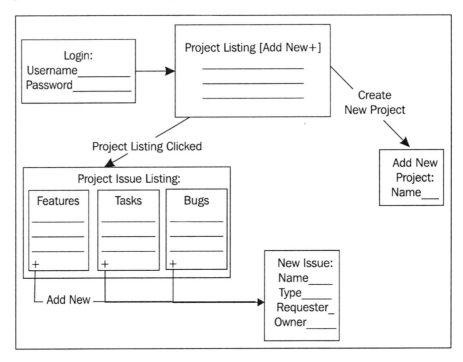

When users first come to the application, they must log in to authenticate themselves before accessing any functionality. Once successfully logged-in, they will be presented with a list of his current projects along with the option to create a new project. Choosing a specific project will take them to the project details page. The project details page will present a list of the issues by type. There will also be the option to add a new issue as well as edit any of the listed issues.

This is all pretty basic functionality, but the figure gives us a little more information on how the application is stitched together and allows us to better identify our needed models, views, and controllers. It also allows something visual to be shared with others so that everyone involved has the same 'picture' of what we are working towards. In my experience, almost everyone prefers pictures over written specifications when first thinking through a new application.

Defining a data scheme

We still need to think a little more about the data we will be working with as we begin to build toward these specifications. If we pick out all the main nouns from our system, we may end up with a pretty good list of domain objects and, by extension of using Active Record, the data we want to model. Our previously outlined user stories seem to dictate the following:

- A User
- A Project
- An Issue

Based on this and the other details provided in the user stories and application workflow diagram, a first attempt at the needed data is shown in the following figure.

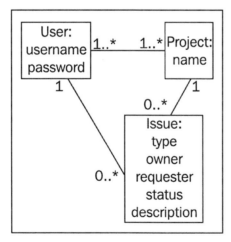

This is a basic object model that outlines our primary data entities, their respective attributes, and some of the relationships between them. The **1..*** on either side of the line between the **Project** and **User** objects represents a many-to-many relationship between them. A user can be associated with one or more projects, and a project has one or more users. Similarly we have represented the fact that a project can have zero or more issues associated with it, whereas an issue belongs to just one specific project. Also, a user can be the owner of (or requester of) many issues, but an issue has just one owner (and also just one requester).

We have kept the attributes as simple as possible at this state. A **User** is going to need a **username** and a **password** in order to get past the login screen. The **Project** has only a **name**

Issues have the most associated information based on what we currently know about them. As discussed briefly in the user stories above, they will have a **type** attribute to distinguish the general category (bug, feature, or task). They will also have a **status** attribute to indicate the progress of the issue being worked on. A user in the system will initially create the issue, this is the **requester**. Once a user in the system has been assigned to work on the issue, they will be the **owner** of the issue. We have also defined the **description** attribute to allow for some descriptive text of the issue to be entered.

Notice that we have not explicitly talked about schemas or databases yet. The fact is, until we think through what is really needed from a data perspective, we won't know the right tool to use to house this data. Would flat files on the filesystem work just as well as a relational database? Do we need a persistent data at all?

The answers to these questions are not needed in this early planning state. It is better to focus more on the features that we want and the type of data needed to support these features. We can turn to the explicit technology implementation details after we have had a chance to discuss these ideas with other project stakeholders to ensure we are on the right track. Other project stakeholders include anyone and everyone involved in this development project. This can include the client, if building an application for someone else, as well as other development team members, product/ project managers, and so on. It is always a good idea to get some feedback from "the team" to help validate the approach and any assumptions being made.

In our case, there is really no one else involved in this development effort. We would certainly consult with you, the reader, if we could, before moving forward. Unfortunately, this book format does not allow for real-time, bi-directional communication. So, as there is no one else to consult, we'll move forward with the outlined approach.

However, before we dive right into building our application, we need to cover our development approach. We will be employing some specific development methodologies and principles, and it makes sense to go over these prior to getting started with coding.

Defining our development methodology

We will be employing an agile inspired process of iterative and incremental development as we build this application. 'Agile' is certainly a loaded term in modern software development and can have varied meanings among developers. Our process will focus on the aspects of an agile methodology that embrace transparent and open collaboration, constant feedback loops, and a strong ability to respond quickly to changing requirements.

We will work incrementally in that we won't wait until every detail of the application has been specified before we start coding. Once the details of a particular feature have been finalized, we can begin work on implementing that feature, even though other features or application details are still in the design/planning stage.

The process surrounding this feature implementation will follow an iterative model. We will do some initial iteration planning, engage in analysis and design, write the code to try out these ideas, test the code, and gather feedback. We then repeat this cycle of design->code->test->evaluation, until everyone is happy. Once everyone is happy, we can deploy the application with the new feature, and then start gathering the specifications on the next feature(s) to be implemented in the next iteration.

Automated software testing

Gathering feedback is of fundamental importance to agile development. Feedback from the users of the application and other project stakeholders, feedback from the development team members, and feedback directly from the software itself. Developing software in a manner that will allow it to tell you when something is broken can turn the fear associated with integrating and deploying applications into boredom. The method by which you empower your software with this feedback mechanism is writing unit and functional tests, and then executing them repeatedly and often.

Unit and functional testing

Unit tests are written to provide the developer with verification that the code is doing the right things. Functional tests are written to provide the developer, as well as other project stakeholders, that the application, as a whole, is doing things the right way.

Unit tests

Unit tests are tests that focus on the smallest units within a software application. In an object-oriented application, (such as a Yii web application) the smallest units are the public methods that make up the interfaces to classes. Unit tests should focus on one single class, and not require other classes or objects to run. Their purpose is to validate that a single unit of code is working as expected.

Functional tests

Functional tests focus on testing the end-to-end feature functionality of the application. These tests exist at a higher level than the unit tests and typically do require multiple classes or objects to run. Their purpose is to validate that a given feature of the application is working as expected.

Benefits of testing

There are many benefits to writing unit and functional tests. For one, they are a great way to provide documentation. Unit tests can quickly tell the exact story of why a block of code exists. Similarly, functional tests document what features are implemented within an application. If you stay diligent in writing these tests, then the documentation continues to evolve naturally as the application evolves.

They are also invaluable as a feedback mechanism to constantly reassure the developer and other project stakeholders that the code and application is working as expected. You run your tests every time you make changes to the code and get immediate feedback on whether or not something you altered inadvertently changed the behavior of the system. You then address these issues immediately. This really increases the confidence that developers have in the application's behavior and translates to fewer bugs and more successful projects.

This immediate feedback also helps to facilitate change and improving the design of the code base. A developer is more likely to make improvements to existing code if a suite of tests are in place to immediately provide feedback as to whether the changes made altered the application behavior. The confidence provided by a suite of unit and functional tests allows developers to write better software, release a more stable application, and ship quality products.

Test-driven development

Test-driven development (TDD) is a software development methodology that helps to create an environment of comfort and confidence by ensuring your test suite grows organically with your application, and is always up-to-date. It does this by stipulating that you begin your coding by first writing a test for the code you are about to write. The following steps sum up the process:

1. Begin by writing a test that will quickly fail.
2. Run the test to ensure it does, indeed, fail.
3. Quickly add just enough code to the class you are testing to get the test to pass.
4. Run the test again to ensure it does, indeed, pass.
5. Refactor the code to remove any repetitive logic or improve any corners cut while you were just trying to get the test to pass.

These steps are then repeated throughout the entire development process.

Even with the best intentions, if you wait to write your tests until after the code is completed, you probably won't. Writing your tests first and injecting the test writing process directly into the coding process will ensure the best test coverage. This depth of coverage will help minimize the stress and fear that can accompany complex software applications and build confidence by constantly providing positive feedback as additions and changes are made.

In order to embrace a TDD process, we need to understand how to test within a Yii application.

Testing in Yii

As of version 1.1, Yii is tightly integrated with the PHPUnit (`http://www.phpunit.de/`) and Selenium Remote Control (`http://seleniumhq.org/projects/remote-control/`) testing frameworks. There is nothing about TDD that presupposes a particular testing framework (or any testing framework at all, for that matter), but using one is strongly recommended.

You may certainly test Yii PHP code with any of the testing frameworks available. However, the tight integration of Yii with the two frameworks mentioned previously makes things even easier. And making things easy is one of our primary goals here. We will be using the testing features of Yii as we proceed.

When we used the `yiic webapp` console command to create our new `Hello World` demo application in *Chapter 2*, we noticed that many files and folders were automatically created for us. The ones among these relevant to writing and performing automated tests are the following:

Name of folder	Use/contents
demo/	
protected	This contains protected application files
tests/	This contains tests for the application
fixtures/	This contains database fixtures
functional/	This contains functional tests
unit/	This contains unit tests
report/	This contains coverage reports
bootstrap.php	The script executed at the very beginning of the tests
phpunit.xml	The PHPUnit configuration file
WebTestCase.php	The base class for Web-based functional tests

We will be placing our tests into three main folders: `fixtures`, `functional`, and `unit`. The `report` folder is used to store the generated code coverage reports.

 Note: The PHP extension, XDebug, must be installed in order to generate reports. It is recommended to use PECL to install XDebug. For details on this installation, see `http://xdebug.org/docs/install`. This is not a requirement if you wish to simply follow along with our examples.

Unit tests

A unit test in Yii is written as a PHP class that extends from the framework class, `CTestCase`. The conventions prescribe it be named `AbcTest` where `Abc` is replaced by the name of the class being tested. For example, if we were to test the `Message` class in our demo application from *Chapter 2*, we would name the test class `MessageTest`. This class is saved in a file called `MessageTest.php` under the folder `protected/tests/unit/`.

The test class primarily has a set of test methods named `testXyz` where `Xyz` is often the same as the method name the test is built for in the class being tested.

Continuing with the `MessageController` example, if we were testing our `actionHelloworld()` method, we would name the corresponding test method in our `MessageTest` class, `testActionHelloworld()`.

Installing PHPUnit

In order to follow along with our unit-testing approach, you will need to install PHPUnit. This should be done using the Pear Installer (for more information on Pear, see http://pear.php.net/) For Mac OS users, this is a simple as issuing two commands from the command line:

```
% sudo pear channel-discover pear.phpunit.de
% sudo pear install phpunit/PHPUnit
```

However, your configuration may differ slightly. For more information on this installation process see: http://www.phpunit.de/manual/3.0/en/installation. html

>
> It is certainly beyond the scope of this book to specifically cover PHPUnit testing features. It is recommended that you take some time to go through the documentation (http://www.phpunit.de/ wiki/Documentation) to get a feel for the jargon and learn how to write basic unit tests.

Functional tests

Much like units tests, functional tests are written as PHP classes. However, they extend from CWebTestCase rather than CTestCase. The conventions are the same in that we name our functional test class AbcTest where Abc is the class being tested, and save the class in a file named AbcTest.php. However, we store these under the folder protected/tests/functional.

In order to run functional tests, you need to install Selenium.

Installing Selenium

In addition to PHPUnit, the Selenium Remote Control Server (Selenium RC) is needed in order to run the functional tests. Installing Selenium RC is very simple.

1. Download Selenium Remote Control (Selenium RC) zip file from http://seleniumhq.org/download/.
2. Unpack the zip file to a preferred location on your system.

The contents of the unzipped folder will have several specific client-based folders and one that contains the actual RC server. It will be named something similar to

```
selenium-server-1.0.x/
```

Where x will be specific to the version downloaded. Starting the server is also simple. Just navigate to this server folder on your system and issue:

```
% java -jar selenium-server.jar
```

This will start the server in that console.

Running a quick example

The TDD approach we will be taking throughout building the TrackStar application will primarily focus on the writing and executing of unit tests. However it would be a shame not to run though at least one functional test example. The site we created for our demo `Hello World` application has an example functional test located at `protected/tests/functional/SiteTest.php`. This file has three test methods created within it. One for testing the main home page, one for testing the contact page, and a third for testing the login and logout functionality.

Before we can run this functional test, we need to make a couple of configuration changes to our application. First we need to alter `protected/tests/WebTestCase. php` to properly define our test URL that Selenium will attempt to open when it runs the tests. Open up that file and make sure the `TEST_BASE_URL` definition matches the URL to your demo application we created in the previous chapter, that is, change the following line: `define('TEST_BASE_URL','http://localhost/testdrive/index-test.php/');`

To: `define('TEST_BASE_URL','http://localhost/demo/index-test.php/');`

The next change may only apply to Mac OS users. Although, if you are using Windows but prefer not to use Internet Explorer as the testing browser, then you may also want to make this change. The file `protected/tests/phpunit.xml` houses some configuration settings for Selenium Server. It is configured to use IE as the primary browser. We can remove the following highlighted line of code to ensure only Firefox will be used when running Selenium:

```
<phpunit bootstrap="bootstrap.php"
    colors="false"
    convertErrorsToExceptions="true"
    convertNoticesToExceptions="true"
    convertWarningsToExceptions="true"
    stopOnFailure="false">

  <selenium>
 <browser name="Internet Explorer" browser="*iexplore" />
    <browser name="Firefox" browser="*firefox" />
  </selenium>

</phpunit>
```

Now, as long as you have installed PHPUnit (see earlier *Unit test* section) and have ensured that Selenium Server is running (mentioned previously), and then we can navigate to our `tests` folder at the command prompt and run this functional test:

```
% cd protected/tests/
% phpunit functional/SiteTest.php
```

What should happen is that you will see your browser being automatically invoked, as the Selenium Server platform is using the browser to access the end-user functionality of the site that we configured in the `WebTestCase.php` file. As it runs through the test methods, it actually automates the behavior of a real user of the site. Pretty cool!

If everything worked, the end results should display back in the command line window where we executed the test. Something similar to the following will be displayed::

Time: 19 seconds, Memory: 10.25Mb

OK (3 tests, 10 assertions)

Being able to automate these end-user functional tests is a fantastic way to begin to automate your quality assurance testing (QA testing). If you have a separate QA team on the project, it would be very beneficial to show them how to use this tool to test the application. As mentioned, we will be focused more on writing unit tests than these end-user browser executed functional tests, as we employ a test-driven approach. However, having a test suite that covers both unit and functional tests is the best approach to ensuing the best quality in the application development.

It might be the case that one of your functional tests failed when running the `SiteTest.php` tests. If the results of your test indicated a failure at line 44 of the `SiteTest.php` file, you may need to slightly alter this line to get your tests to pass. This depends on the way the logout link in the main menu displays. The autogenerated test might expect the link read just **Logout** rather than **Logout (demo)**. If your functional test fails for this reason, simply change that line to read just as the logout link would read if you had logged in as **demo/demo**, like this:

```
$this->clickAndWait('link=Logout (demo)');
```

Hello TDD!

Let's briefly revisit `Hello World!` demo application that we built in the previous chapter to provide an example of testing in Yii following a TDD approach.

As a reminder, we have a working application that displays **Hello World!** and **Goodbye, Yii Developer**. The two action methods handling the requests to display these messages are in our `MessageController` class.

Let's add some new behavior to `MessageController.php`. Let's enhance it be able to take in any message string, and simply return that exact message string back to the caller. That sounds simple enough. We should just open up `MessageController.php` and add a new public method, maybe called `repeat()` and have it do what we just described, right? Well, not quite. As we are taking a TDD approach, we should start by writing a test for this new behavior.

As we are testing the behavior of a class method, we need to write a unit test. Following the Yii defaults, this unit test should reside in the `protected/tests/unit/` folder and be called `MessageTest.php`. Taking small steps, let's just add a new class by this name and have it extend the base Yii Framework class for unit tests, `CTestCase`.

Create the new file, `protected/tests/unit/MessageTest.php` and add to it the following code:

```php
<?php
class MessageTest extends CTestCase
{
}
```

Now we can navigate to our tests folder and execute the command to run this test:

```
%cd /WebRoot/demo/protected/tests
```

```
%phpunit unit/MessageTest.php
```

The following will be displayed after execution:

```
phpunit unit/MessageTest.php
PHPUnit 3.3.17 by Sebastian Bergmann.

F

Time: 0 seconds

There was 1 failure:

1) Warning(PHPUnit_Framework_Warning)
No tests found in class "MessageTest".

FAILURES!
Tests: 1, Assertions: 0, Failures: 1.
```

Our test failed. It tells us we don't have a test defined in our test class. This is certainly true, as we have not coded one yet. But we have started down the first step of TDD, which is to quickly write a test that fails (though one could argue we have not really written an actual test as of yet).

Let's add a test method. As we are writing a test to validate our `MessageController`'s ability to repeat back a string fed to it, let's call this test `testRepeat`. Add the following code so that our test class looks like:

```
class MessageTest extends CTestCase
{
        public function testRepeat()
        {
        }
}
```

If we rerun the test now, we will get the following results:

```
OK (1 test, 0 assertions)
```

This is certainly a step in the right direction. We have followed the TDD second step, which is writing just enough code to get the test to pass. Of course, it passed because the method does not test anything at all, so this is not terribly useful. Nonetheless, is a small step in the right direction. As there is nothing to really refactor here, let's repeat the TDD process back at the top: Quickly write a test that fails.

This time, we will add to the test so it does something. That "something" will be testing the specific repeat behavior of `MessageController`. In order to do that, we need to:

1. Create a new instance of our `MessageController` class in the test method.
2. Call a method on it by feeding it a string of text.
3. Verify that the returned string is the same as the input string.

Let's add the code to do that now. Alter the `testRepeat()` method to be:

```
public function testRepeat()
{
        $message = new MessageController('messageTest');
        $yell = "Hello, Any One Out There?";
        $returnedMessage = $message->repeat($yell);
        $this->assertEquals($returnedMessage, $yell);
}
```

We have created a new `MessageController` class by providing a required controllerId to its constructor. We then built a string called `$yell` that we want repeated back. We call the repeat() method with this input string and capture the returned output in the variable `$returnedMessage`.

As we expect the returned message to contain the exact same string as was sent, we use the phpUnit API method `assertEquals()` that will compare the first string to the second and result in true or false depending on whether or not they are indeed equal. Now that we have a test written, let's try running it:

```
%phpunit unit/MessageTest.php

PHPUnit 3.4.12 by Sebastian Bergmann.

E

Time: 0 seconds, Memory: 10.00Mb

There was 1 error:

1) MessageTest::testRepeat
include(MessageController.php): failed to open stream: No such file or
directory

...

FAILURES!
Tests: 1, Assertions: 0, Errors: 1.
```

I realize this may feel like we have taken a step backward. But, this is really within the nature of TDD. Small steps, testing all the time, and working to quickly get the test to first fail, and then pass. The error is telling us it is trying to create a new instance of `MessageController`, but it can't find the class in the classpath. We need to include the class as part of the unit test file. As we are running this within the context of the application, we can use the **Yii::import** syntax to include the class we want to test.

> The `Yii::import` method allows us to quickly include the definition of a class. It differs from `include` and `require` in that it is more efficient. The class definition being imported is actually not included, until it is referenced for the first time. Importing the same namespace multiple times is also much faster than `include_once` and `require_once`. Also, it is good to note that when referring to a class defined by the Yii Framework, we do not need to import or include it. All core Yii classes are pre-imported.

Alter the `MessageTest.php` file to include the following line at the top:

```php
<?php
Yii::import('application.controllers.MessageController');
class MessageTest extends CTestCase
{
```

Saving and running the test again does seem to get us past the previous error, but we are met with another. Now it fails due to the fact that we are calling a method named `repeat()` on our `MessageController` class, but this class does not have such a method. This certainly makes sense, as we have not added this method yet. Finally, it is time to code our new method, and get this test to pass.

Add the following method to the `MessageController` class:

```
public function repeat($inputString)
{
    return $inputString;
}
```

Save and run the test again:

```
% phpunit unit/MessageTest.php

...

OK (1 test, 1 assertion)
```

Bingo! We have a passing test. We can clean up our test code and refactor just a little by being a bit more compact in our writing and move some things inline:

```
public function testRepeat()
  {
      $message = new MessageController('messageTest');
      $this->assertEquals($message->repeat("Any One Out There?"),
"Any One Out There?");
  }
```

You should run the test one last time to ensure it still passes, as expected.

If TDD is new to you, all of this may seem a little strange, especially given all of the small, at times excruciatingly small, steps we took to achieve such a trivial method implementation. This was mostly to help underscore the rhythm of TDD. The size of the steps you take when using TDD is more of an art than a science. Start out super small and then take bigger steps as you become more confident and comfortable.

In several of the testing frameworks available to developers, the test results are displayed as color-coded. Tests that pass are displayed in green, and tests that fail are displayed in red. This also follows the familiar stoplight metaphor. For this reason, TDD is often summed up as: Red, Green, Refactor, Repeat. This refers to the basic rhythm that the previous example underscored:

1. **Red**: Quickly add a new test and then run all the tests and see the new one fail.
2. **Green**: Make a little change, just enough to get the failed test to pass.

3. **Refactor**: If necessary, remove any duplication in the code or things you did just to make the test pass quickly, but otherwise makes you feel icky.

4. **Repeat**: Start over with #1.

Summary

This chapter introduced the task tracking application, TrackStar, which we will be developing throughout the rest of this book. We talked about what the application is and what it does and provided some high-level requirements for the application in the form of informal user stories. We then identified some of the main domain objects we will need to create as well as worked through some of the data we will need to be able to house and manage.

Not only did we discuss what we are going to be building, but we also outlined how we are going to be building it. We covered a basic *agile-inspired* development methodology and how we will be applying it to our process. We also introduced Test Driven Development (TDD) as one of the agile methodologies we will be embracing. We covered what TDD is in the abstract, but also how to implement it within the testing framework provided by Yii.

In the next chapter, we will finally leave our world of fake demo applications and begin coding something we can really sink our programming teeth into.

4
Iteration 1: Creating the Initial TrackStar Application

In the previous chapter, we introduced our development methodology, which embraces an incremental and iterative approach. Within this methodology there is the concept of an *iteration*. For our purposes, an iteration can be thought of as an opportunity for a development team to create working, tested, and production-ready features of an application within a specified time constraint. The development team and other project stakeholders decide which features will be worked on within this fixed amount of time. Creating such a *timebox* around our desired features cannot really be done in a book. So, we will let the scope of each chapter define our iteration.

From now on, we'll treat each of our chapters as a new iteration, and begin each chapter with the iteration planning section. In this section we will:

- Identify the features and functionality that we want to focus on within the iteration
- Provide a little upfront design and analysis if necessary, and then quickly break the items into more granular tasks for implementation

Iteration planning

From what we learned in the previous chapter about our task tracking application, we know that we are going to be building a web-based application. We also learned in *Chapter 2, Getting Started*, just how easy it is to create a new working Yii web application using the `yiic` command-line tool.

We also talked about data in *Chapter 3, The Trackstar Application*, but did not talk specifically about how we want to handle that data. Now is the time to provide some explicit implementation answers to the questions posed in *Chapter 3*. Do we need persistent data at all? Would flat files on the filesystem work just as well as a relational database?

Based on this being a web-based application and the nature of the information that we need to store, retrieve, and manipulate, we can safely say that we need to persist the data in this application. Also, based on the relationships that exist between the types of data we want to capture and manage, we feel that the best approach to storing this data would be in a relational database. Because of its ease of use, excellent price point, general popularity among PHP application developers and its compatibility with the Yii Framework, we will be using MySQL as the specific database server.

Getting a basic, working skeleton application in place and successfully connected to a database is all we want to attempt in this first iteration. So in this first iteration, we will focus only on the following basic tasks:

- Creating a new Yii web application to be the foundation to the `TrackStar` application
- Creating a new MySQL database
- Configuring the new web application to connect to the newly created database

In *Chapter 2, Getting Started*, we saw how easy it is to create a new application. Even though this first iteration will be a short one, at the end, we will have a working, tested, and deployable web application.

Creating the new application

First things first, let's create the initial Yii web application. We have already seen how easy this is to accomplish in *Chapter 2*. As we did there, we will assume the following:

- `YiiRoot` is the folder where you have installed Yii
- `WebRoot` is configured to be the document root of your web server (that is, to where `http://localhost/` resolves)

So, from the command line, change to your `WebRoot` folder, and execute the following:

```
% cd WebRoot
% YiiRoot/framework/yiic webapp trackstar
Create a Web application under '/Webroot/trackstar'? [Yes|No] Yes
```

This provides us with our skeleton folder structure and our out of the box working application. You should be able to view the homepage of this new application by navigating to:

```
http://localhost/trackstar/index.php?r=site/index
```

Connecting to the database

Now that we have our skeleton application up and running, let's work on getting it properly connected to a database. Although this is more a matter of configuration than writing code, we will maintain a test-first approach, so that basic database connectivity becomes a part of our routine test suite.

Testing the connection

Chapter 3, introduced us to the testing framework provided by Yii. So, we know we add our unit tests under `protected/tests/unit/`. Let's create a simple database connectivity test file under this folder called `DbTest.php`. Create this new file with the following contents:

```php
<?php
class DbTest extends CTestCase
{
    public function testConnection()
    {
        $this->assertTrue(true);
    }
}
```

Here we have added a fairly trivial test. The `assertTrue()` method, which is part of `phpUnit`, is an assertion that will pass if the argument passed to it is `true`, and it will fail if it is `false`. So, in this case, it will pass if `true` is `true`. Of course it is, so this test will pass. We are doing this to make sure our new application is working as expected for testing. Navigate to the `tests` folder and execute this new test:

```
%cd /WebRoot/trackstar/protected/tests
%phpunit unit/DbTest.php
...
```

```
Time: 0 seconds, Memory: 10.00Mb
```

```
OK (1 test, 1 assertion)
```

...

>
>
> **Configuring the test suite**
>
> If for some reason this test failed on your system, you many need to change `protected/tests/bootstrap.php` so that the variable `$yiit` properly points to your `/YiiRoot/yiit.php` file.

Confident that our testing framework is working as expected within our newly created `TrackStar` application, we can actually test for a `db` connection.

Change the trivial `assertEquals(true)` statement in the `testConnection()` test method to:

```
$this->assertNotEquals(NULL, Yii::app()->db);
```

And rerun the test:

```
%phpunit unit/DbTest.php
There was 1 error:
1) DbTest::testConnection
CDbException: CDbConnection failed to open the DB connection: could not find driver
```

...

```
FAILURES!
Tests: 1, Assertions: 0, Errors: 1.
```

Now we have a failing test. The test is assuming the application has been configured with a database connection application component called `db`. (We'll talk a little more about application components later). The test is written to assert that when the application is asked for a `db` connection, the result is not a null value.

In fact, the skeleton application was auto-configured to use a database. A by-product of using the `yiic` tool is that our new application is configured to use an SQLite database. If you take a peek into the main application configuration file, located at `protected/config/main.php`, you will see the following declaration about halfway down:

```
'db'=>array('connectionString' => 'sqlite:'.dirname(__FILE__).'/../
data/testdrive.db',
    ),
```

And you can also verify the existence of `protected/data/testdrive.db`, which is the SQLite database it is configured to use.

In our case, this test fails because we don't have an SQLite driver configured in our development environment. This test may not have failed for you if you happen to have the correct driver available. Before we change the configuration to use a MySQL database server, let's briefly talk about Yii and databases more generally.

Yii and databases

Yii provides great support for database programming. Yii **Data Access Objects** (**DAO**) is built on top of the **PHP Data Objects** (**PDO**) extension (http://php.net/pdo). This is a database abstraction layer that enables the application to interact with the database independent of the specific choice of database server. All supported **database management systems** (**DBMS**) are encapsulated behind a single uniform interface. This way, the code can remain database independent, and applications developed using Yii DAO can be easily switched to use a different DBMS without the need for modification.

To establish a connection with a supported DBMS, one can simply create a new `CDbConnection` class and instantiate it:

```
$connection=new CDbConnection($dsn,$username,$password);
```

Here the format of the `$dsn` variable depends on the specific PDO database driver being used. Some common formats include:

- SQLite: `sqlite:/path/to/dbfile`
- MySQL: `mysql:host=localhost;dbname=testdb`
- PostgreSQL: `pgsql:host=localhost;port=5432;dbname=testdb`
- SQL Server: `mssql:host=localhost;dbname=testdb`
- Oracle: `oci:dbname=//localhost:1521/testdb`

`CDbConnection` also extends from `CApplicationComponent`, which allows it to be configured as an application component. This means that we can add it to the components property of the application, and customize the class and property values that are there in the configuration file. This is our preferred approach.

Adding a db connection as an application component

To take a quick step back. When we created the initial application, we specified the application type to be a web application. Doing so actually specified that the application singleton class that is created upon each request should be of type `CWebApplication`. This Yii application singleton is the execution context within which all request processing is run. Its main task is to resolve the user request and route it to an appropriate controller for further processing. This was represented as the Yii Application Router back in our *Chapter 1, Meet Yii* diagrams, when we covered the request routing. It also serves as the central place for keeping application-level configuration values.

To customize our application configuration, we normally provide a configuration file to initialize its property values when the application instance is being created. The main application configuration file is located in `/protected/config/main.php`. This is actually a PHP file containing an array of key-value pairs. Each key represents the name of a property of the application instance, and each value is the corresponding property's initial value. If you open up this file, you will see that a few settings have already been configured for us by the `yiic` tool.

Adding an application component to the configuration is easy. Open up the main `config` file and locate the components property.

We see that there are already entries specifying a log and a user application component. These will be covered in subsequent chapters. We also see (as we noted previously) that there is a db component there as well, configured to use an SQLite connection to an SQLite database located at `protected/data/testdrive.db`. We are going to replace that connection with one for a MySQL database. It can be defined as follows:

```
// application components
  'components'=>array(
    ...
    'db'=>array(
'connectionString' => 'mysql:host=127.0.0.1;dbname=trackstar_dev',
      'emulatePrepare' => true,
      'username' => 'your_db_user_name',
      'password' => 'your_db_password',
      'charset' => 'utf8',
    ),
  ),
```

This assumes that a MySQL database has been created called `trackstar_dev` and is available to connect to the localhost IP of `127.0.0.1`. One of the great benefits of making this an application component is that from now on, we can reference the database connection simply as a property of the main Yii application: `Yii::app()->db` anywhere throughout our application. Similarly, we can do this for any of the components defined in the `config` file.

All of our examples will be using the MySQL database. However, we will be providing the low-level DDL statements for the table structures, and we will try to keep things generic from a database implementation perspective. It is entirely possible to follow along using any Yii-compatible database of your choice. At the time of writing, Yii has Active Record support for MySQL, PostgresSQL, SQLite, SQL Server, and Oracle.

> The `charset` property set to `utf8` sets the character set used for database connection. This property is only used for MySQL and PostgreSQL databases. We are setting it here to ensure proper `utf8` unicode character support for our PHP application.
>
> The `emulatePrepare => true` configuration sets a PDO attribute (`PDO::ATTR_EMULATE_PREPARES`) to `true` which is recommended if you are using PHP 5.1.3 or higher.

So, we have specified a MySQL database called `trackstar_dev` as well as the username and password needed to connect to this database. We did not show you how to create such a database in MySQL. We assume you have a favorite database you are going to use as you follow along and know how to create a new database. Please refer to your specific database documentation if you are unsure of how to create a new database called `trackstar_dev`, and define a username and password for connectivity.

Once the database is in place, we can test it again by running our unit test again:

```
%phpunit unit/DbTest.php
PHPUnit 3.3.17 by Sebastian Bergmann.
Time: 0 seconds
OK (1 test, 1 assertion)
```

Our test now passes

Summary

We have completed our first iteration, and we have a working and tested application that is ready to be deployed if necessary. However, our application certainly does not do much of anything. All we have is the functionality that comes out of the box from the autogenerated code when we created the application, and a valid connection to a database. This is certainly far from what we have described when we introduced the TrackStar application. But we are taking small, incremental steps towards achieving our desired functionality, and this first iteration was a great milestone towards that end.

In the next chapter, we will finally get to sink our teeth into more meaningful features. We will begin to do some actual coding as we implement the needed functionality to manage our *project* entities within the application.

5
Iteration 2: Project CRUD

Now that we have a basic application in place and configured to communicate with our database, we can begin to work on some real features of our application. We know that the *project* is one of the most fundamental components in our application. A user cannot do anything useful with the TrackStar application without first either creating or choosing an existing project within which to add tasks and other issues. For this reason, we want to use our second iteration to focus on getting the project entity wired into the application.

Iteration planning

This iteration is fairly straightforward. At the end of this iteration, our application should allow users to create new projects, select from a list of existing projects, update/edit existing projects, and delete existing projects.

In order to achieve this goal, we need to identify all the more granular tasks on which to focus. The following list identifies a more granular list of tasks we aim to accomplish within this iteration:

- Design the database schema to support projects
- Build the needed tables and all other database objects indentified in the schema
- Create the Yii AR model classes needed to allow the application to easily interact with the created database table(s)
- Create the Yii controller class(es) that will house the functionality to:
  - Create new projects
  - Fetch a list of existing projects for display
  - Update metadata on existing projects
  - Delete existing projects

- Create the Yii view files and present their logic in a way that will:

  ○ Display the form to allow for new project creation

  ○ Display a list of all the existing projects

  ○ Display the form to allow a user to edit an existing project

  ○ Add a delete button to the project listing to allow for project deletion

This is certainly enough to get us started. We will soon be able to put these tasks into our `TrackStar` application, and manage them from there. For now, I guess we will just have to jot them down in a notebook.

Running our test suite

Before we jump right into development, we should run our existing test suite and make sure all of our tests pass. We only have one test thus far. The test we added in *Chapter 4, Iteration 1: Creating the Initial TrackStar Application* tests for a valid database connection. So, it certainly won't take too long to quickly run our test suite. Open up your command prompt and from the `/protected/tests` folder, run all of the following unit tests at once:

```
%phpunit unit/
PHPUnit 3.3.17 by Sebastian Bergmann.
Time:
::0 seconds
OK (1 test, 1 assertion)
```

With all of our tests passing, our confidence is boosted. Now we can begin to make changes

Creating the project table

Back in *Chapter 3, The TrackStar Application* we talked about the basic data that represents a project, and in *Chapter 4* we decided that we would use a MySQL relational database to build out the persistence layer of this application. Now we need to turn the idea of project content into a real database table.

We know projects need to have a name and a description. We are also going to keep some basic table auditing information on each table by tracking the time a record was created and updated as well as who created and updated the record. This is enough to get us started and meet the goals of this first iteration.

Based on these desired properties, here is how the project table looks:

```
CREATE TABLE tbl_project
(
id INTEGER NOT NULL PRIMARY KEY AUTO_INCREMENT,
name VARCHAR(128),
description TEXT,
create_time DATETIME,
create_user_id INTEGER,
update_time DATETIME,
update_user_id INTEGER
);
```

Covering third-party database administration tools is outside of the scope of this book. We also want to allow you to follow along while potentially using something other than MySQL. For these reasons, we are going to simply provide the low-level **Data Definition Language (DDL)** statements for the structures that we create. So, go ahead and open up your favorite database editor within your preferred Yii-supported database server and create this table in the `trackstar_dev` database that you created in *Chapter 4*.

Depending on the particular database you choose to use, there are many available tools that help with the maintenance of a database schema and assist in database administration We recommend using a tool that will make things easier when it comes to database administration. We are actually using MySQLWorkbench (`http://dev.mysql.com/downloads/workbench/5.1.html`) to design, document, and manage our database schema. We are also using phpMyAdmin (`http://www.phpmyadmin.net/home_page/downloads.php`) to help with general administration. There are many similar tools available. The small amount of time it takes to become familiar with how to use them can save you a lot of time in the long run.

Naming conventions

You may have have noticed that we defined our database table as well as all of the column names in lowercase. Throughout our development, we will use lowercase for all table names and column names. This is primarily because different DBMS handle case-sensitivity differently. As one example, **PostgreSQL** treats column names as case-insensitive by default, and we must quote a column in a query condition if the column contains mixed-case letters. Using lowercase would help eliminate this problem.

You may have also noticed that we used a `tbl_` prefix in naming our projects table. As of version 1.1.0, Yii provides integrated support for using table prefix. Table prefix is a string that is pre-pended to the names of the tables. It is often used in shared hosting environments where multiple applications share a single database and use different table prefixes to differentiate from each other. For example, one application could use `tbl_` as a prefix while another could use `yii_`. Also, some database administrators use this as a naming convention to prefix database objects with an identifier as to what type of entity they are, or otherwise to use a prefix to help organize objects into similar groups.

In order to take full advantage of the integrated table prefix support in Yii, one must appropriately set the `CDbConnection::tablePrefix` property to be the desired table prefix. Then, in SQL statements used throughout the application, one can use `{{TableName}}` to refer to table names, where `TableName` is the name of the table, but without the prefix. For example, if we were to make this configuration change we could use the following code to query about all projects:

```
$sql='SELECT * FROM {{project}}';
$projects=Yii::app()->db->createCommand($sql)->queryAll();
```

But this is getting a little ahead of ourselves. Let's leave our configuration as it is for now, and revisit this topic when we get into database querying a little later in our application development.

Creating the AR model class

Now that we have the `tbl_project` table created, we need to create the Yii model class to allow us to easily manage the data in that table. We introduced Yii's **Object -relational Mapping (ORM)** layer and **Active Record (AR)**, back in *Chapter 1, Meet Yii*. Now we will see a concrete example of that in the context of this application.

Previously, we used the `yiic shell` command to help with some autogeneration of code. As we saw in *Chapter 2, Getting Started* when we were using the `shell` command to create our first controller, there are many other `shell` commands you can execute to help auto create application code. However, as of version 1.1.2 of Yii, there is a new and more sophisticated interface available called **Gii**. Gii is a highly customizable and extensible web-based code generation platform that takes the `yiic shell` command to new heights. We will be using this new platform to create our new model class.

Configuring Gii

Before we can start using Gii, we have to configure it for use within our application. At this point you probably know enough to guess we would do that in our main application configuration file, `protected/config/main.php`. This is correct. To configure Gii for use, open this file and add the following highlighted code to the returned array:

```
return array(
  'basePath'=>dirname(__FILE__).DIRECTORY_SEPARATOR.'..',
  'name'=>'My Web Application',

  // preloading 'log' component
  'preload'=>array('log'),

  // autoloading model and component classes
  'import'=>array(
    'application.models.*',
    'application.components.*',
  ),

  'modules'=>array(
      'gii'=>array(
            'class'=>'system.gii.GiiModule',
            'password'=>'[add_your_password_here]',
      ),
  ),
```

This configures Gii as an application module. We will cover Yii modules in detail later in the book. The important thing at this point is to make sure this is added to the configuration file and that you provide your password. Now, navigate to the tool at: `http://localhost/trackstar/index.php?r=gii`.

The following screenshot shows the authentication form you will be presented with:

Using Gii to create our Project AR class

Go ahead and enter the password you provided during the configuration. A successful entry will take you to the following main menu page of Gii:

As you may recall, these choices are similar to the options we received back in *Chapter 2* when typing `help` within the `yiic shell` command-line tool. As we want to create a new model class for our `tbl_project` table, the **Model Generator** option seems like the right choice. Clicking that link takes us to the following page:

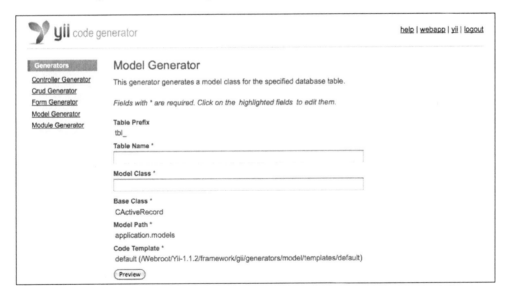

The **Table Prefix** field is primarily used to help Gii determine how to name the AR class we are generating. If you are using a prefix, you can add this here. This way, it won't use that prefix when naming the new class. In our case, we are using the **tbl_** prefix, which also just happens to be what this form field defaults to. So, specifying this value will mean that our newly generated AR class will be named Project, rather than `tbl_project`.

The next two fields are asking for our **Table Name** and the name of the class file we want it to generate. Type in the name of our table, **tbl_project**, and watch as the model class name auto-populates. The convention for the **Model Class** name is the name of the table, minus the prefix, and starting with an uppercase letter. So, it will assume a name of Project for our **Model Class** name, but of course you can customize this.

The next few fields allow for further customization. The **Base Class** field is used to specify the class from which our **Model Class** will extend. This will have to be `CActiveRecord` or a child class thereof. The `Model Path` field allows you to specify where in the application folder structure to output the new file. The default is `protected/models/` (also known as **application.models**). The last field allows us to specify a template on which the generated code is based. We can customize the default one to meet any specific needs we have that might be common to all such class files. For now, the default values for these fields meet our needs just fine.

Proceed by clicking on the **Preview** button. This will result in the following table that is displayed at the bottom of the page:

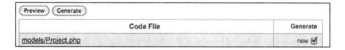

This link allows you to preview the code that will be generated. Before you hit **Generate**, click on the **models/Project.php** link. The following screenshot displays what this preview looks like:

```php
<?php

/**
 * This is the model class for table "{{project}}".
 */
class Project extends CActiveRecord
{
    /**
     * The followings are the available columns in table '{{project}}':
     * @var integer $id
     * @var string $name
     * @var string $description
     * @var string $create_time
     * @var integer $create_user
     * @var string $update_time
     * @var integer $update_user
     */

    /**
     * Returns the static model of the specified AR class.
     * @return Project the static model class
     */
    public static function model($className=__CLASS__)
    {
        return parent::model($className);
    }
```

/Webroot/trackstar/protected/models/Project.php

It provides a nice scrollable popup, so that we can preview the whole file that will be generated.

Okay, close this popup and go ahead and click on the **Generate** button. Assuming all went well, you should see the following screenshot displayed at the bottom of the page:

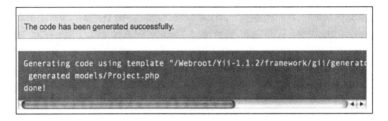

> Ensure that /protected/models (or whatever folder you specified in the **Model Path** form field) is writable by your web server process prior to attempting to generate your new model class. Otherwise, you will receive a permissions error.

Gii has created for us a new Yii AR model class, named (as we instructed it to) as Project.php, and placed it (as we instructed it to) in the default Yii location for model classes, protected/models/. This class is a wrapper class for our tbl_project database table. All of the columns in the tbl_project table are accessible as properties of the Project AR class.

Let's get familiar with our newly created AR class by writing some tests.

Testing out our newly generated code

A great way to get familiar with new code or functionality is to write tests against it. Starting with some unit tests is a great way to get a general feel of how AR classes work in Yii. As this iteration is focused on **Creating**, **Reading**, **Updating**, and **Deleting (CRUD)** projects, we'll write some tests for these operations on the Project AR class. The public methods for each of these CRUD functionalities are already present in our new Project.php AR class, so we won't need to code for those. We can just focus on writing the tests.

Creating the unit test file

First we need to create a new unit test file. Let's create that file here: `protected/tests/unit/ProjectTest.php`, and have it contain the following code:

```php
<?php
class ProjectTest extends CDbTestCase
{
    public function testCRUD()
    {
    }
}
```

The class we have added extends `CDbTestCase`, which is the Yii Framework base class for unit test classes specifically intended to test database related functionality. This database specific base class provides fixture management, which we will cover in more detail.

We'll use the `testCRUD()` method for testing all CRUD operations against the Project AR class. We'll start with testing a new Project creation.

> We are not actually engaging in TDD as this point. The reason for this is that we are not writing any of the code we are testing. We are using this testing approach to help you get familiar with both AR classes in Yii as well as with writing some basic tests. As this is not really TDD, we will not exactly follow the TDD steps closely as outlined in *Chapter 3*. For example, because the code we are going to be testing is core Yii Framework code, which works very well, we don't have to do things such as first writing a failing test.

Testing create

Add the following code to the `testCRUD()` method that creates a new Project AR class, sets its project attributes, and then saves it:

```php
public function testCRUD()
{
    //Create a new project
    $newProject=new Project;
    $newProjectName = 'Test Project 1';
    $newProject->setAttributes(
        array(
                    'name' => $newProjectName,
                    'description' => 'Test project number one',
                    'create_time' => '2010-01-01 00:00:00',
```

```
                    'create_user_id' => 1,
                    'update_time' => '2010-01-01 00:00:00',
                    'update_user_id' => 1,
               )
         );
      $this->assertTrue($newProject->save(false));
   }
```

This code first creates a new Project AR instance by invoking new. We then use the setAttributes() method of the AR class to set the AR class attributes in a bulk way based on an input array. We see that the class properties are the keys to this input array, and they will be set to the values specified in this array.

After setting the attributes, we save the new Project by invoking its save() method. We pass the optional false parameter into the save() method to tell it to bypass any data validation of the attributes (we'll cover model data validation in the section, *Adding a required field to our form*). We then test to make sure the returned value from saving the new record is true, which indicates a successful save.

Now toggle to the command line to execute this new test to ensure success:

```
% cd Webroot/protected/tests
% phpunit unit/ProjectTest.php
PHPUnit 3.3.17 by Sebastian Bergmann.

.

Time:
::0 seconds
OK (1 test, 1 assertion)
```

Great, it passed. So we have successfully added a new project. You can verify this by querying your database directly. Using your preferred database maintenance tool, select back everything from the **Project** table. You will see that you have a new row with the details that match the attributes we set for the Project AR class. In the following example we used MySQL command line as follows:

```
mysql> select * from tbl_project\G
*************************** 1. row ***************************
           id: 1
         name: Test Project 1
  description: Test project number one
  create_time: 2010-01-01 00:00:00
create_user_id: 1
  update_time: 2010-01-01 00:00:00
update_user_id: 1
1 row in set (0.00 sec)
```

You may have noticed that we did not specify the id column when setting the attributes of the Project AR class. This is because the column is defined to be an auto-increment Primary Key. The database automatically assigns this value when inserting new rows. Once the insert is successful, this attribute is properly set in the AR class itself. You could easily access the newly auto-assigned id attribute in the following manner:

```
$newProject->id
```

We'll use this in our next test.

Testing read

Now that we have verified the create functionality by testing the save() method of our new Project AR class, let's move on to the read. Add the following highlighted code to the same testCRUD() method, just below where we saved the new record:

```
public function testCRUD()
{
  //Create a new project

  //READ back the newly created project
  $retrievedProject=Project::model()->findByPk($newProject->id);
  $this->assertTrue($retrievedProject instanceof Project);
  $this->assertEquals($newProjectName,$retrievedProject->name);
}
```

Here we use the static method model() that must be defined in every AR class. This method returns an instance of the Project AR class that is further used to call other class-level methods. We are calling the findByPk() method to retrieve a specific instance of Project.

This method (as you might expect) takes in the Primary Key value and returns the specific row that matches the unique identifier. We feed it the newly created auto increment id attribute of the Project instance we created previously. This way, we are attempting to read back the exact row we inserted when we saved $newProject. We then have two assertions. We first verify that the entity we read back is an instance of the Project AR class. We then verify that the project name of the record read back is the same as the name we gave the project when we initially saved it.

Once again, let's toggle to the command line and run the following test:

```
% phpunit unit/ProjectTest.php

...

OK (1 test, 3 assertions)))  )
```

Very nice! We have verified that the "R" in CRUD is working as we expect.

Let's move a little more quickly now and test `Update` and `Delete` at the same time.

Testing update and delete

Now add the following code at the bottom of the same `testCRUD()` method we have been using, just after the tests we added for `create` and `read` previously:

```
//Create a new project
...

//READ back the newly created project
...

//UPDATE the newly created project
$updatedProjectName = 'Updated Test Project 1';
$newProject->name = $updatedProjectName; $this-
>assertTrue($newProject->save(false));

//read back the record again to ensure the update worked
$updatedProject=Project::model()->findByPk($newProject->id);
$this->assertTrue($updatedProject instanceof Project);
$this->assertEquals($updatedProjectName,$updatedProject->name);

//DELETE the project
$newProjectId = $newProject->id;
$this->assertTrue($newProject->delete());
$deletedProject=Project::model()->findByPk($newProjectId);
$this->assertEquals(NULL,$deletedProject);
```

Here we have added the tests for updating and deleting a Project. First we gave the `$newProject` instance a new and updated name and then saved the project again. As we are dealing with an existing AR instance this time, our AR class knows to do an `Update`, rather than inserting a new record, whenever we invoke `->save()`. We then read back the row to ensure the name was updated.

To test the `Delete`, we saved the project id into a local variable `$newProjectId`. We then called the `->delete()` method on our AR instance which (as you probably guessed) deletes the record from the database and destroys the AR instance. We then used our local variable holding the project id to attempt to read back the row by this Primary Key. As the record should have been deleted, we expect this result to be NULL. The test asserts that we do get a NULL value returned.

Let's make sure these tests pass. Run the test once again to ensure success:

```
% phpunit unit/ProjectTest.php
...
OK (1 test, 8 assertions)
```

Thus we have verified that all of our Project AR class CRUD operations are working as expected.

Was all that testing really necessary?

When taking a TDD approach to software development, one is constantly faced with making a decision of what to test and, sometimes more importantly, what parts not to test.

These are questions you have to answer for yourself. You want to test enough to provide maximum confidence in the code, but obviously testing every single line of code in an application can be overkill.

 One general rule of thumb is not to worry about testing code in external libraries you did not write (unless you have a specific reason to distrust it).

The CRUD operations we just wrote tests for, against the Project AR class, fall into this category. The code behind them is part of the Yii Framework, and not code that we wrote. We did not write these tests because we distrust the framework code, but rather to get a feel for using Active Record in Yii. A great by-product of this exercise is that we now have this as part of our test suite. However, it is unnecessary to go through this testing exercise for every AR model class we create, and thus we won't be doing so for other AR classes we create.

Enabling CRUD operations for users

The previously mentioned tests introduced us to using AR class instances. It showed us how to use them to create new records, retrieve back existing records, update existing records, and delete existing records. We spent a lot of time testing these lower-level operations on the AR class instance for the Project table, but our TrackStar application does not yet expose this functionality to users. What we really need is a way for users to Create, Read, Update, and Delete projects within the application. Now that we know our way around AR a little, we could start coding this functionality in some controller class. Luckily, we don't have to.

Creating CRUD scaffolding for projects

Once again, the Gii code generation tool is going to rescue us from having to write common, tedious and often time-consuming code. CRUD operations are such a common need of database tables created for applications that the developers of Yii decided to provide this for us. If you are familiar with other frameworks, you may know this by the term **scaffolding**. Let's see how to take advantage of this in Yii.

Navigate back to the main Gii menu located at `http://localhost/trackstar/index.php?r=gii`, and choose the **Crud Generator** link. You will be presented with the following screen:

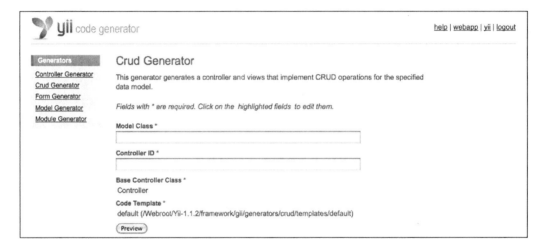

Here we are presented with two input form fields. The first one is asking for us to specify the **Model Class** against which we would like all of the CRUD operations generated. In our case, this is our `Project.php` AR class we created earlier. So enter **Project** in this field. As we do this, we notice that the **Controller ID** field is auto-populated with the name **project**, based on convention. We'll stick with this default for now.

With these two fields filled in, clicking the **Preview** button will result in the following table being added to the bottom of the page:

Preview	Generate		

Code File	Generate ☐
controllers/ProjectController.php	new ☑
views/project/_form.php	new ☑
views/project/_search.php	new ☑
views/project/_view.php	new ☑
views/project/admin.php	new ☑
views/project/create.php	new ☑
views/project/index.php	new ☑
views/project/update.php	new ☑
views/project/view.php	new ☑

We can see that quite a few files are going to be generated, which include a new
`ProjectContrller.php` controller class that will house all of the CRUD action
methods and many separate `view` files. There is a separate `view` file for each of the
operations as well as one that will provide the ability to search project records. You
can, of course, choose not to generate some of these by changing the checkboxes in
the corresponding **Generate** column in the table. However, for our purposes, we
would like Gii to create all of these for us.

Go ahead and click the **Generate** button. You should see the following success
message at the bottom of the page:

The controller has been generated successfully. You may try it now.

```
Generating code using template "/Webroot/Yii-1.1.2/framework/gii/generat
 generated controllers/ProjectController.php
 generated views/project/_form.php
 generated views/project/_search.php
 generated views/project/_view.php
 generated views/project/admin.php
 generated views/project/create.php
 generated views/project/index.php
 generated views/project/update.php
 generated views/project/view.php
done!
```

You may need to ensure that both /protected/controllers, as well as, /protected/views under the root application folder are both writable by the web server process. Otherwise, you will receive permission errors, rather than this success result.

We can now click on the **try it now** link to take our new functionality for a test drive.

Doing so takes you to the project listing page. This is the page that displays all of the projects currently in the system. You might not expect any to be in there yet, as we have not explicitly created any using our new Create functionality. However, our project listing page does have a few projects displayed as shown in the following screenshot. (For reference, the page can be found here: http://localhost/trackstar/index.php?r=project)

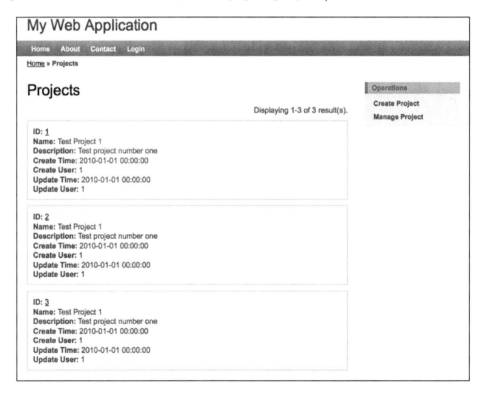

So, where did these projects come from? You might even have more or less than these three that are listed in the preceding screenshot depending on the number of times you reran the unit tests mentioned previously. The unit tests we wrote to test the CRUD operations of our new Project AR class were actually creating new records in the database every time we ran them. These are all of the records that were created before we finished writing our test for deletion, as that test eventually deleted the same record created in the test for creation. In this particular case, it is nice to have a few projects in the system so we can see how they are displayed. However, in general it is a bad idea to run the unit and functional tests against the development database. Soon, we'll cover how to change these tests to run against a separate dedicated test database. For now, let's just keep playing with our newly generated code.

Creating a new project

You'll notice on this project listings page (displayed in the previous screenshot) a little navigation column in the right column block. Go ahead and click on on the **Create Project** link. You'll discover this actually takes us to the **Login** page, rather than a form to create a new project. The reason for this is that the code Gii has generated applies a rule that stipulates that only properly authenticated users (that is, logged-in users) can create new projects. Any anonymous user that attempts to access the functionality to create a new project will be redirected to the **Login** page. Go ahead and log in using the credentials username as **demo** and password as **demo**.

A successful login should redirect you to the following URL:

```
http://localhost/trackstar/index.php?r=project/create
```

This page displays a nice input form for adding a new project, as shown in the following figure:

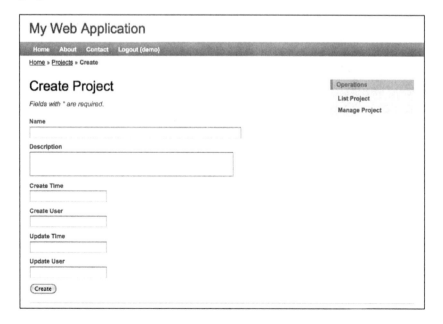

Let's quickly fill out this form to create a new project. Even though none of the fields are marked as required, let's fill in the **Name** field as **Test Project** and the **Description** field as **Test project description**. Hitting the **Create** button will post the form data back to the server, and attempt to add a new project record. If there are any errors, a simple error message will display that highlights each field in error. A successful save will redirect to the specific listing for the newly created project. Ours was successful, and we were redirected to the page with the URL `http://localhost/trackstar/index. php?r=project/view&id=4`, as shown in the following screenshot:

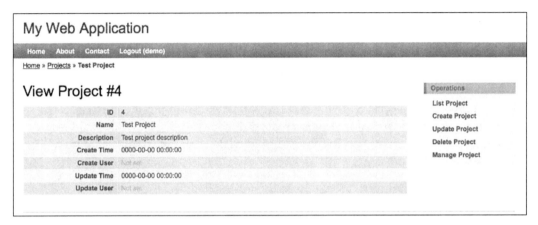

As was mentioned previously, one thing we notice about our new project creation form is that none of the fields are currently marked as being required. We can successfully submit the form without any data at all. However, we know that every project needs to have at least a name. Let's make this a required field.

Adding a required field to our form

When working with AR model classes within forms in Yii, setting validation rules around form fields is a snap. This is done by specifying values in an array set in the `rules()` method within the Project AR model class.

Opening up the `/protected/models/Project.php` class reveals that this `public` method has already been defined, and that there are already a few rules in there:

```
/**
 * @return array validation rules for model attributes.
 */
public function rules()
{
```

```
    // NOTE: you should only define rules for those attributes that
    // will receive user inputs.
    return array(
       array('create_user_id, update_user_id', 'numerical',
'integerOnly'=>true),
       array('name', 'length', 'max'=>128),
       array('create_time, update_time', 'safe'),
       // The following rule is used by search().
       // Please remove those attributes that should not be searched.
       array('id, name, description, create_time, create_user_id,
update_time, update_user_id', 'safe', 'on'=>'search'),
       );
```

The `rules()` method returns an array of rules. Each rule is of the following general format:

`Array(`**'Attribute List'**`, `**'Validator'**`, `**'on'**`=>`**'Scenario List'**`, `...**additional options**`);`

The `Attribute List` is a string of comma separated class property names to be validated according to the `Validator`. The **Validator** specifies what kind of rule should be enforced. The `on` parameter specifies a list of scenarios in which the rule should be applied.

> Scenarios allow you to restrict the application of a validation to special contexts. A typical example for an active record would be insert or update. For example, if 'on'=>'insert' is specified, this would indicate that the validation rule should only be applied when the model's scenario attribute is insert. The same holds true for 'update' or any other scenario you wish to define. You can set a model's scenario attribute either directly, or by passing it to the constructor when creating a new instance."

If this is not set, the rule is applied in all scenarios when `save()` is called. Finally, the additional options are name/value pairs, which are used to initialize the Validator's properties.

The `Validator` can be either a method in the model class, or a separate `Validator` class. If defined as a model class method, it must have the following signature:

```
/**
 * @param string the name of the attribute to be validated
 * @param array options specified in the validation rule
 */
public function ValidatorName($attribute,$params) { ... }
```

If we use a separate class to define the Validator, that class must extend from CValidator. There are actually three ways to specify the Validator in the previously mentioned general format:

1. One is to specify a method name in the model class itself.
2. A second is to specify a separate class that is of a Validator type (that is, a class that extends CValidator).
3. The third manner in which you can define the Validator is by specifying a predefined alias to an existing Validator class in the Yii Framework.

Yii provides many predefined Validator classes for you and also provides aliases with which to reference these when defining rules. The complete list of predefined Validator class aliases as of Yii version 1.1 is as follows:

- boolean: Alias of CBooleanValidator, ensuring the attribute has a value that is either true or false
- captcha: Alias of CCaptchaValidator, ensuring the attribute is equal to the verification code displayed in a CAPTCHA
- compare: Alias of CCompareValidator, ensuring the attribute is equal to another attribute or constant
- email: Alias of CEmailValidator, ensuring the attribute is a valid e-mail address
- default: Alias of CDefaultVAlidator, assigning a default value to the specified attributes
- exist: Alias of CExistValidator, ensuring the attribute value can be found in the specified table column
- file: Alias of CFileValidator, ensuring the attribute contains the name of an uploaded file
- filter: Alias of CFilterValidator, transforming the attribute with a filter
- in: Alias of CRangeValidator, ensuring the data is among a pre-specified list of values
- length: Alias of CStringValidator, ensuring the length of the data is within certain range
- match: Alias of CRegularExpressionValidator, ensuring the data matches a regular expression
- numerical: Alias of CNumberValidator, ensuring the data is a valid number
- required: Alias of CRequiredValidator, ensuring the attribute is not empty
- type: Alias of CTypeValidator, ensuring the attribute is of a specific data type

- unique: Alias of CUniqueValidator, ensuring the data is unique in a database table column

- url: Alias of CUrlValidator, ensuring the data is a valid URL

As we want to make the project name attribute a required field, it looks like the required alias will meet our needs. Let's add a new rule specifying this alias as the Validator to validate our project name attribute. We'll append it to the existing rules:

```
public function rules()
    {
      // NOTE: you should only define rules for those attributes that
      // will receive user inputs.
      return array(
        array('create_user_id, update_user_id',   'numerical','integerO
nly'=>true),
        array('name', 'length', 'max'=>128),
        array('create_time, update_time', 'safe'),
        // The following rule is used by search().
        // Please remove those attributes that should not be searched.
        array('id, name, description, create_time, create_user_id,
update_time, update_user_id', 'safe', 'on'=>'search'),
        array('name', 'required'),
      );
    }
```

By saving this file and viewing the new Project form again at: `http://localhost/trackstar/index.php?r=project/create`, we see a little red asterisk next to the **Name** field. This indicates that this field is now required. Try submitting the form without this field filled in. You should see an error message indicating that the **Name** field cannot be blank, as shown in the following screenshot:

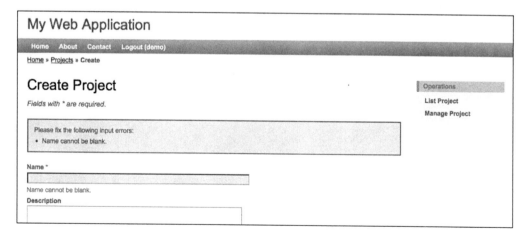

While we are making these changes, let's go ahead and make the **Description** field required as well. All we have to do is add the **Description** field to the list of fields specified in the new rule we just added, as such:

```
array('name, description', 'required'),
```

So, we see we can specify multiple fields in the attribute list by comma separating them. With this in place, you will see that our form now indicates that both the name and the description are required. Attempting to submit either one without a value will result in a form validation error.

If we had stipulated the name and description columns as NOT NULL as part of the SQL when initially creating the table, then this rule would have been autogenerated for us when we created the model class using the Gii code generation tool. It will automatically add rules based on the definitions of the columns in the table. For example, columns with NOT NULL constraints will be added as required. As another example, columns that have length restrictions, like our name column being defined as varchar(128), will have character limit rules automatically applied. We notice by taking another look at our rules() method in the Project AR class that Gii auto created the rule array('name', 'length', 'max'=>128) for us based on its column definition.

Reading the project

Viewing the detail listing of our new project: http://localhost/trackstar/index.php?r=project/view&id=4, does, basically, demonstrate the "R" in CRUD. However, to view the entire listing, we can click on the **List Project** link in the right column. This takes us back to where we started, except now we have our newly created project in the project list. So, we have the ability to retrieve a listing of all of the projects in the application, as well as view the details of each project individually.

Updating and deleting projects

Navigating back to a project details page can be done by clicking the little project **ID** link on any of the projects in the listing. Let's do this for our newly created project, which is **ID: 4** in our case. Clicking this link takes us to the project details page for this project. This page has a number of action operations in the right-hand column, as the next screenshot shows:

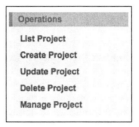

We see both of the **Update Project** and **Delete Project** links which provide us with the "U" and "D" in our CRUD operations respectively. We'll leave it up to you to verify that these links do work as expected.

Managing projects in admin mode

The last link we have not covered in the previous screenshot depicting our project operations is the **Manage Project** link. Go ahead and click on this link. It will most likely result in an authorization error, as shown in the following screenshot:

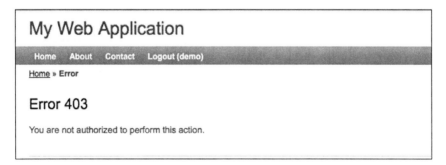

The reason for this error is that when we had to log into the application in order to create a new project, we used **demo/demo** as our **username/password** combination. The code generated by Gii restricts the access to this functionality to administrators.

An administrator in this context is simply someone who has logged in with the **username/password** combination of **admin/admin**. Go ahead and log out of the application by clicking **Logout (demo)** from the main, top, navigation. Then log in again, but this time, use these administrator credentials. Once successfully logged in as admin (you can verify this by ensuring the logout link reads **Logout (admin)**. Navigate back to a specific project listing page, for example: `http://localhost/ trackstar/index.php?r=project/view&id=4`, and try the **Manage Projects** link again .We should now see what is shown in the following screenshot:

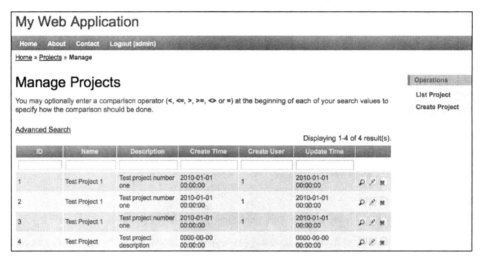

What we now see is a highly interactive version of our project listing page. It displays all the projects in an interactive data table. Each row has inline links, to view, update and delete each project. Clicking on any of the column header links sorts the project list by that column value. The little input boxes in the second row allow you to search this project list by keywords within those individual column values. The **Advanced Search** link exposes an entire search form providing the ability to specify multiple search criteria, to submit against one search. The next screenshot displays this **Advanced Search** form:

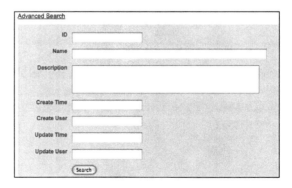

Wow! We have basically implemented all of the functionality we set out to achieve in this iteration, and haven't really had to code much of anything. In fact, with the help of Gii, we have implemented basic project searching functionality that we were not expecting to achieve. Though basic, we have a fully functional application with features specific to a project task tracking application, and have done very little coding to achieve it.

But don't hit the beach just yet. All of this scaffolding code is not really intended to fully replace application development. Rather, it is there to help support us as we work to build the real application. As we work through all the details and nuances of how the project functionality should work, we can rely on this autogenerated code to keep things moving forward. We'll keep as much of it as we can, depending on project requirements as we move forward, but this type of autogenerated code scaffolding is not intended to be a complete solution for all the functionality we will need to manage the projects in our application.

More on testing—fixtures

Before we move on to adding more functionality into our TrackStar application, we need to briefly revisit our testing configuration. As we previously discussed, our unit tests actually added new projects to our application in our development environment. Also, even after we completed our tests by deleting the row we created, the database will reuse that same project identifier on subsequent inserts. So, as we continue to run our tests, we will notice gaps in our project ID sequence (which could be confusing during normal development).

The problem is that the unit tests are run against the same database that the web form uses when creating new projects. As a result, there is potential for some issues to arise. What we need to do is to configure our tests to run against a separate, mirrored database, that is dedicated just to testing. What we also need is a way to ensure that our tests are always run in the same manner, against the same data. The former is an easy change in a configuration file, which we will make shortly. The latter is achieved through the use of **fixtures**.

A test fixture is a system state or context in which tests are run. We want to run our tests a multiple number of times, and each time they run, we want to be able to have them return repeatable results. A fixture is intended to provide a well-known and fixed environment in which to run our tests. Typically, a fixture's job is to ensure that all of the objects involved in the testing are consistently initialized to a particular state. One typical example of a fixture is the loading of a database table with a fixed and known set of data.

Fixtures in yii are PHP files that return an array specifying the initial data configuration. They are typically named the same as the database table they represent, and are located under the protected/tests/fixtures/ folder. So, to specify project fixture data, we will need to create a new file in this directory called tbl_project.php. This file holds the fixed and known set of data that will initialize our Project database table before any tests in the /tests/unit/ProjectTest.php file are run. This fixture file is specified at the top of the ProjectTest.php test file:

```
class ProjectTest extends CDbTestCase
{
  public $fixtures=array
    (
      'projects'=>'Project',
    );
}
```

Configuring the fixture manager

Setting up these types of database fixtures can be an extremely time consuming part of the testing process. Yii comes, once again, to rescue us from this tedium by the providing CdbFixtureManager class. When configured as an application component, it will provide the following functionality:

- Before all tests are run, it resets all the relevant tables to a known data state
- Before a single test is run, it can reset specified tables to a known data state
- During the execution of a test, it provides access to the rows of data that are part of the fixed data state

To use the fixture manager, we configure it in the application configuration files. This was actually already done for us when we created the initial application. If you open up the application configuration file specific to testing, protected/config/test.php, you will see the following application component defined:

```
'fixture'=>array(
'class'=>'system.test.CDbFixtureManager', ),
```

So the application has already been configured to use this fixture manager. Now we need to create a new fixture.

Creating a fixture

A fixture in Yii is implemented as a PHP file that returns an array representing the initial rows of data for a particular table. The filename is the same as the table name. By default, these fixture files are expected to be placed in the folder protected/

tests/fixtures. You can use the CDbFixtureManager::basePath property in the application configuration to customize this location if desired. Let's provide an example by creating a new fixture for our tbl_project database table. Create a new file, protected/tests/fixtures/tbl_project.php, with the following contents:

```php
<?php

return array(
    'project1'=>array(
        'name' => 'Test Project 1',
        'description' => 'This is test project 1',
        'create_time' => '',
        'create_user_id' => '',
        'update_time' => '',
        'update_user_id' => '',
    ),
    'project2'=>array(
        'name' => 'Test Project 2',
        'description' => 'This is test project 2',
        'create_time' => '',
        'create_user_id' => '',
        'update_time' => '',
        'update_user_id' => '',
    ),
    'project3'=>array(
        'name' => 'Test Project 3',
        'description' => 'This is test project 3',
        'create_time' => '',
        'create_user_id' => '',
        'update_time' => '',                    'update_user_id' => '',
    ),
);
```

As we can see, our fixture array has keys that represent entries in our table. The value of these keys are themselves arrays with a key=>value pair for each column in the table. We have added three rows, but you can add as many as you like. For simplicity, we have only filled out the values we have previously stipulated cannot be NULL, that is, the name and description fields. This will be enough data for us to demonstrate the use of fixtures.

You may have also noticed that the id column was not specified in the previous fixture data. This column is defined to be an auto-increment field. The value for this column will be handled by the database itself when we insert new rows.

Configuring this fixture for use

We still need to tell our unit tests to actually use this fixture we just created. We do this in the unit test file. In this case, we will need to add our fixture declaration to the top of our test file `protected/tests/unit/ProjectTest.php` as such:

```php
<?php
class ProjectTest extends CDbTestCase
{
  public $fixtures=array
    (
       'projects'=>'Project',
    );
}
```

So, what we have done is specified the `$fixtures` member variable to be an array that specifies which fixtures will be used by this test. The array represents a mapping from fixture names that will be used in the tests to model class names or fixture table names (for example, from fixture name `projects` to model class `Project`). When using a model class name, as in this case, the underlying tables that correspond to the model class will be considered as fixture tables. As we described earlier, it is the fixture manager that will manage these underlying tables and reset the data to some known state each time a test method is executed.

If you need to use a fixture for a table that is not represented by an AR class, you need to prefix table name with a colon (for example, `:tbl_project`) to differentiate it from the model class name.

Fixture names allow us to access the fixture data in test methods in a convenient way. So, for example, now that we have defined this in our `ProjectTest` class, we can access our fixture data in the following ways:

```php
// return all rows in the 'Project' fixture table
$projects = $this->projects;
// return the row whose alias is 'project1' in the `Project` fixture
table
$projectOne = $this->projects['project1'];
// If our fixture is associated with an active record, return the AR
instance representing
// the 'project1' fixture data row
$project = $this->projects('project1');
```

We'll provide more concrete examples when we change some of our actual unit tests to take advantage of this fixture data. First we need to make another change to our testing environment.

Specifying a test database

As we previously mentioned, we need to separate our development database from our testing database so that our testing will not continue to interfere with our development.

The test specific application configuration file provides a place for us to do just that. We need to create another new database, call it `trackstar_test`. We also need to replicate the schema we have in our current `trackstar_dev` database. This is easy as we just have the one `tbl_project` table at the moment. Please proceed as you did in *Chapter 4* to create this new database with the `tbl_project` table. Once created, we can add the database connection information as an application component to our test specific configuration file located at `protected/config/test.php`. You can copy the db component from your `main.php` `config` file that we added back in *Chapter 4*. For MySQL users, like us, we add the following highlighted code to our test `config` file:

```
return CMap::mergeArray(
    require(dirname(__FILE__).'/main.php'),
    array(
        'components'=>array(
            'fixture'=>array(
                'class'=>'system.test.CDbFixtureManager',
            ),
            'db'=>array(
                'connectionString' =>
'mysql:host=localhost;dbname=trackstar_test',
                'emulatePrepare' => true,
                'username' => '[your db username]',
                'password' => '[your db password]',
                'charset' => 'utf8',
            ),
        ),
    )
);
```

When we run our tests, this test `config` is loaded, rather than the main `config` file. This file actually merges the array from the main `config` file with the array defined in this test config file. If the same components or `config` values are defined in both, the values in the test file will take precedence. Now when we run our unit tests, we will be manipulating this test database rather than our development one, and won't run the risk of having our test suite negatively impact our development progress.

Using fixtures

Now that we have adjusted our test environment to use a separate database, we should take advantage of what fixtures have to offer. When we initially wrote the unit tests for the CRUD operations against the Project AR class, we put all of the `Create`, `Read`, `Update` and `Delete` tests all into one test method we called `testCRUD()`. This has the disadvantage of lumping all these discrete tests into one big test. If the first `create` fails, then the execution of that entire test method stops, and the tests for `Read`, `Update` and `Delete` are never even run. Ideally, we should separate these so that one test does not have to depend on the others. The main reason we wrote the test this way was to avoid the need to ensure the order in which the test methods must run. If we separated the create test from the read test, there is a potential for the read method to be executed prior to the create method, which would result in a failed test, as no rows would have been created to read back. However, we can avoid this issue if we use the fixture data.

Now that our new test environment configured to use a new dedicated database, and our fixture data defined, we can decouple our CRUD unit tests. This will give us some concrete examples of how to use our fixture data.

Let's start with `Read`. Open up the `ProjectTest.php` unit test file and add the following test method:

```
public function testRead()
{
$retrievedProject = $this->projects('project1');
$this->assertTrue($retrievedProject instanceof Project);
$this->assertEquals('Test Project 1',$retrievedProject->name);
}
```

We know that before this test is run, the fixture manger will reset the `tbl_project` table, in the `trackstar_test` database, to the known state defined by the fixture data. Here, we are simply reading back the first row of data, referencing the row alias, `project1`, which returns a Project AR instance based on that first row of data defined in our `protected/tests/fixtures/tbl_project.php` fixture file. We then test that the returned entity is an instance of Project and test to make sure its name is what we established in the fixture data.

We can similarly add separate `testCreate()`, `testUpdate()`, and `testDelete()` methods. The entire test file after making the needed change to decouple all of these CRUD tests into separate methods is shown below:

```
<?php

class ProjectTest extends CDbTestCase
{
```

```
    public $fixtures=array(
    'projects'=>'Project',
);
    public function testCreate()
{
    //CREATE a new Project
    $newProject=new Project;
    $newProjectName = 'Test Project Creation';
    $newProject->setAttributes(array(
    'name' => $newProjectName,
    'description' => 'This is a test for new project creation',
    'createTime' => '2009-09-09 00:00:00',
    'createUser' => '1',
    'updateTime' => '2009-09-09 00:00:00',
    'updateUser' => '1',
    )
);
    $this->assertTrue($newProject->save(false));
    //READ back the newly created Project to ensure the creation
    worked
    $retrievedProject=Project::model()->findByPk($newProject->id);
    $this->assertTrue($retrievedProject instanceof Project);
    $this->assertEquals($newProjectName,$retrievedProject->name);
}
    public function testRead()
{
    $retrievedProject = $this->projects('project1');
    $this->assertTrue($retrievedProject instanceof Project);
    $this->assertEquals('Test Project 1',$retrievedProject->name);
}
    public function testUpdate()
{
    $project = $this->projects('project2');
    $updatedProjectName = 'Updated Test Project 2';
    $project->name = $updatedProjectName;
    $this->assertTrue($project->save(false));
    //read back the record again to ensure the update worked
    $updatedProject=Project::model()->findByPk($project->id);
    $this->assertTrue($updatedProject instanceof Project);
    $this->assertEquals($updatedProjectName,$updatedProject->name);
}
    public function testDelete()
{
    $project = $this->projects('project2');
    $savedProjectId = $project->id;
    $this->assertTrue($project->delete());
    $deletedProject=Project::model()->findByPk($savedProjectId);
    $this->assertEquals(NULL,$deletedProject);
}
}
```

Now, if any one of these fails when we run the tests, the rest will still execute providing us more granular feedback on each distinct operation.

Summary

Even though we did not do a ton of actual coding in this chapter, we accomplished quite a lot. We created a new database table, which allowed us to see Yii AR in action. We used the Gii code generation tool to first create an AR class to wrap our tbl_project database table. We then wrote tests to try out this new class and got a lot of exposure to using these AR class types.

We then demonstrated how to use the Gii code generation tool to generate actual CRUD functionality in the Web application. With this amazing tool, we achieved most of application functionality that we outlined for this iteration. We made one small change to enforce the project name and description on form submission, which showcased the form validation functionality.

Finally, we introduced testing fixtures in Yii, and made some adjustments to our testing environment to take advantage of this feature.

In the next iteration, we will build on what we have learned here and dive more deeply into Active Record in Yii as we introduce related entities in our data model.

6

Iteration 3: Adding Tasks

In the previous iteration, we delivered the basic functionality around the project entity. The project is the foundation of the TrackStar application. However, projects by themselves are not very useful. Projects are the basic containers of the issues we want this application to manage. As managing project issues is the main purpose of this application, we want to spend the next iteration adding some basic issue management functionality.

Iteration planning

We already have the ability to create and list projects, but these projects are not yet able to contain anything. At the end of this iteration, we want the application to expose all CRUD operations on the project issues or tasks (we tend to use the terms *issue* and *task* interchangeably, but in our data model, a task will actually be just one type of issue). We also want to restrict all CRUD operations on issues to be within the context of a specific Project. That is, issues belong to projects. The user must have selected an existing project to work within prior to being able to perform any CRUD operations on the project issues.

In order to achieve the preceding outlined goals, we need to identify all the granular items that we will work on within this iteration. The following list outlines these items:

- Design the database schema, and build the objects to support project issues
- Create the Yii model classes that allow the application to easily interact with the database table(s) that we created
- Create the controller class that will house the functionality to allow us to:
  - Create new issues
  - Fetch a list of existing issues within a project from the database
  - Update/edit existing issues
  - Delete existing issues
- Create views to render user interfaces for these (preceding) actions

This is enough information to allow us to get started. After we run our tests, we'll get started on making the necessary database changes.

Running the test suite

It is always a good idea to run our existing test suite prior to diving into development. Our test suite grew a little with the previous iteration's work. We now have tests for our db connection as well as all CRUD operations for projects. Once again, we'll run them all at once. Navigate to the test folder, /protected/tests/ unit, and run all unit tests:

```
%phpunit unit/
PHPUnit 3.3.17 by Sebastian Bergmann.

. . . . .
Time: 0 seconds
OK (5 tests, 11 assertions)
```

Everything passes. Let's start making some changes.

Designing the schema

Back in *Chapter 3,The TrackStar Application* we proposed some initial ideas about the `issue` entity. We proposed it have a *type*, an *owner*, a *requester*, a *status*, and a *description*. We also mentioned when we created the `tbl_project` table that we would be adding basic audit history information to each table we create to track the dates, times and users who update tables. Nothing has changed in the requirements that would alter this approach, so we can move ahead with that initial proposal. However, types, owners, requesters, and statuses are themselves, their own entities. To keep our model flexible and extensible, we'll model some of these separately. Owners and requesters are both users of the system, and will be referenced to the rows in a table called `tbl_user`. We have already introduced the idea of a user in the `tbl_project` table, as we added the columns `create_user_id` and `update_user_id` to track the identification of the user who initially created the project, as well as, the user who was responsible for last updating the project details. Even though we have not formally introduced that table yet, these fields were modeled to be foreign keys to another table in the database for storing the user data table. The `owner_id` and `requestor_id` in the our `tbl_issue` table will also be foreign keys that relate back to the `tbl_user` table.

We could similarly model the `type` and `status` attributes in the same manner. However, until our requirements demand this extra complexity in the model, we can keep things simple. The `type` and `status` columns in the `tbl_issue` table will remain integer values that map to named types and statuses. Instead of complicating our model by using separate tables, we will model these as basic class constant (`const`) values within the `AR model` class we create for the `issue` entity. Don't worry if all of this is a little fuzzy, it will make more sense in the coming sections.

Defining some relationships

As we are going to be introduced to the `tbl_user` table, we need to go back and define the relationship between users and projects. Back when we introduced the `TrackStar` application in *Chapter 3*, we specified that users (we called them project members) would be associated with one or more projects. We also mentioned that projects can also have many (zero or more) users. As projects can have many users, and users can be associated with many projects, we call this a *many-to-many* relationship between projects and users. The easiest way to model a many-to-many relationship in a relational database is to use an association or assignment table. So, we need to add this table to our model as well.

The following figure outlines a basic entity relationship we need to model among users, projects, and issues. Projects can have zero to many users. A user needs to be associated with at least one project, but can also be associated with many. Issues belong to one and only one project, while projects can have zero to many issues. Finally, an issue is assigned to (or requested by) a single user.

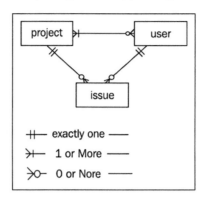

Building the database and the relationships

So, we need to create three new tables: `tbl_issue`, `tbl_user`, and our association table, `tbl_project_user_assignment`. For your convenience we have provided the basic **Data Definition Language (DDL)** statements for the tables as well as their relationships. We also provided a little *seed* data for the users table, so we have a couple of rows populated for immediate use because basic user management is not a part of this iteration. Please proceed as you have done in previous iterations to create the following tables and relationships. The exact syntax of the following statements assumes a MySQL database:

```
CREATE TABLE IF NOT EXISTS 'tbl_issue'
(
'id' INTEGER NOT NULL PRIMARY KEY AUTO_INCREMENT,
'name' varchar(256) NOT NULL,
'description' varchar(2000),
'project_id' INTEGER,
'type_id' INTEGER,
'status_id' INTEGER,
'owner_id' INTEGER,
'requester_id' INTEGER,
'create_time' DATETIME,
'create_user_id' INTEGER,
'update_time' DATETIME,
'update_user_id' INTEGER
) ENGINE = InnoDB
;
```

```
CREATE TABLE IF NOT EXISTS 'tbl_user'
(
  'id' INTEGER NOT NULL PRIMARY KEY AUTO_INCREMENT,
  'email' Varchar(256) NOT NULL,
  'username' Varchar(256),
  'password' Varchar(256),
  'last_login_time' Datetime,
  'create_time' DATETIME,
  'create_user_id' INTEGER,
  'update_time' DATETIME,
  'update_user_id' INTEGER
) ENGINE = InnoDB
;

CREATE TABLE IF NOT EXISTS 'tbl_project_user_assignment'
(
  'project_id' Int(11) NOT NULL,
  'user_id' Int(11) NOT NULL,
  'create_time' DATETIME,
  'create_user_id' INTEGER,
  'update_time' DATETIME,
  'update_user_id' INTEGER,
 PRIMARY KEY ('project_id','user_id')
) ENGINE = InnoDB
;

-- The Relationships
ALTER TABLE 'tbl_issue' ADD CONSTRAINT 'FK_issue_project' FOREIGN KEY
('project_id') REFERENCES 'tbl_project' ('id') ON DELETE CASCADE ON
UPDATE RESTRICT;

ALTER TABLE 'tbl_issue' ADD CONSTRAINT 'FK_issue_owner' FOREIGN KEY
('owner_id') REFERENCES 'tbl_user' ('id') ON DELETE CASCADE ON UPDATE
RESTRICT;

ALTER TABLE 'tbl_issue' ADD CONSTRAINT 'FK_issue_requester' FOREIGN
KEY ('requester_id') REFERENCES 'tbl_user' ('id') ON DELETE CASCADE ON
UPDATE RESTRICT;

ALTER TABLE 'tbl_project_user_assignment' ADD CONSTRAINT 'FK_project_
user' FOREIGN KEY ('project_id') REFERENCES 'tbl_project' ('id') ON
DELETE CASCADE ON UPDATE RESTRICT;

ALTER TABLE 'tbl_project_user_assignment' ADD CONSTRAINT 'FK_user_
project' FOREIGN KEY ('user_id') REFERENCES 'tbl_user' ('id') ON
DELETE CASCADE ON UPDATE RESTRICT;

-- Insert some seed data so we can just begin using the database
INSERT INTO 'tbl_user'
  ('email', 'username', 'password')
VALUES
  ('test1@notanaddress.com','Test_User_One', MD5('test1')),
  ('test2@notanaddress.com','Test_User_Two', MD5('test2'))
;
```

Creating the Active Record model classes

Now that we have these tables created, we need to create the Yii AR model classes to allow us to easily interact with these tables within the application. We did this when creating the `Project.php` model class in *Chapter 5, Iteration 2: Project CRUD* using the Gii code generation tool. We'll remind you of the steps again here, but spare you of all the screenshots. Please refer back to *Chapter 5* for a more detailed walkthrough of using the Gii tool.

Creating the Issue model class

Navigate to the Gii tool via `http://localhost/trackstar/index.php?r=gii`, and choose the **Model Generator** link. Leave the table prefix as **tbl_**. Fill in the **Table Name** field as **tbl_issue**, which will auto-populate the **Model Class** field as **Issue**.

Once the form is filled out, click the **Preview** button to get a link to a popup that will show you all of the code about to be generated. Then click the **Generate** button to actually create the new **Issue.php** model class in the /protected/models/ folder. The full listing of the generated code is as follows:

```php
<?php

/**
 * This is the model class for table "tbl_issue".
 */
class Issue extends CActiveRecord
{
  /**
   * The followings are the available columns in table 'tbl_issue':
   * @var integer $id
   * @var string $name
   * @var string $description
   * @var integer $project_id
   * @var integer $type_id
   * @var integer $status_id
   * @var integer $owner_id
   * @var integer $requester_id
   * @var string $create_time
   * @var integer $create_user_id
   * @var string $update_time
   * @var integer $update_user_id
   */

  /**
   * Returns the static model of the specified AR class.
   * @return Issue the static model class
```

```php
     */
    public static function model($className=__CLASS__)
    {
      return parent::model($className);
    }

    /**
     * @return string the associated database table name
     */
    public function tableName()
    {
      return 'tbl_issue';
    }

    /**
     * @return array validation rules for model attributes.
     */
    public function rules()
    {
      // NOTE: you should only define rules for those attributes that
      // will receive user inputs.
      return array(
        array('name', 'required'),
        array('project_id, type_id, status_id, owner_id, requester_id,
create_user_id, update_user_id', 'numerical', 'integerOnly'=>true),
        array('name', 'length', 'max'=>256),
        array('description', 'length', 'max'=>2000),
        array('create_time, update_time', 'safe'),
        // The following rule is used by search().
        // Please remove those attributes that should not be searched.
        array('id, name, description, project_id, type_id, status_id,
owner_id, requester_id, create_time, create_user_id, update_time,
update_user_id', 'safe', 'on'=>'search'),
      );
    }

    /**
     * @return array relational rules.
     */
    public function relations()
    {
      // NOTE: you may need to adjust the relation name and the related
      // class name for the relations automatically generated below.
      return array(
        'owner' => array(self::BELONGS_TO, 'User', 'owner_id'),
        'project' => array(self::BELONGS_TO, 'Project', 'project_id'),
        'requester' => array(self::BELONGS_TO, 'User', 'requester_id'),
      );
    }

    /**
     * @return array customized attribute labels (name=>label)
```

```php
    */
    public function attributeLabels()
    {
      return array(
        'id' => 'ID',
        'name' => 'Name',
        'description' => 'Description',
        'project_id' => 'Project',
        'type_id' => 'Type',
        'status_id' => 'Status',
        'owner_id' => 'Owner',
        'requester_id' => 'Requester',
        'create_time' => 'Create Time',
        'create_user_id' => 'Create User',
        'update_time' => 'Update Time',
        'update_user_id' => 'Update User',
      );
    }

    /**
     * Retrieves a list of models based on the current search/filter
    conditions.
     * @return CActiveDataProvider the data provider that can return the
    models based on the search/filter conditions.
     */
    public function search()
    {
      // Warning: Please modify the following code to remove attributes
    that
      // should not be searched.

      $criteria=new CDbCriteria;

      $criteria->compare('id',$this->id);

      $criteria->compare('name',$this->name,true);

      $criteria->compare('description',$this->description,true);

      $criteria->compare('project_id',$this->project_id);

      $criteria->compare('type_id',$this->type_id);

      $criteria->compare('status_id',$this->status_id);

      $criteria->compare('owner_id',$this->owner_id);

      $criteria->compare('requester_id',$this->requester_id);

      $criteria->compare('create_time',$this->create_time,true);

      $criteria->compare('create_user_id',$this->create_user_id);

      $criteria->compare('update_time',$this->update_time,true);

      $criteria->compare('update_user_id',$this->update_user_id);
```

```
        return new CActiveDataProvider(get_class($this), array(
            'criteria'=>$criteria,
        ));
    }
}
```

Creating the User model class

This is probably getting to be old-hat for you at this point, so we are going to leave the creation of the User AR class as an exercise for you. This particular class becomes much more important in the next chapter, when we dive into user authentication and authorization.

What about the AR class for the `tbl_project_user_assignment` **table?**

Although one could create an AR class for this table, it is not necessary. The AR model provides an **Object Relational Mapping (ORM)** layer to our application to help us work easily with our domain objects. However, `ProjectUserAssignment` is not a domain object of our application. It is simply a construct in a relational database to help us model and manage the many-to-many relationship between projects and users. Maintaining a separate AR class to handle the management of this table is extra complexity, and we can avoid this for the time being. We will avoid the additional maintenance and slight performance overhead by managing the inserts, updates, and deletes on this table using Yii's DAO directly.

Creating the Issue CRUD operations

Now that we have our AR classes in place, we can turn to building the functionality required to manage our project issues. As the CRUD operations on project issues are the main goal of this iteration, we'll again lean on the Gii code generation tool to help create the basics of this functionality. We did this in detail for the projects in *Chapter 5*. We'll remind you of the basic steps for issues again here.

Navigate to the Gii generator menu at `http://localhost/trackstar/index.php?r=gii`, and choose the **Crud Generator** link. Fill out the form using **Issue** as the value for the **Model Class** field. This will auto-populate the **Controller ID** to also be **Issue**. The **Base Controller Class** and **Code Template** fields can remain their predefined default values. Click the **Preview** button to get a list of all of the files that the Gii tool is proposing to create. The following screenshot shows this list of files:

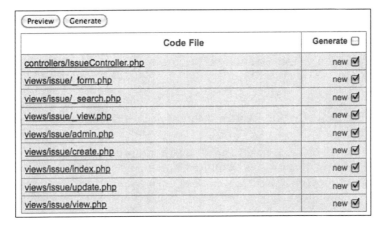

You can click each individual link to preview the code to be generated. Once satisfied, click the **Generate** button to have all of these files created. You should receive the following success message:

Using the Issue CRUD operations

Let's try this out. Either click the **try it now** link shown in the previous screenshot or simply navigate to `http://localhost/trackstar/index.php?r=issue`. You should be presented with something similar to what is shown in the following screenshot:

Creating a new Issue

As we have not added any new issues as yet, there are none to list. So, let's create a new one. Click on the **Create Issue** link (if this takes you to the login page, then log in using either **demo/demo** or **admin/admin**), you should now see a new issue input form similar to what is shown in the following screenshot:

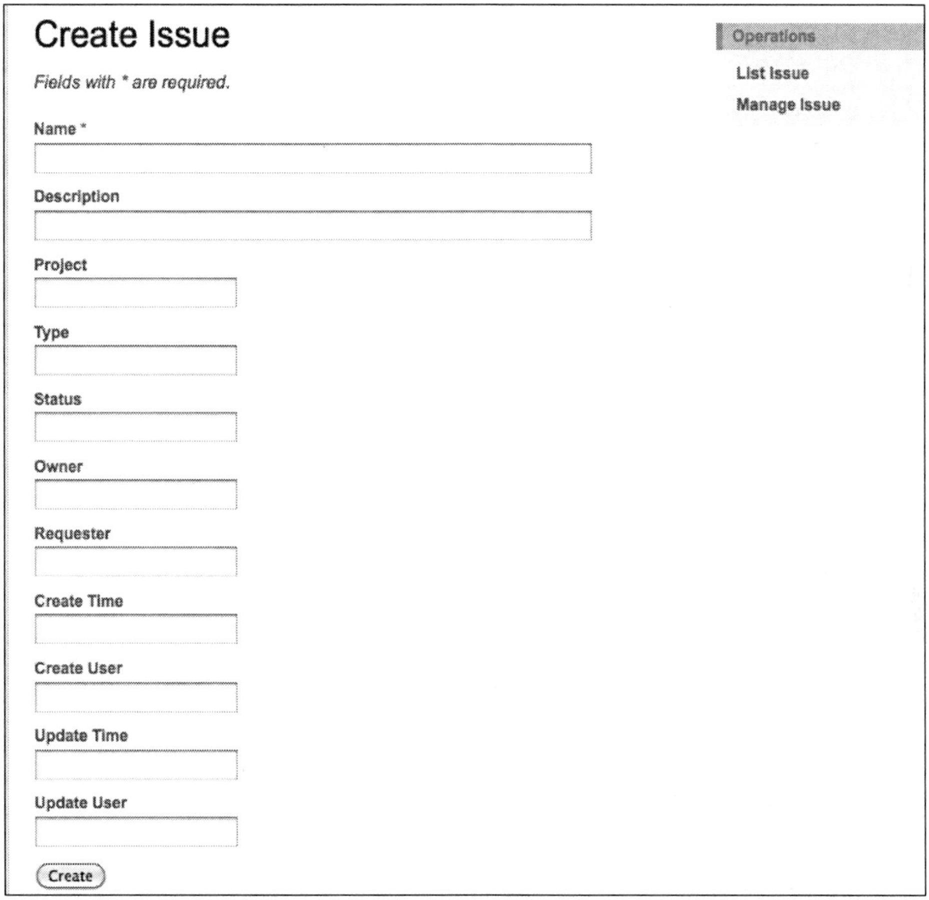

Create Issue

*Fields with * are required.*

Operations

List Issue

Manage Issue

Name *

Description

Project

Type

Status

Owner

Requester

Create Time

Create User

Update Time

Update User

(Create)

When looking at this input form, we notice that it has an input field for every column in the database table, just as it is defined in the database table. However, as we know from when we designed our schema and built our tables, some of these fields are not direct input fields, but rather represent relationships to other entities. For example, rather than having a **Type** free-form input text field on this form, we should use a drop-down input form field that is populated with choices of allowed issue types. A similar argument could be made for the **Status** field. The **Owner** and **Requester** fields should also be drop-downs exposing choices of the names of users who have been assigned to work on the project under which the issue resides. Also all issue management should be taking place within the context of a specific project. Therefore, the **Project** field should not even be a part of this form at all. Lastly, the **Create Time**, **Create User**, **Update Time**, and **Update User** fields are all values that should be calculated and determined once the form is submitted, and should not be available to the user to directly manipulate.

Okay, so we have identified a number of corrections we would like to make on this initial input form. As we mentioned in *Chapter 5*, the auto-created CRUD *scaffolding* code that is generated by the Gii tool is just the starting point. Rarely is it enough on its own to meet all the specific functionality needs of an application. We have certainly identified many changes we need to make to this issue creation process. We'll take them on, one at a time.

Adding the types drop-down menu

We'll start with adding a dropdown menu for the issue types.

Issues have just the following three types:

- *Bugs*
- *Features*
- *Tasks*

What we would like to see when creating a new issue is a drop-down menu input type form field with these three choices. We will achieve this by having the Issue model class itself provide a list of its available types. As you might have guessed, we'll add this new functionality to the Issue model AR class by first writing a test.

As you remember, back in *Chapter 5*, we added a new database to run our tests against called `trackstar_test`. We did this to ensure our testing environment would not have an adverse impact on our development environment. So please make sure that you have updated your test database with the new tables, `tbl_issue` and `tbl_user`, which we created earlier.

Getting the test in the "Red"

As we know, the first step in our TDD process is to quickly write a test that fails. Create a new unit test file `protected/tests/unit/IssueTest.php` and add to it the following:

```
public function testGetTypes()
{
  $options = Issue::model()->typeOptions;
  $this->assertTrue(is_array($options));
}
```

Now toggle to the command line and run the test from with the `/protected/tests` folder

```
phpunit unit/IssueTest.php
PHPUnit 3.3.17 by Sebastian Bergmann.
.E
Time: 0 seconds
There was 1 error:
1) testGetTypes(IssueTest)
CException: Property "Issue.typeOptions" is not defined.
/YiiRoot/framework/base/CComponent.php:131
/YiiRoot/yii-read-only/framework/db/ar/CActiveRecord.php:107
/Webroot/tasctrak/protected/tests/unit/IssueTest.php:6

FAILURES!
Tests: 1, Assertions: 0, Errors: 1.
```

Okay, so we have accomplished the first step in TDD (that is, quickly writing a test that fails). The test fails for obvious reasons. There is no method `Issue::typeOptions()` in the model class. We need to add one.

Moving From "Red" To "Green"

Now open the AR model class, in the `protected/models/Issue.php` folder, and add the following method to the class:

```
/**
 * @return array issue type names indexed by type IDs
 */
public function getTypeOptions()
{
  return array();
}
```

We have added a simple method, named appropriately, that returns an array type (albeit still empty at the moment).

Now if we run our test again:

```
phpunit unit/IssueTest.php
PHPUnit 3.3.17 by Sebastian Bergmann.

..

Time: 0 seconds
OK (1 tests, 1 assertion)
```

 It should be noted that Yii Framework base classes make use of the PHP __get *magic* function. This allows us in our child classes to write methods such as getTypeOptions(), and yet reference those methods like class properties using >typeOptions syntax.

So now our test will pass, and we are in the "green". This is great, but we don't actually have any values returned yet. We certainly can't add our drop-down menu based on this empty array. For our basic three issue types, we are going to use class constants to map these to integer values, and then we will use our getTypeOptions() method to return user friendly descriptions to be used in the drop-down menu.

Moving Back To "Red"

Before adding this to the Issue class, let's get our test to fail again. Let's add one more assertion that interrogates the returned array and verifies that its contents are as expected. We'll test to ensure that the returned array has three elements, and that these values correspond to our issue types: Bug, Feature, and Task. Alter the test to be:

```
public function testGetTypes()
{
  $options = Issue::model()->typeOptions;
  $this->assertTrue(is_array($options));
  $this->assertTrue(3 == count($options));
$this->assertTrue(in_array('Bug', $options));
  $this->assertTrue(in_array('Feature', $options));
  $this->assertTrue(in_array('Task', $options));
}
```

As the getTypeOptions() method still returns a blank array, our assertions are sure to fail. So, we are back in the red. Let's add the code to the Issue.php class to get these new assertions to pass.

Getting back to "Green" once again

At the top of the Issue class, add the following three constant definitions:

```
const TYPE_BUG=0;
const TYPE_FEATURE=1;
const TYPE_TASK=2;
```

Then, alter the `Issue::getTypeOptions()` method to return an array based on these defined constants:

```
public function getTypeOptions()
{
  return array(
    self::TYPE_BUG=>'Bug',
    self::TYPE_FEATURE=>'Feature',
    self::TYPE_TASK=>'Task',
  );
}
```

Now if we run our tests again, all five of our assertions pass, and we are back in the green.

```
phpunit unit/IssueTest.php

PHPUnit 3.3.17 by Sebastian Bergmann.

..

Time: 0 seconds

OK (1 tests, 5 assertions)
```

We now have our model class returning our issue types as needed, but we don't yet have a drop-down field in the input form that takes advantage of these values. Let's add that now.

Adding the issue type dropdown

Open up the file containing the new issue creation form, `protected/views/issue/_ form.php`, and find the lines that correspond to the **Type** field on the form:

```
<div class="row">
  <?php echo $form->labelEx($model,'type_id'); ?>
  <?php echo $form->textField($model,'type_id'); ?>
  <?php echo $form->error($model,'type_id'); ?>
</div>
```

These lines need a little clarification. In order to understand this, we need to refer to some code at the top of the `_form.php` file which is as follows:

```php
<?php $form=$this->beginWidget('CActiveForm', array(
    'id'=>'issue-form',
    'enableAjaxValidation'=>false,
)); ?>
```

This is defining the `$form` variable using the CActiveForm widget in Yii. *Widgets* are going to be covered in much more detail in *Chapter 9*. For now, we can comprehend this code by better understanding CActiveForm. It can be thought of as a `helper` class that provides a set of methods to help us to create a data entry form that is associated with a data model class. In this case, it is represented by the Issue model class.

To fully understand the variables in our `view` file, let's also review our controller code that is rendering the `view` file(s). As you recall, one way to pass data from the controller to the view is by explicitly declaring an array, the keys of which will be the names of available variables in the `view` files. As this is the `create` action for a new issue, the `controller` method rendering the form is `IssueController::actionCreate()`. This method is listed as follows:

```php
public function actionCreate()
{
    $model=new Issue;

    // Uncomment the following line if AJAX validation is needed
    // $this->performAjaxValidation($model);

    if(isset($_POST['Issue']))
    {
        $model->attributes=$_POST['Issue'];
        if($model->save())
        $this->redirect(array('view','id'=>$model->id));
    }

    $this->render('create',array(
        'model'=>$model,
    ));
}
```

Here, we see that when the view is being rendered, it is being passed an instance of the Issue model class, that will be available in a variable called `$model`.

Okay, so now let's go back to the code that is responsible for rendering the **Type** field on the create new issue entry form. The first line is:

```
$form->labelEx($model,'type_id');
```

This line is using the `CActiveForm::labelEx()` method to render an HTML label for a the Issue model attribute, `type_id`. It takes in an instance of the model class, and the corresponding model attribute for which we want a label generated. The model class' `Issue::attributeLabels()` method will be used to determine the label. If we take a look at this method, we see that the attribute `type_id` is mapped to a label of `Type`, which is exactly what we see rendered as the label to this form field

```php
public function attributeLabels()
  {
    return array(
      'id' => 'ID',
      'name' => 'Name',
      'description' => 'Description',
      'project_id' => 'Project',
      'type_id' => 'Type',
      'status_id' => 'Status',
      'owner_id' => 'Owner',
      'requester_id' => 'Requester',
      'create_time' => 'Create Time',
      'create_user_id' => 'Create User',
      'update_time' => 'Update Time',
      'update_user_id' => 'Update User',
    );
  }
```

The next line of code is as follows:

```php
<?php echo $form->textField($model,'type_id'); ?>
```

It uses the `CActiveForm::textField()` method to render a text input field for our Issue model attribute, `type_id`. Any of the validation rules defined for `type_id` in the model class `Issue::rules()` method will be applied as form validation rules to this input form.

The final line of code is as follows:

```php
<?php echo $form->error($model,'type_id'); ?>
```

It uses the `CActiveForm::error()` method to render any validation errors associated with the specific `type_id` attribute of the Issue model class on submission. Used in this way, the error message will display directly below the field.

You can try out this validation with the **Type** field. As the `type_id` column is defined as an integer type in our MySQL schema definition, the Gii generated `Issue model` class has a validation rule in the `Issue::rules()` method to enforce this constraint:

```
public function rules()
{
    // NOTE: you should only define rules for those attributes that
    // will receive user inputs.
    return array(
        array('name', 'required'),
        array('project_id, type_id, status_id, owner_id, requester_id,
create_user_id, update_user_id', 'numerical', 'integerOnly'=>true),
```

So, if we attempt to submit a string value in our **Type** form field, we will receive an inline error, right under the field, as depicted in the following screenshot:

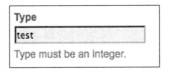

Now that we understand exactly what we have , we are in a better position to change it. What we need to do is change this field from a free-form text input field to a drop-down entry type. It probably comes as little surprise that the `CActiveForm` class has a `dropDownList()` method that will generate a drop-down list for a model attribute. So, let's replace the line that calls `$form->textField`, with the following:

```
<?php echo $form->dropDownList($model,'type_id', $model-
>getTypeOptions()); ?>
```

This still takes in the same model as the first argument and the model attribute as the second. The third argument specifies the list of drop-down choices. This should be an array of `value=>display` pairs. We already created our `getTypeOptions()` method in the `Issue model` class to return an array of this format, so we can use it directly. Save your work and look again at our issue input form. You should see a nice drop-down menu of issue type choices in place of the free-form text field, as displayed in the following screenshot:

Adding the status drop-down menu: Do it yourself

We are going to take the same approach for the issue status. As mentioned back in *Chapter 3* when we introduced the application, issues can be in one of three statuses:

- Not yet started
- Started
- Finished

We are going to leave the implementation of the status dropdown to the reader. After following the same approach we took for the types (and we hope you take a test-first approach), and both the **Type** and **Status** form field should be dropdown lists. The form should look similar to what is shown in the following screenshot:

Fixing the owner and requester fields

Another problem that we previously noticed with the issue creation form is that the **Owner** and **Requester** fields were also free-form input text fields. However, we know these are integer values in the issue table that hold foreign key identifiers to the `tbl_user` table. So, we also need to add drop-down fields for these fields. We won't take the exact same approach we took for the `Type` and `Status` attributes, as issue owners and requesters need to be taken from the `tbl_user` table. To complicate things a bit further, because not every user in the system will be associated with the project under which the issue resides, these cannot be dropdowns populated with data taken from the entire `tbl_user` table. We need to restrict the list to just those users associated with this project.

This brings up another thing we need to address. As mentioned in the *Iteration planning* section, we need to manage our issues within the context of a specific project. That is, a specific project should be chosen before you are even able to view the form for creating a new issue. Currently, our application functionality does not enforce this workflow.

Let's address these issues in turn. First we will alter the application to enforce a valid project that should be identified first, prior to using any functionality to manage the issues associated with that project. Once a project is chosen, we'll make sure both our **Owner** and **Requester** dropdown choices are restricted to only users that are associated with that project.

Enforcing a project context

We want to ensure a valid project context is present before we allow any issue-related functionality. To do this, we are going to implement what is called a **filter**. A filter in Yii is bit of code that is configured to be executed either before or after a controller action is executed. One common example is if we want to ensure a user is logged in prior to executing a controller action method, then we could write a simple access filter that would check this requirement before the action is executed. Another example is if we want to perform some extra logging or other auditing logic after an action has executed. We could write a simple audit filter to provide this post-action processing.

In this case, we want to ensure a valid project has been chosen prior to creating a new issue. So, we'll add a project filter to our `IssueController` class to accomplish this.

Implementing a filter

A filter can be defined as a controller class method or it can be a separate class. When using the simple method approach, the method name must begin with word `filter` and have a specific signature. For example, if we were going to create a `filter` method called `SomeMethodName`, our full filter method would look like:

```
public function filterSomeMethodName($filterChain)
{
    ...
}
```

The other approach is to write a separate class to perform the filter logic. When using the separate class approach, the class must extend `CFilter` and then override at least one of the `preFilter()` or `postFilter()` methods depending on whether the logic should be executed before the action is invoked, or after.

Adding a filter

So, let's add a filter to our `IssueController` class to handle the valid project. We'll take the simplest approach for now, and add a method that begins with the word `filter` directly to the class. As the invocation of this method is done by the Yii Framework itself, it is hard for us to take a test-first approach with this implementation. We'll break from our preferred approach a little bit in this case, and add this method to the `IssueCcontroller` without first writing a test.

Open up `protected/controllers/IssueController.php` and add the following method to the bottom of the class:

```
public function filterProjectContext($filterChain)
{
    $filterChain->run();
}
```

Okay, we now have a filter defined, but it does not do much yet. It simply executes `$filterChain->run()`, which continues the filtering process and allows execution of the action methods that are being filtered by this method. This brings up another point. How do we define for which action methods we should use this filter?

Specifying the filtered actions

`CController`, the Yii Framework base class for our controller classes has a `filters()` method that needs to be overridden in order to specify the actions on which to apply filters. In fact, this method has already been overridden in our `IssueController` class. This was done for us when we used the Gii tool to autogenerate this class. It already added a simple `accessControl` filter, which is defined in the `CController` base class, to handle some basic authorization to ensure that the user has sufficient permission to perform certain actions. We'll be covering user authentication and authorization in the next chapter. For now, we just need to add to this filter configuration array. To specify that our new filter should apply to the `create` action, alter the `IssueController::filters()` method by adding the following highlighted code :

```
/**
 * @return array action filters
 */
public function filters()
{
  return array(
    'accessControl', // perform access control for CRUD operations
    'projectContext + create', //check to ensure valid project context
  );
}
```

The `filters()` method should return an array of filter configurations. The previous method returns a configuration that specifies that the `projectContext` filter, which is defined as a method within the class, should apply to the `actionCreate()` method. The configuration syntax allows for '+' and '-' symbols to be used to specify whether or not a filter should or apply. For example, if we decided that we wanted this filter to apply to all the actions except the `actionUpdate()` and `actionView()` action methods, we could specify:

```
return array(
        'projectContext - update, view' ,
  );
```

You should not specify both the plus and the minus operator at the same time. Only one should be used for any given filter configuration. The plus operator means 'Only apply the filter to the following actions'. The minus operators means 'Apply the filter to all actions except the following'. If neither the '+' nor the '-' is in the configuration, the filter will be applied to all actions.

At the moment, we'll keep this restricted to just the `create` action. So, as defined previously with the + `create` configuration, our filter method will be called when any user attempts to create a new issue.

Adding some filter logic

Okay, so now we have a filter defined and we have configured it to be called upon every attempted `actionCreate()` method call within the Issuecontroller class. However, it still does not perform the needed logic. As we want to ensure the project context before the action is attempted, we need to put the logic in the filter method before the call to `$filterChain->run()`.

We'll add a project property to the `controller` class itself. We'll then use a `querystring` parameter in our URLs to indicate the project identifier. Our pre-action filter will check to see if the existing project attribute is `null`. If so, it will use the `querystring` parameter to attempt to select the project based on the Primary Key identifier. If successful, the action will execute, and if it fails an exception will be thrown. Here is the code that is required in the `IssueController` class to perform all of this:

```
class IssueController extends CController
{
    ....
    /**
     * @var private property containing the associated Project model
instance.
     */
    private $_project = null;

    /**
     * Protected method to load the associated Project model class
         * @project_id the primary identifier of the associated Project
     * @return object the Project data model based on the primary key
     */
    protected function loadProject($project_id)    {
    //if the project property is null, create it based on input id
    if ($this->_project===null)
    {
      $this->_project=Project::model()->findbyPk($project_id);
      if ($this->_project===null)
            {
          throw new CHttpException(404,'The requested project does not
exist.');
            }
```

```
        }

    return $this->_project;
}


/**
 * In-class defined filter method, configured for use in the above
filters() method
 * It is called before the actionCreate() action method is run in
order to ensure a proper project context
 */
public function filterProjectContext($filterChain)
{
        //set the project identifier based on either the GET or POST
input
                //request variables, since we allow both types for
our actions
        $projectId = null;
        if(isset($_GET['pid']))
            $projectId = $_GET['pid'];
        else
            if(isset($_POST['pid']))
                $projectId = $_POST['pid'];

    $this->loadProject($projectId);

        //complete the running of other filters and execute the
requested action
        $filterChain->run();
}
...
}
```

With this in place, now attempt to create a new issue by clicking the **Create Issue** link from the issue listing page at this URL, `http://hostname/tasctrak/index.php?r=issue/list`

You should be met with an **Error 404** error message which also displays the error text we specified previously, **The requested project does not exist**.

This is good. It shows we have properly implemented the code to prevent a new issue from being created when no project has been identified. The quickest way to get past this error is to simply add a `pid` querystring parameter to the URL used for creating new issues. Let's do that so we can supply the filter with a valid project identifier, and proceed to the form to create a new issue.

Adding the project ID

Back in *Chapter 5*, we added several new projects to the application as we were
testing and implementing the CRUD operations on Projects. So, it is likely that
you still have a valid project in your development database. If not, simply use the
application to create a new project again. Once complete, take note of the project ID
created, as we need to add this ID to the new issue URL.

The link we need to alter is in the `view` file for the issue listing page: `/protected/`
`views/issue/index.php`. At the top of that file you will see the **create new** link
specified in the menu as shown in the following highlighted code:

```
$this->menu=array(
  array('label'=>'Create Issue', 'url'=>array('create')),
  array('label'=>'Manage Issue', 'url'=>array('admin')),
);
```

To add a `querystring` parameter to this link, we simply append a `name=>value`
pair in the array defined for the `url`. The code we added for the filter is expecting
the `querystring` parameter to be `pid` (for project ID). Also, as we are using the first
(project ID = 1) project for this example, we alter the **Create Issue** link as follows:

```
array('label'=>'Create Issue', 'url'=>array('create', 'pid'=>1)),
```

Now when you view the issue listing page, you will see that the **Create Issue**
hyperlink opens a URL with a `querystring` parameter appended to the end:

```
http://localhost/trackstar/index.php?r=issue/create&pid=1
```

This `querystring` parameter allows the filter to properly set the project context. So,
this time when you click the link, rather than getting the 404 error, the create new
issue form will be displayed.

Altering the project details page

Adding the project ID to the URL for the create new issue link was a good first step
to ensure our filter was working as expected. However, now we have hard-coded the
link to always associate a new issue with the project ID '=' 1. Of course, this is not what
we want. What we want to do is to have the menu option for creating a new issue be
a part of the project details page. This way, once you have chosen a project from the
project listing page, the specific project context will be known, and we can dynamically
append that project ID to the create new issue link. Let's make that change.

Open up the project details view, `/protected/views/project/view.php`. At the top of this file, you will notice the menu items contained within the `$this->menu` array. We need to add another create a new issue link to the end of this list of defined menu links:

```
$this->menu=array(
  array('label'=>'List Project', 'url'=>array('index')),
  array('label'=>'Create Project', 'url'=>array('create')),
  array('label'=>'Update Project', 'url'=>array('update',
'id'=>$model->id)),
  array('label'=>'Delete Project', 'url'=>'#', 'linkOptions'=>array('s
ubmit'=>array('delete','id'=>$model->id),'confirm'=>'Are you sure you
want to delete this item?')),
  array('label'=>'Manage Project', 'url'=>array('admin')),
  array('label'=>'Create Issue', 'url'=>array('issue/create',
'pid'=>$model->id)),
);
```

What we have done is moved the menu option to create a new issue to the page that lists the details for a specific project. We used a link similar to the one before, but this time we had to specify the full `controllerId/actionId` pair (`issue/create`). Also, rather than hardcode the project ID to be 1, we have used the `$model` variable within the `view` file, which is the AR class for the specific project. This way, regardless of the project we choose, this variable will always reflect the correct project `id` attribute for that project.

Removing the project input form field

Now that we have the project context properly set when creating a new issue, we can remove the **Project** field as a user input form field. However, we do still need the project ID to be submitted with the form. As we know the project ID before we render this input form, we can set the `project model` attribute in the `create` action. This way, the `$model` instance that is passed to the `view` file will already have the proper project ID set.

First, let's alter the `IssueController::actionCreate()` method to set the `project_id` property of the Issue model instance just after it is created:

```
public function actionCreate()
{
  $model=new Issue;
      $model->project_id = $this->_project->id;
  ...
}
```

Now the `project_id` property is set and will be available in the `form` file.

Open up the `view` file for the new issue form, `/protected/views/issue/_form.php`. Remove the following lines that are associated with the **Project** input field:

```
<div class="row">
        <?php echo $form->labelEx($model,'project_id'); ?>
        <?php echo $form->textField($model,'project_id'); ?>
        <?php echo $form->error($model,'project_id'); ?>
</div>
```

Replace them with a hidden field:

```
<div class="row">
        <?php echo $form->hiddenField($model,'project_id'); ?>
</div>
```

Now when we submit the form, the `project_id` attribute will be correctly set. Even though we don't have our Owner and Requester drop-down menu set yet, we can submit the form and a new issue will be created with the proper project ID set.

Returning back to the owner and requester dropdowns

Finally, we can turn back to what we set out to do, which is to change the **Owner** and **Requester** fields to be dropdown choices of valid members of that project. In order to do this properly, we need to associate some users with a project. As user management is the focus of *Chapter 7* and *Chapter 8,* we will do this quickly by adding the association directly to the database via SQL. We already added two new test users as part of our *seed* data in our earlier DDL statements. As a reminder, that `insert` statement was as follows:

```
INSERT INTO 'tbl_user'
   ('email', 'username', 'password')
VALUES
   ('test1@notanaddress.com','Test_User_One', MD5('test1')),
   ('test2@notanaddress.com','Test_User_Two', MD5('test2'))
 ;
```

This created two new users in our system with ID's 1 and 2. Let's manually assign these two users to Project #1.

To do so, run the following `insert` statement against your `trackstar_dev` and `trackstar_test` databases:

```
INSERT INTO 'tbl_project_user_assignment' ('project_id', 'user_id')
VALUES (1,1), (1,2);
```

After running the preceding SQL, we have two valid members assigned to Project #1.

One of the wonderful features of relational Active Record within Yii, is the ability to access valid members of a project to which an issue belongs directly from the issue `$model` instance itself. When we used the Gii tool to initially create our issue model class, it was smart enough to look at the underlying database and build in the relevant relationships. This can be seen in the `relations()` method within `/protected/models/Issue.php`. As we created this class after adding the appropriate relationships to the database, the method should look similar to this:

```
    /**
     * @return array relational rules.
     */
    public function relations()
    {
      // NOTE: you may need to adjust the relation name and the related
      // class name for the relations automatically generated below.
      return array(
        'owner' => array(self::BELONGS_TO, 'User', 'owner_id'),
        'project' => array(self::BELONGS_TO, 'Project', 'project_id'),
        'requester' => array(self::BELONGS_TO, 'User', 'requester_id'),
      );
    }
```

As the NOTE suggests, you may have slightly different attributed names and may want to adjust them as needed. This array configuration defines properties on the model instance that are themselves other AR instances. With these relations in place, we can access the related AR instances incredibly easily. For example, say we want to access the Project model class to which an issue is associated. We can do so by using the following syntax:

```
//create the model instance by primary key:
$model = Issue::model()->findbyPk(1);
//access the associated Project AR instance
$project = $model->project;
```

Now, because we created our Project model class prior to having other tables and relationships defined in our database, there are no relations defined yet. However, now that we have some relationships defined, we need to add these to the `Project::relations()` method. Open the Project AR class in /protected/models/ Project.php, and replace the entire `relations()` method with the following:

```
/**
 * @return array relational rules.
 */
public function relations()
{
    // NOTE: you may need to adjust the relation name and the
related
    // class name for the relations automatically generated below.
    return array(
        'issues' => array(self::HAS_MANY, 'Issue', 'project_id'),
        'users' => array(self::MANY_MANY, 'User', 'tbl_project_
user_assignment(project_id, user_id)'),
    );
}
```

With these in place, we can easily access all of the issues and/or users associated with a project with incredibly easy syntax as follows:

```
//create the Project model instance by primary key:
$model = Project::model()->findbyPk(1);
//get an array of all associated Issue AR instances
$allIssues = $model->issues;
//get an array of all associated User AR instance
$allUsers = $model->users;
//get the User AR instance representing the owner of
//the first issue associated with this project
$ownerOfFirstIssue = $model->issues[0]->owner;
```

Normally we would have to write complicated SQL `join` statements to access such related data. Using relational AR in Yii saves us from this complexity and tedium. We can now access these relationships in a very elegant and concise object oriented manner.

Generating the data to populate the drop-down menu

Now, there are a couple of ways by which we could use this data to populate our needed dropdowns for the **Requester** and **Owner** fields. We'll follow a similar approach as we did for the **Status** and **Type** drop-down data, and place the logic inside a model class. In this case, the Project AR class makes the most sense, as valid users are associated with a project, and not with an issue.

As we are going to add a new `public` method to the Project AR class, we can once again use our TDD approach. So, let's quickly write a test that fails.

 Once again, remember that we have now setup a `trackstar_test` database against which to test. If you are following along, please ensure this database schema is in sync with the `trackstar_dev` database.

Open the `/protected/tests/unit/ProjectTest.php` file and add the following test:

```
public function testGetUserOptions()
{
  $project = $this->projects('project1');
  $options = $project->userOptions;
  $this->assertTrue(is_array($options));
}
```

Now run the test.

```
>>phpunit unit/ProjectTest.php

PHPUnit 3.3.17 by Sebastian Bergmann.

....E

Time: 0 seconds

There was 1 error:

1) ProjectTest::testGetUserOptions

CException: Property "Project.userOptions" is not defined....

FAILURES!

Tests: 5, Assertions: 10, Errors: 1.
```

Okay, we have a test that fails. It is failing for obvious reasons, as we are testing a method in the Project AR class that does not yet exist. So let's add it. Open up the file `/protected/models/Project.php`, and add the following method to the bottom of the class:

```
/**
 * @return array of valid users for this project, indexed by user IDs
 */
public function getUserOptions()
{
  $usersArray = array();
  return $usersArray;
}
```

If we run our tests again, we see we are back in the "green". However, we only have a method that returns an empty array. What we need is a valid user array that can be used to populate the form dropdowns. Let's get our test back in the "red" by testing to ensure the count of the returned array is > 0.

Alter the test method to be:

```
public function testGetUserOptions()
{
  $project = $this->projects('project1');
  $options = $project->userOptions;
  $this->assertTrue(is_array($options));
  $this->assertTrue(count($options) > 0);
}
```

Running the test again should now result in the following error:

```
There was 1 failure:
1) ProjectTest::testGetUserOptions
Failed asserting that <boolean:false> is true.
```

So, let's toggle back to the `Project::getUserOptions()` method and return some actual users. Alter that method to be:

```
public function getUserOptions()
{
  $usersArray = CHtml::listData($this->users, 'id', 'username');
    return $usersArray;
}}
```

Here we are using Yii's CHtml helper class to help us create an array of
id=>username pairs from each user associated with the project. Remember that the
users property in the Project class maps to an array of User AR instances. The
CHtml::listData() method can take in this list and product a valid array suitable for
CActiveForm::dropDownList(). Now, as long as we remember to populate our test
database with our two users and associate them with Project #1, our tests will pass.

Adding User and ProjectUserAssignment fixtures

Our tests are now passing, but only because we explicitly added users, and we also
explicitly added the related entries to the project association table. What happens
if someone comes along and removes these entries? We need to fix this fragile
relationship. We already know that test fixtures are exactly what we need to
ensure that our tests involving database data can be repeatedly run in a consistent
manner. We did this before for our project data. We need to do it again for data
related to both the tbl_user and tbl_project_user_assignment tables.

Create a new file, /protected/tests/fixtures/tbl_user.php, and add to it
the following:

```php
<?php

return array(
  'user1'=>array(
    'email' => 'test1@notanaddress.com',
    'username' => 'Test_User_One',
    'password' => MD5('test1'),
    'last_login_time' => '',
    'create_time' => '',
    'create_user_id' => '',
    'update_time' => '',
    'update_user_id' => '',
  ),
  'user2'=>array(
    'email' => 'test2@notanaddress.com',
    'username' => 'Test_User_Two',
    'password' => MD5('test2'),
    'last_login_time' => '',
    'create_time' => '',
    'create_user_id' => '',
    'update_time' => '',
    'update_user_id' => '',
  ),
);
```

This is the same data we added manually via explicit SQL earlier, but here it is represented as fixture data.

We need to do the same for our association table. Create another new file, /protected/tests/fixtures/tbl_project_user_assignment.php and add the following content:

```php
<?php

return array(
    'user1ToProject1'=>array(
        'project_id' => 1,
        'user_id' => 1,
        'create_time' => '',
        'create_user_id' => '',
        'update_time' => '',
        'update_user_id' => '',
    ),
    'user2ToProject1'=>array(
        'project_id' => 1,
        'user_id' => 2,
        'create_time' => '',
        'create_user_id' => '',
        'update_time' => '',
        'update_user_id' => '',
    ),
);
```

This is also the same data as we added to the tbl_project_user_assignment table manually, but represented as fixture data.

Now we need to add the fixture to the unit test. Open up the ProjectTest file, /protected/tests/unit/ProjectTest.php, and add it to the fixtures definition at the top of that file with the following highlighted code:

```php
public $fixtures=array(
    'projects'=>'Project',
    'users'=>'User',
    'projUsrAssign'=>':tbl_project_user_assignment',
    );
```

Notice that we had to add the : when mapping to the tbl_project_user_assignment table. This is needed to indicate that this is a database table, and not an AR model class.

Now that this has been added, each time we run the `ProjectTest.php` unit test, our `tbl_user` and `tbl_project_user_assignment` tables will be reset to a consistent state using the data defined in the corresponding fixture data files.

Now let us run our project-related tests again:

```
>> unit/ProjectTest.php
PHPUnit 3.4.12 by Sebastian Bergmann.

. . . . .

Time: 0 seconds
OK (5 tests, 12 assertions)
```

We still have passing tests, but now they are using this new `fixture` data.

Now that we have our `getUserOptions()` method working as expected, we need to implement the dropdown to display that returned data. We already added a `private $_project` attribute to our `IssueController` class. This attribute contains the valid project context. We need to access this same `project` attribute in our `view` file that displays the input form. So, we need to add a simple `getter` method to expose this `private` attribute. Add the following method to the bottom of the `IssueController` class:

```
/**
  * Returns the project model instance to which this issue belongs
  */
public function getProject()
{
  return $this->_project;
}
```

Now, open up the `view` file containing the input form elements, /protected/views/ issue/_form.php, and find where the two text field input forms element definitions for `owner_id` and `requester_id`.

Replace

```
<?php //echo $form->textField($model,'owner_id'); ?>
```

with this:

```
<?php echo $form->dropDownList($model,'owner_id', $this->getProject()->getUserOptions()); ?>
```

Also replace this line:

```
<?php echo $form->textField($model,'requester_id'); ?>
```

with this:

```
<?php echo $form->dropDownList($model,'requester_id', $this-
>getProject()->getUserOptions()); ?>
```

Now if we view our issue creation form again, we see two nicely populated dropdown fields for the **Owner** and **Requester**.

Making one last change

As we already have the **Create Issue** form `view` file open, let's quickly make one last change. The creation time and user as well as the last updated time and user fields that we have on every table for basic history and auditing purposes should not be exposed to the user. Later, we will alter the application logic to automatically populate these fields upon inserts and updates. For now, let's just remove them as inputs on the form.

Just completely remove the following lines from `/protected/views/issue /_form.php`:

```
<div class="row">
    <?php echo $form->labelEx($model,'create_time'); ?>
    <?php echo $form->textField($model,'create_time'); ?>
    <?php echo $form->error($model,'create_time'); ?>
</div>

<div class="row">
    <?php echo $form->labelEx($model,'create_user_id'); ?>
    <?php echo $form->textField($model,'create_user_id'); ?>
    <?php echo $form->error($model,'create_user_id'); ?>
</div>

<div class="row">
    <?php echo $form->labelEx($model,'update_time'); ?>
    <?php echo $form->textField($model,'update_time'); ?>
    <?php echo $form->error($model,'update_time'); ?>
</div>

<div class="row">
    <?php echo $form->labelEx($model,'update_user_id'); ?>
    <?php echo $form->textField($model,'update_user_id'); ?>
    <?php echo $form->error($model,'update_user_id'); ?>
</div>
```

The following screenshot shows what our new issue creation form now looks like with all of these changes:

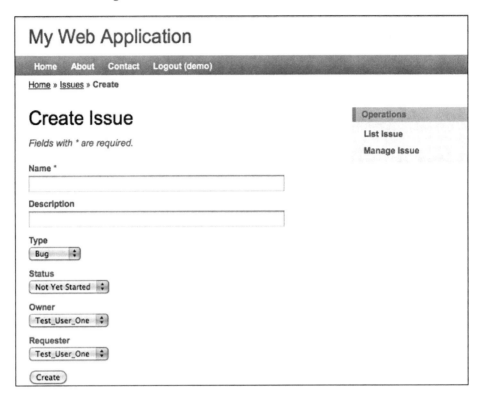

Finishing the rest of the CRUD

The goal of this iteration is to implement all the CRUD operations for issues. We have finalized the create functionality, but we still need to complete the read, update and delete of issues. Luckily, most of the foundation has already been laid by using the Gii CRUD generation functionality. However, as we want to manage issues all within the context of a project, we need to make some adjustments to how you access this functionality.

Listing the issues

Even though there is the actionIndex() method in the IssueController class that displays a list of all issues in the database, we don't have a need for this functionality as it is currently coded. Rather than a separate standalone page that lists all the issues in the database, we want to only list the issues that are associated with a specific project. So, we'll alter the application to display the listing of issues as part of the project details page. As we are taking advantage of the relational AR model in Yii, it will be a snap to make this change.

Altering the ProjectController

First, let's alter the actionView() method in the ProjectController class. As we want to display a list of the issues associated with a specific project, we can do this on the same page as the project details page. The method actionView() is the method that displays the project details.

Alter that method to be:

```
/**
 * Displays a particular model.
 */
public function actionView()
{
  $issueDataProvider=new CActiveDataProvider('Issue', array(
    'criteria'=>array(
      'condition'=>'project_id=:projectId',
      'params'=>array(':projectId'=>$this->loadModel()->id),
    ),
    'pagination'=>array(
      'pageSize'=>1,
    ),
  ));

  $this->render('view',array(
    'model'=>$this->loadModel(),
    'issueDataProvider'=>$issueDataProvider,
  ));
}
```

Here we are using the `CActiveDataProvider` framework class to provide data in terms of `ActiveRecord` objects. It will use the associated AR model class to retrieve data from the database in a manner that can be used very easily with the Zii widget `CListView` to display items in a list rendered in a manner specified in a `view` file. We have used the `criteria` property to specify the condition that it should only retrieve issues associated with the project being displayed. We also used the `pagination` property to limit the issue list to just one issue per page. We set this very low so we can quickly demonstrate the paging features by just adding two issues. We'll demonstrate this soon.

The last thing we did was add this data provider to the array defined in the `render()` to make it available to the `view` file in a `$issueDataProvider` variable.

Altering the project view file

We'll use the Zii widget `CListView` to display our list of issues on the project details page. Open up `/protected/views/project/view.php`, and add this to the bottom of that file:

```
<br>
<h1>Project Issues</h1>

<?php $this->widget('zii.widgets.CListView', array(
   'dataProvider'=>$issueDataProvider,
   'itemView'=>'/issue/_view',
)); ?>
```

Here we are setting the `dataProvider` property of `CListView` to be our issue data provider we created above. And then we are configuring it to use the `protected/views/issue/_view.php` file as a template for rendering each item in the data provider. This file was already created for us by the Gii tool when we generated our CRUD for issues. We are just using it here to display issues on the project details page.

We need to also make a couple of changes to the `/protected/views/issue/_view.php` file that we specified as a layout template for each issue. Alter the entire contents of that file to be the following:

```
<div class="view">

   <b><?php echo CHtml::encode($data->getAttributeLabel('name'));
?>:</b>
   <?php echo CHtml::link(CHtml::encode($data->name), array('issue/
view', 'id'=>$data->id)); ?>
   <br />
```

```
   <b><?php echo CHtml::encode($data->getAttributeLabel('descripti
on')); ?>:</b>
   <?php echo CHtml::encode($data->description); ?>
   <br />

   <b><?php echo CHtml::encode($data->getAttributeLabel('type_
id')); ?>:</b>
   <?php echo CHtml::encode($data->type_id); ?>
<br />

   <b><?php echo CHtml::encode($data->getAttributeLabel('status_
id')); ?:</b>
   <?php echo CHtml::encode($data->status_id); ?>

</div>
```

Now if we save and view our results by looking at the project details page for
Project # 1 (`http://localhost/tasctrak/index.php?r=project/view&id=1`),
and assuming you have created a couple of test issues under that project, you
should see a page like the one in the following screen:

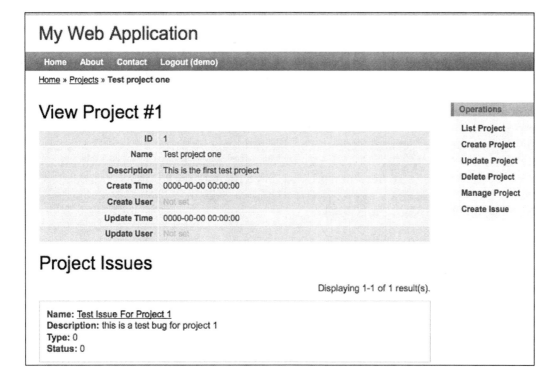

As we set the `pagination` property of our data provider very low (remember we set it to just 1), we can add one more issue to demonstrate the built-in paging functionality. Adding one more issue changes the display of issues to have links that allow us to go from page to page within our **Project Issues** listing, as depicted in the following screenshot:

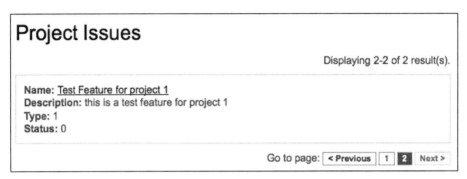

Making some final tweaks

We now have a list of our issues associated with a project that are displayed from within the project details page. We also have the ability to view the details of an issue "R"ead, as well as links to "U"pdate and "D"elete issues. So, for the most part our CRUD operations are in place.

However, there are still a few items that need to be addressed before we can close out this iteration. One thing we notice is that the issues display list is showing numeric ID numbers for the **Type**, **Status**, **Owner** and **Requester** fields. We should change this so that the text values for those are displayed instead. Also, as issues are under a specific project already, it is a bit redundant to have the project ID displayed as part of the issue list data. So, we can remove that. Finally, we need to address some of the navigational links that are displayed on the various other issue related forms to ensure we are always returning to this project details page as the starting place for all of our issue management.

We'll tackle these one at a time.

Getting the status and type text to display

Previously we added public methods to the `Issue` AR class to retrieve the **Status** and **Type** options to populate our dropdowns on the issue creation form. We need to add similar methods on this AR class to return the text for the specific identifier for display on our issues listing.

As these will be `public` methods on the issue AR class, we should implement it using our TDD approach. To speed things up a bit, we'll do both of these at the same time. Also, as we get a hang of TDD a little bit, we'll start to take bigger steps. We can always return to a more granular approach.

First we need to add some `fixture` data to ensure we have a couple of issues associated with a project. We also need to make sure our issue tests are using the project `fixture` data as well as issues belong to projects.

First, add a new `fixtures` data file for issues, `/protected/tests/fixtures/tbl_issue.php` and add to it the following content:

```php
<?php

return array(
  'issueBug'=>array(
    'name' => 'Test Bug 1',
    'description' => 'This is test bug for project 1',
    'project_id' => 1,
    'type_id' => 0,
    'status_id' => 1,
    'owner_id' => 1,
    'requester_id' => 2,
    'create_time' => '',
    'create_user_id' => '',
    'update_time' => '',
    'update_user_id' => '',
  ),
  'issueFeature'=>array(
    'name' => 'Test Bug 2',
    'description' => 'This is test bug for project 2',
    'project_id' => 2,
    'type_id' => 1,
    'status_id' => 0,
    'owner_id' => 2,
    'requester_id' => 1,
    'create_time' => '',
    'create_user_id' => '',
    'update_time' => '',
    'update_user_id' => '',
  ),
);
```

Now we need to configure our `IssueTest` class to use some fixture data. Add the following fixtures array at the top of the issue test class:

```
public $fixtures=array(
    'projects'=>'Project',
    'issues'=>'Issue',
);
```

With our fixture data in place, we can add two new tests to the `IssueTest` unit test class for testing the status and type text:

```
public function testGetStatusText()
{
    $this->assertTrue('Started' == $this->issues('issueBug')-
>getStatusText());
}
And also this test:
public function testGetTypeText()
{
    $this->assertTrue('Bug' == $this->issues('issueBug')-
>getTypeText());
}
```

Now if we run the test, we should get a failure due to the fact that we have not yet added these `public` methods to our AR class:

```
>>phpunit unit/IssueTest.php

PHPUnit 3.4.12 by Sebastian Bergmann.

..EE

Time: 2 seconds, Memory: 12.25Mb

There were 2 errors:

1) IssueTest::testGetStatusText
Exception: Unknown method 'issues' for class 'IssueTest'.

...

2) IssueTest::testGetTypeText
Exception: Unknown method 'issues' for class 'IssueTest'.

...

FAILURES!
Tests: 4, Assertions: 10, Errors: 2.
```

So, we've got our failing test, let's add the necessary code to our /protected/ models/Issue.php file to get them to pass. Add the following two new public methods to the Issue class to retrieve the status and type text for the current issue:

```
/**
* @return string the status text display for the current issue
*/
public function getStatusText()
{
    $statusOptions=$this->statusOptions;
    return isset($statusOptions[$this->status_id]) ?
$statusOptions[$this->status_id] : "unknown status ({$this->status_
id})";
}


/**
* @return string the type text display for the current issue
*/
public function getTypeText()
{
    $typeOptions=$this->typeOptions;
    return isset($typeOptions[$this->type_id]) ? $typeOptions[$this-
>type_id] : "unknown type ({$this->type_id})";
}
```

Now let's run our tests again:

```
>>phpunit unit/IssueTest.php

....

Time: 1 second, Memory: 12.25Mb

OK (4 tests, 12 assertions)
```

We have both tests passing and back in the 'green'.

Adding the text display to the form

Now we have our two new `public` methods that will return the valid status and type text for our listing to display, we need to make use of them. Alter the following lines of code in `/protected/views/issue/_view.php`:

Change the following command:

```
<?php echo CHtml::encode($data->type_id); ?>
```

to:

```
<?php echo CHtml::encode($data->getTypeText()); ?>
```

and change this command:

```
<?php echo CHtml::encode($data->status_id); ?>
```

to this:

```
<?php echo CHtml::encode($data->getStatusText()); ?>
```

After these changes, our **Issues** listing page, `http://localhost/trackstar/index.php?r=issue` no longer displays integer values for our issue **Type** and **Status** fields. It now looks like what is displayed in the following screenshot:

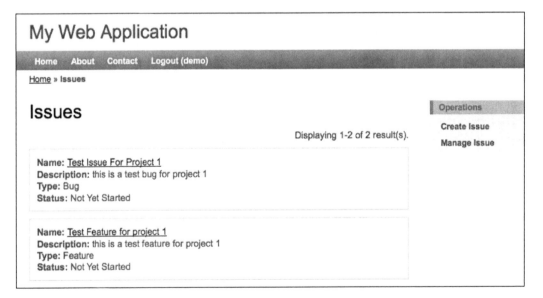

As we are using the same `view` file to display our **Issues** listing on our project detail pages, these changes are reflected there as well.

Changing the issue detail view

We also need to make these and a few other changes to the detailed view of the Issue. Currently, if we view the **Issue** details, it should look like the following screenshot:

```
View Issue #1

               ID   1
             Name   Test Issue For Project 1
      Description   this is a test bug for project 1
          Project   1
             Type   0
           Status   0
            Owner   1
        Requester   1
      Create Time   0000-00-00 00:00:00
      Create User   Not set
      Update Time   0000-00-00 00:00:00
      Update User   Not set
```

This is using a `view` file we have not altered at all as of yet. It is still displaying the project ID, which we don't need to display, as well as the type and status as integer values, rather than their associated text values. Opening the `view` file used to render this display, `/protected/views/issue/view.php`, we notice that it is using the Zii extension widget, `CDetailView`, which we have not seen before. This is similar to the `CListView` widget used to display the listing, but is used to display the details of a single data model instance (or associative array), rather than for displaying a list view of many. The relevant code from this file showing the use of this widget is as follows:

```php
<?php $this->widget('zii.widgets.CDetailView', array(
  'data'=>$model,
  'attributes'=>array(
      'id',
      'name',
      'description',
      'project_id',
      'type_id',
      'status_id',
      'owner_id',
      'requester_id',
```

```
            'create_time',
            'create_user_id',
            'update_time',
            'update_user_id',
        ),
)); ?>
```

Here we are setting the data model of the CDetailView widget to be the Issue model class and then setting a list of attributes of the model to be displayed in the rendered detail view. An attribute can be specified as a string in the format of Name:Type:Label, of which both Type and Label are optional, or as an array itself. Here, just the name of the attributes are specified.

If we specify an attribute as an array, we can customize the display further by declaring a value element. We will take this approach in order to specify the model class methods getTypeText() and getStatusText() be used as the values for the **Type** and **Status** fields respectively.

Let's change this use of CDetailView to use the following configuration:

```
<?php $this->widget('zii.widgets.CDetailView', array(
    'data'=>$model,
    'attributes'=>array(
        'id',
        'name',
        'description',
        array(
            'name'=>'type_id',
            'value'=>CHtml::encode($model->getTypeText())
        ),
        array(
            'name'=>'status_id',
            'value'=>CHtml::encode($model->getStatusText())
        ),
        'owner_id',
        'requester_id',
        ),
)); ?>
```

Here we have removed a few attributes from displaying at all. The project_id, create_time, update_time, create_user_id, and update_user_id. We will handle the population and display of some of these later, but for now we can just remove them from the detail display.

We also changed the declaration of the `type_id` and `status_id` attributes to use an array specification so that we could use the `value` element. We have specified that the corresponding `Issue::getTypeText()` and `Issue::getStatusText()` methods be used for getting the values of these attributes. With these changes in place, the **Issue** details page looks like the following:

View Issue #1	
ID	1
Name	Test Issue For Project 1
Description	this is a test bug for project 1
Type	Bug
Status	Not Yet Started
Owner	1
Requester	1

Okay, we are getting much closer to what we want, but there are still a couple of changes we need to make.

Getting the owner and requester names to display

Things are looking better, but we still see integer identifiers displaying for the owner and requester, rather than the actual user names. We'll take a similar approach to what we did for the type and status text displays. We'll add two new `public` methods on the Issue model class to return the names of these two properties.

Using relational AR

As the *issues* and *users* are represented as separate database tables and related through a foreign key relationship, we an actually access the owner and requester username directly from `$model` in the `view` file. Utilizing the power of Yii's relational AR model features, displaying the username attribute of the related `User` model class instance is a snap.

As we have mentioned, the model class `Issue::relations()` method is where the relationships are defined. If we take a peek at this method, we see the following:

```
/**
    * @return array relational rules.
    */
   public function relations()
   {
       // NOTE: you may need to adjust the relation name and the
related
       // class name for the relations automatically generated below.
       return array(
           'owner' => array(self::BELONGS_TO, 'User', 'owner_id'),
           'project' => array(self::BELONGS_TO, 'Project', 'project_
id'),
           'requester' => array(self::BELONGS_TO, 'User', 'requester_
id'),
       );
   }
```

The highlighted code is what is most relevant for our needs. There are both `owner` and `requester` attributes defined as relations to the `User` model class. These definitions specify that the values of these attributes are `User` model class instances. The `owner_id` and the `requester_id` specify the unique Primary key of their respective `User` class instances. So, we can access these just as we do for other attributes of the `Issue` model class.

So, to display the username of the owner and requester `User` class instances, we once again change our `CDetailView` configuration to be:

```
<?php $this->widget('zii.widgets.CDetailView', array(
   'data'=>$model,
   'attributes'=>array(
       'id',
       'name',
       'description',
       array(
           'name'=>'type_id',
           'value'=>CHtml::encode($model->getTypeText())
       ),
       array(
           'name'=>'status_id',
           'value'=>CHtml::encode($model->getStatusText())
       ),
       array(
```

```
            'name'=>'owner_id',
            'value'=>CHtml::encode($model->owner->username)
        ),
        array(
            'name'=>'requester_id',
            'value'=>CHtml::encode($model->requester->username)
        ),
    ),
)); ?>
```

After making these changes, our **Issues** detail listing is starting to look pretty good. The following figure shows the progress thus far:

View Issue #1	
ID	1
Name	Test Issue For Project 1
Description	this is a test bug for project 1
Type	Bug
Status	Not Yet Started
Owner	Test_User_One
Requester	Test_User_One

Making some final navigation tweaks

We are very close to completing the functionality we set out to implement within this iteration. The only thing left is to clean up our navigation just a little. You may have noticed that there are still some options available that allow the user to navigate to an entire listing of issues, or to create a new issue, outside of a project context. For the purposes of the TrackStar application, everything we do with issues should be within the context of a specific project. Earlier, we enforced this project context for creating a new issue (which is a good start), but we still need to make a few changes.

One thing that we notice is that the application still allows the user to navigate to a listing of all issues, across all projects. For example, on an **Issue** detail page, like http://localhost/trackstar/index.php?r=issue/view&id=1, we see in the right column menu navigation there are the links **List Issue** and **Manage Issue**, corresponding to http://localhost/trackstar/index.php?r=issue/index and http://localhost/trackstar/index.php?r=issue/admin respectively (remember that to access the **admin** page, you have to be logged in as **admin/admin**). These still display all issues, across all projects. So, we need to limit this list to a specific project.

As these links originate from the **Issue** details page, and that specific issue has an associated project, we can first alter the links to pass in a specific project ID, and thehe uof that project ID as both the `IssueController::actionIndex`, and `IssueController::actionAdmin()` methods.

First let's alter the links. Open up `/protected/views/issue/view.php` file and locate the array of menu items at the top of the file. Change the menu configuration to be:

```
$this->menu=array(
    array('label'=>'List Issue', 'url'=>array('index', 'pid'=>$model-
>project->id)),
    array('label'=>'Create Issue', 'url'=>array('create',
'pid'=>$model->project->id)),
    array('label'=>'Update Issue', 'url'=>array('update', 'id'=>$model-
>id)),
    array('label'=>'Delete Issue', 'url'=>'#', 'linkOptions'=>array('s
ubmit'=>array('delete','id'=>$model->id),'confirm'=>'Are you sure you
want to delete this item?')),
    array('label'=>'Manage Issue', 'url'=>array('admin', 'pid'=>$model-
>project->id)),
);
```

The changes made are highlighted. We have added a new querystring parameter to the new **Create Issue** link, as well as to the **Issue** listing page and the **issue admin** listing page. We already knew we had to make this change for the Create link, as we have previously implemented a filter to enforce a valid project conssue. We won't have to make any further changes relative to this link. But for the **index** and **admin** links, we will need to alter their corresponding action methods to make use of this new `querystring` variable.

As we have already configured a filter to load the associated project using the `querysting` variable, let's take advantage of this. We'll need to change the filter configuration so that our `filter` method is called prior to execution of both the `IssueController::actionIndex()` and `IssueController::actionAdmin()` methods. Change the filters method as shown:

```
public function filters()
    {
        return array(
            'accessControl', // perform access control for CRUD
    operations
            'projectContext + create index admin', //perform a check to
    ensure valid project context
        );
    }
```

With this in place, the associated project will be loaded and available for use. Let's use it in our `IssueController::actionIndex()` method. Alter that method to be:

```
    public function actionIndex()
    {
$dataProvider=new CActiveDataProvider('Issue', array(
        'criteria'=>array(
            'condition'=>'project_id=:projectId',
            'params'=>array(':projectId'=>$this->_project->id),
        ),
    ));
    $this->render('index',array(
        'dataProvider'=>$dataProvider,
    ));
    }
```

Here, as we have done before, we are simply adding a condition to the creation of the model data provider to only retrieve issues associated with the project. This will limit the list of issues to just the ones under the project.

We need to make the same change to the **admin** listing page. However, this `view` file, `/protected/views/issue/admin.php` is using the results of the model class `Issue::search()` method to provide the listing of issues. So, we actually need to make two changes to enforce the project context with this listing.

First, we need to alter the `IssueController::actionAdmin()` method to set the correct `project_id` attribute on the model instance it is sending to the view. The following highlighted code shows this change:

```
    public function actionAdmin()
    {
        $model=new Issue('search');
        if(isset($_GET['Issue']))
            $model->attributes=$_GET['Issue'];

        $model->project_id = $this->_project->id;

        $this->render('admin',array(
            'model'=>$model,
        ));
    }
```

Then we need to add to our criteria in the `Issue::search()` model class method. The following highlighted code identifies the change we need to make to this method:

```
public function search()
{
    // Warning: Please modify the following code to remove
attributes that
    // should not be searched.

    $criteria=new CDbCriteria;

    $criteria->compare('id',$this->id);

    $criteria->compare('name',$this->name,true);

    $criteria->compare('description',$this->description,true);

    $criteria->compare('type_id',$this->type_id);

    $criteria->compare('status_id',$this->status_id);

    $criteria->compare('owner_id',$this->owner_id);

    $criteria->compare('requester_id',$this->requester_id);

    $criteria->compare('create_time',$this->create_time,true);

    $criteria->compare('create_user_id',$this->create_user_id);

    $criteria->compare('update_time',$this->update_time,true);

    $criteria->compare('update_user_id',$this->update_user_id);

    $criteria->condition='project_id=:projectID';

    $criteria->params=array(':projectID'=>$this->project_id);

    return new CActiveDataProvider(get_class($this), array(
        'criteria'=>$criteria,
    ));
}
```

With these changes in place, the issues listed on the admin page are now restricted to be only those associated with the specific project.

There are several places throughout the `view` files under `/protected/views/issues/` that contain links that require a `pid querystring` to be added in order to work properly. We leave it as an exercise to the reader to make the appropriate changes following the same approach as provided in these examples. As we proceed with our application's development, we'll assume all links to create a new issue or to display a list of issues are properly formatted to contain the appropriate `pid querystring` parameter.

Summary

We were able to cover a lot of different topics in this iteration. Based on the relationship between issues, projects, and users within our application, the implementation of our issue management functionality was significantly more complicated than our project entity management we worked on in the previous iteration. Fortunately, Yii was able to come to our rescue many times to alleviate the pain of having to write all of the code needed to address this complexity.

Specifically, we covered:

- Using the `Gii` code generator tool for Active Record model creation as well as for the initial implementation of all basic CRUD operations against the `Issue` entity
- Designing and building database tables with explicit relationships
- Using relational Active Record
- Adding drop-down menu input type form elements
- Controller filters

We have made a lot of progress on our basic application thus far, and have done so without having to write a lot of code. The Yii Framework itself has done most of the heavy lifting. We now have a working application that allows us to manage projects and also manage issues within those projects. This is the heart of what our application is trying to achieve. We should feel proud of the accomplishments thus far.

However, we still have a long way to go before this application is truly ready for production use. A major missing piece is all of the needed functionality around user management. This is going to be the focus of the next two iterations.

7
Iteration 4: User Management and Authentication

We have made a lot of progress in a short amount of time. The basic functionality foundations for our TrackStar application have been laid. We now have the ability to manage projects and issues within projects, and this is the primary purpose of this application. Of course, there is still much left to do.

Back in *Chapter 3*, when we were introducing this application, we described it as a user-based application that allows for the creation of user accounts, and grants access to the application features once a user has been authenticated and authorized. In order for this application to be useful to more than one person we need to add the ability to manage users within projects. This is going to be the focus of the next two iterations.

Iteration planning

When we used the `yiic` command line tool to initially create our TrackStar application, we noticed that basic login functionality was automatically created for us. The login page allows for two username/password credential combinations, **demo/demo** and **admin/admin**. You may recall that we had to log in to the application in order to perform some of our CRUD operations on our project and issue entities.

This basic authentication skeleton code does provide a good start, but we need to make a few changes in order to support any number of users. We also need to add user CRUD functionality to the application to allow us to manage these multiple users. This iteration is going to focus on extending the authentication model to use the User table and add the needed functionality to allow for basic user data management.

In order to achieve the above outlined goals, we should identify all the more granular items we will work on within this iteration. The following list identifies these items:

- Create the controller classes that will house the functionality to allow us to:
  - Create new users
  - Fetch a list of existing users from the database
  - Update/edit existing users
  - Delete existing users

- Create the view files and presentation tier logic that will:
  - Display the form to allow for new project creation
  - Display a listing of all the existing projects
  - Display the form to allow for a user to edit an existing project
  - Add a delete button to the project listing to allow for project deletion

- Make adjustments to the create new user form so that it can be used by external users as a self-registration process
- Alter the authentication process to use the database to validate the login credentials

Running the test suite

It's always best to run our test suite before we start adding new functionality. With each iteration, as we add to our application functionality, we add to our test suite. As our test suite grows, so does our application's ability to provide us feedback on its general health. Making sure everything is still working as expected will boost our confidence as we begin making changes. From the tests folder, `/protected/tests/`, run all unit tests as once:

```
% phpunit unit/
PHPUnit 3.4.12 by Sebastian Bergmann.

. . . . . . . . . .

Time: 0 seconds

OK (10 tests, 26 assertions)
```

Everything looks good, so let's dive in to this iteration.

Creating our User CRUD

As we are building a user-based web application, we must have the means to add and manage users. We added a `tbl_user` table to our database model in *Chapter 6*. You may recall that we left it as an exercise for the reader to create the associated AR model class. If you are following along and did not create the needed user model class, you will need to do so now.

As a brief reminder on using the Gii code creation tool to create the model class. Navigate to the Gii tool via `http://localhost/trackstar/index.php?r=gii` and choose the **Model Generator** link. Leave the table prefix as **tbl**. Fill in the **Table Name** field as **tbl_user**, which will auto-populate the **Model Class** name field as **User**.

Once the form is filled out, click the **Preview** button to get a link to a popup that will show you all of the code about to be generated. Then click the **Generate** button to actually create the new `User.php` model class file in the `/protected/models/` directory

With the `User` AR class in place, creating the CRUD scaffolding is a snap. As we have done previously, we will once again we lean on the Gii code generation tool for this. As a reminder, here are the necessary steps:

1. Navigate to the tool via `http://localhost/trackstar/index.php?r=gii`.

2. Choose the **Crud Generator** link from the list of available generators.

3. Type in **User** for the **Model Class** name field. The corresponding **Controller ID** will auto-populate with **user.**

4. You will then be presented with options to preview each file prior to generating. When satisfied, click the **Generate** button, which will generate all of the associated CRUD files in their proper locations.

With this in place, we can view our user listing page at `http://localhost/trackstar/index.php?r=user`. In the previous iteration, we manually created a couple of users in our system, so that we could properly handle the relationships between projects, issues and users. So, we should see a couple of users listed on this page.

The following screenshot shows how this page is displaying for us:

We can also view the new **Create User** form by visiting `http://localhost/tasctrak/index.php?r=user/create`. If you are not currently logged in, you will be routed to the login page before being able to view the form. So you might have to log in using **demo/demo** or **admin/admin** to view this form.

Having created and used our CRUD operation functionality first on our `project` entity, and then again with `Issues`, we are very familiar at this point with how these features are initially implemented by the Gii code generation tool. The input forms provided for creating and updating are a great start, but often need some adjusting to meet the specific application requirements. The form generated for creating a new user is no exception. It has an input form field for every single column that has been defined in the `tbl_user` table. We don't want to expose all of these fields for user input. The columns for last login time, creation time and user, and update time and user should all be set programmatically after the form is submitted.

Updating our common audit history columns

Back in *Chapters 5* and *6*, when we introduced our `Project` and `Issue` CRUD functionality, we also noticed that our forms had more input fields than they should. As we have defined all of our database tables to have the same creation and update time and user columns, every one of our auto-created input forms has these fields exposed. We completely ignored these fields when dealing with the project creation form back in *Chapter 5*. Then, with the new issue creation form in *Chapter 6*, we removed the fields from in the form, but we never added the logic to properly set these values when a new row is added.

Let's take a minute to add this logic. As all of our entity tables—tbl_project, tbl_issue, and tbl_user—have the same columns defined, we will add the required logic to a common base class and then have each of the individual AR classes extend from this new base class.

As you might have guessed, we'll write a test first before we start adding in the needed application code. We already have a test in place ProjectTest::testCreate(), in tests/unit/ProjectTest.php, for testing the creation of a new project. We'll alter this existing test method to test our new process of updating our common audit history columns.

The first thing we need to change in our ProjectTest::testCreate() method is to remove the explicit setting of these columns when we call the setAttributes() method for the newly created project:

```
$newProject->setAttributes(array(
        'name' => $newProjectName,
        'description' => 'This is a test for new project creation',
    // - remove - 'createTime' => '2009-09-09 00:00:00',
    // - remove - 'createUser' => '1',
    // - remove - 'updateTime' => '2009-09-09 00:00:00',
    // - remove - 'updateUser' => '1',
    ));
```

Now we need to add in the explicit setting of the user ID and remove the false parameter sent when saving the Active Record, as we now want the validation to be triggered. The reason we want to trigger the AR validation is because we are going to tap into the validation workflow in order to update these fields. The code below shows the entire method with the new changes highlighted:

```
public function testCreate()
  {
    //CREATE a new Project
      $newProject=new Project;
      $newProjectName = 'Test Project Creation';
      $newProject->setAttributes(array(
        'name' => $newProjectName,
          'description' => 'This is a test for new project creation',
      ));

      //set the application user id to the first user in our users
fixture data
      Yii::app()->user->setId($this->users('user1')->id);
      //save the new project, triggering attribute validation
      $this->assertTrue($newProject->save());
```

```
        //READ back the newly created Project to ensure the creation
worked
        $retrievedProject=Project::model()->findByPk($newProject->id);
        $this->assertTrue($retrievedProject instanceof Project);
        $this->assertEquals($newProjectName,$retrievedProject->name);

        //ensure the user associated with creating the new project is
the same as the applicaiton user we set
        //when saving the project
        $this->assertEquals(Yii::app()->user->id, $retrievedProject-
>create_user_id);
    }
```

The new assertion added is testing that the create_user_id column of the Project was properly updated with the current application's user ID. This should be enough to confirm that our approach is working. If you now run this test from the command line, you should see the test fail, which is what we expect. The test fails because we have yet to add in the logic required to set this field.

Now let's get this test to pass. We are going to create a new class to house the logic needed to update our common audit history fields. This class is going to be a base class from which all our application AR classes can extend. The reason we are creating this new class, rather than just adding the logic directly to our Project model class, is because our other model classes, Issue and User, also need this logic. Rather than duplicate the code in every AR model class, this approach will allow us to properly set these fields for every AR model class in just one place. We will also make this new class abstract, as it should not be instantiated directly.

We need to manually create a new file, protected/models/ TrackStarActiveRecord.php, and add the following code::

```php
<?php
abstract class TrackStarActiveRecord extends CActiveRecord
{
  /**
  * Prepares create_time, create_user_id, update_time and update_user_
id attributes before performing validation.
  */
  protected function beforeValidate()
  {
      if($this->isNewRecord)
    {
      // set the create date, last updated date and the user doing the
creating
      $this->create_time=$this->update_time=new
CDbExpression('NOW()');
```

```
            $this->create_user_id=$this->update_user_id=Yii::app()-
    >user->id;
            }
        else
        {
            //not a new record, so just set the last updated time and last
    updated user id
            $this->update_time=new CDbExpression('NOW()');
            $this->update_user_id=Yii::app()->user->id;
        }

        return parent::beforeValidate();
        }
    }
```

Here we are overriding the CActiveRecord::beforeValidate() method. This is
one of the many events that CActiveRecord exposes to allow customization of its
process workflow. As a quick reminder, if you do not explicitly send false as a
parameter when calling the save() method on an AR class, the validation process
will be triggered. This process performs the validations as specified in the rules()
method within the AR class. There are two methods exposed that allow us to tap in
to the validation workflow and perform any necessary logic either right before or
right after the validation is performed: beforeValidate() and afterValidate().
In this case, we have decided to explicitly set our audit history fields just prior to
performing the validation.

You probably noticed the use of CDbExpression in the previous code to set the
timestamp for both the creation and update time. Starting from version 1.0.2 of Yii,
an attribute can be assigned a value of CDbExpression type before the record is
saved. That database expression will then be executed to provide the value for the
attribute during the saving process.

Using NOW() in the previous code is specific to MySQL. This may
not work if you are following along using a different database.
You can always take a different approach for setting this value. For
example, using the PHP time function and formatting it appropriately
for the column's data type: $this->createTime=$this-
>updateTime=date('Y-m-d H:i:s', time());

We determine whether or not we are dealing with a new record (that is, an insert) or
an existing record (that is, an update) and set our fields appropriately. We then make
sure to invoke the parent implementation by returning parent::beforeValidate()
to ensure it has a chance to do everything it needs to do.

To try this out, we now need to alter each of the three existing AR classes — Project. php, User.php, and Issue.php — to extend from this new abstract class rather than directly from CActiveRecord. So, for example, rather than the following:

```
class Project extends CActiveRecord
{
```

We need to change it to:

```
class Project extends TrackStarActiveRecord
{
```

And similarly for our other model classes. Once you have done this for the Project model AR class, rerun the tests to ensure they pass.

With this now in place, we can remove these fields from each of the forms for creating new projects, issues, and users (we already removed them from the issues form in the previous iteration). The HTML for these form fields are defined in protected/views/project/_form.php, protected/views/issue/_form.php, and protected/views/user/_form.php respectively. The lines we need to remove from each of these files are the following:

```
<div class="row">
  <?php echo $form->labelEx($model,'create_time'); ?>
  <?php echo $form->textField($model,'create_time'); ?>
  <?php echo $form->error($model,'create_time'); ?>
</div>

<div class="row">
  <?php echo $form->labelEx($model,'create_user_id'); ?>
  <?php echo $form->textField($model,'create_user_id'); ?>
  <?php echo $form->error($model,'create_user_id'); ?>
</div>

<div class="row">
  <?php echo $form->labelEx($model,'update_time'); ?>
  <?php echo $form->textField($model,'update_time'); ?>
  <?php echo $form->error($model,'update_time'); ?>
</div>

<div class="row">
  <?php echo $form->labelEx($model,'update_user_id'); ?>
  <?php echo $form->textField($model,'update_user_id'); ?>
  <?php echo $form->error($model,'update_user_id'); ?>
</div>
```

And from the user creation form, `protected/views/user/_form.php`, we can also remove the last login time field:

```
<div class="row">
    <?php echo $form->labelEx($model,'last_login_time'); ?>
    <?php echo $form->textField($model,'last_login_time'); ?>
    <?php echo $form->error($model,'last_login_time'); ?>
</div>
```

As we are removing these from being form inputs, we should also remove the validation rules defined for these fields in the associated rules method. These validation rules are defined to ensure the data submitted by the user is correctly formatted. As these fields are not going to be filled in by the user, we can remove the rules.

In the `User::rules()` method, the two rules we should remove are:

```
array('create_user_id, update_user_id', 'numerical',
'integerOnly'=>true),
array('last_login_time, create_time, update_time', 'safe'),
```

The Project and Issue AR classes have similar rules defined, but not identical. When removing those rules, be sure to leave in the rules that do still apply to the user input fields.

> The removal of the rule for the `last_login_time` attribute above was intentional. We should prevent this from being shown as a user input field as well. This field needs to be updated automatically upon a successful login. As we had the `view` file open and were removing the other fields, we decided to remove this one now as well. However, we will wait to add the necessary application logic until after we make a few other changes and cover a few other topics.

Actually, while we still have our hands in this validation rules method for the `User` class, we should make another change. We want to ensure that the e-mail, as well as the username, for every user is unique. We should validate this requirement when the form is submitted. We can add these two rules by adding the following line of code to this `rules()` method:

```
array('email, username', 'unique'),
```

The entire `User::rules()` method should now look like the following:

```
public function rules()
  {
     // NOTE: you should only define rules for those attributes that
     // will receive user inputs.
     return array(
        array('email', 'required'),
array('email, username, password', 'length', 'max'=>256),
array('email, username', 'unique'),
        // The following rule is used by search().
        // Please remove those attributes that should not be searched.
        array('id, email, username, password, last_login_time,
create_time, create_user_id, update_time, update_user_id', 'safe',
'on'=>'search'),
     );
  }
```

The unique declaration in the previous rule is an alias that refers to the Yii's built-in validator, `CUniqueValidator`. This validates the uniqueness of the model class attribute against the underlying database table. With the addition of this validation rule, we will receive an error when attempting to enter either an e-mail and/or username that has already been entered. When we first created our `tbl_user` table in *Chapter 6*, we added two test users, so we would have some data to play with. The first of these two users has an e-mail address of `test1@notanaddress.com`. Try to add another user using the same e-mail address. The following screenshot shows the error message received and the highlighting of the field in error after such an attempt:

Adding a password confirmation field

We should add a new field to force the user to confirm the password they entered. This is a standard practice on new user registration forms and helps the user avoid making a mistake when entering this important piece of information. Fortunately, Yii comes with another built-in validator, CCompareValidator, which does exactly what you think it might do. It compares the values of two attributes, and returns an error if they are not equal.

In order to take advantage of this built-in validation, we need to add a new attribute to our model class. Add the following attribute to the top of the User model AR class:

```
public $password_repeat;
```

We named this attribute by appending _repeat to the name of the attribute we want to compare against. The compare validator will allow you to specify any two attributes to compare, or compare an attribute to a constant value. If no comparison attribute or value is specified when declaring the compare rule, it will default to looking for an attribute beginning with the same name as the one being compared with the addition of _repeat appended to the end. This is why we named the attribute in this manner. Now we can add a simple validation rule to the User::rules() method as follows:

```
array('password', 'compare'),
```

We want to mark all of the fields on the form as being required. Currently, our required rule is being applied to the e-mail field only. While we are making changes to this User::rules() method, let's add username and password to this list as well:

```
array('email, username, password', 'required'),
```

As we have explicitly added the $password_repeat attribute to the User AR class, and it is not a column in the underlying database table, we need to also tell the model class to allow this field to be set in a bulk manner when the setAttributes() method is called. We do this by explicitly adding our new attribute to the *safe* attributes list for our User model class. To do this, add the following to the User::rules() array:

```
array('password_repeat', 'safe'),
```

To explain this in a little more detail. When our form is submitted back to the UserController::actionCreate() method, it uses the following code to set the User model class attributes in a bulk manner:

```
$model->attributes=$_POST['User'];
```

What happens here is that for every key in the $_POST['User'] array that matches the name of a *safe* attribute in the $model class, that class attribute's value is set to the corresponding value in the array. By default, for a CActiveRecord model class, all underlying database columns, except the Primary Key, are considered *safe*. As our new $password_repeat is not a column of tbl_user, we need to explicitly add it to this list of safe attributes.

We still need to add this password confirmation field to the form, so let's do that now.

To add this new field to the HTML form, open up protected/views/user/_form. php, and add the following code block below the password field:

```
<div class="row">
    <?php echo $form->label($model,'password_repeat'); ?>
    <?php echo $form->passwordField($model,'password_repeat',array('si
ze'=>60,'maxlength'=>256)); ?>
    <?php echo $form->error($model,'password_repeat'); ?>
</div>
```

With all of these form changes in place, the create new user form should look as depicted in the following screen:

Create User

*Fields with * are required.*

Email *

Username *

Password *

Password Repeat

(Create)

Now, if we attempt to submit the form with different values in the **Password** and **Password Repeat** fields, we will be met with an error as shown in the following screenshot:

Create User

*Fields with * are required.*

> Please fix the following input errors:
> * Password must be repeated exactly.

Email *

testagain@thisisatest.com

Username *

test_again

Password *

••••

Password must be repeated exactly.

Password Repeat

(Create)

Adding password encryption

One last change we should make before we leave the new user creation process is to encrypt the password before we store it. It is the least we can do, from a security standpoint, to perform a one-way encryption algorithm on sensitive user information before we add it to persistent storage. We will add this logic to the `User.php` AR class by taking advantage of another one of `CActiveRecord`'s methods that allow us to customize the default active record workflow. This time we'll override the `afterValidate()` method and apply a simple MD5 encryption to the password before we save the record.

Open the User AR class and add the following to the bottom of the class:

```
    /**
     * perform one-way encryption on the password before we store it in
    the database
     */
    protected function afterValidate()
    {
      parent::afterValidate();
      $this->password = $this->encrypt($this->password);
    }
    public function encrypt($value)
    {
      return md5($value);
    }
```

With this in place, it will encrypt the password using a simple one-way **MD5** encryption just after all of the other attribute validations are performed.

This approach works fine for brand new records, but for updates, it runs the risk of encrypting an already encrypted value. We could handle this a number of ways, but to keep things simple for now, we will need to ensure we ask the user to supply a valid password every time they desire to update their user data.

We now have the ability to add new users to our application. As we initially created this form using the Gii tool's **Crud Generator** command, we also have read, update, and delete functionality for users. Try it out by adding some new users, viewing a list of those users, updating their information, and then deleting a few of the entries to ensure everything is working as expected. Remember that you will need to be logged in as **admin**, as opposed to **demo**, in order to perform the deletes.

Authenticating users using the database

As we know, a basic login form and user authentication process was created for us simply by using the `yiic` command to create our new application. This authentication scheme is very simple. It interrogates the input form username/password values, and if they are either **demo/demo** or **admin/admin**, the authentication passes, otherwise it fails. This is obviously not intended to be the long term solution, but rather a foundation on which to build. We are going to build upon this by altering the authentication process to use our user database table that we already have as part of our model. But before we start changing the default implementation, let's take a closer look at how Yii implements an authentication model.

Introducing the Yii authentication model

Central to the Yii authentication framework is an application component, called user, which, in the most general case, is an object implementing the `IWebUser` interface. The specific class used by our default implementation is the framework class, `CWebUser`. This user component encapsulates all the identity information for the current user of the application. This component was configured for us as part of the auto-generated application code when we initially created our application using the `yiic` tool. The configuration can be seen in the `protected/config/main.php` file, under the `components` array element:

```
'user'=>array(
  // enable cookie-based authentication
  'allowAutoLogin'=>true,
),
```

As it is configured as an application component, with the key 'user', we can access it at any place throughout our application using Yii::app()->user.

We also notice that the class property, allowAutoLogin, is being set here as well. This property is false by default, but setting it to true enables user information to be stored in persistent browser cookies. This data is then used to automatically authenticate the user upon subsequent visits. This is what will allow us to have a **Remember Me** checkbox on the login form so that, if the user chooses, they can be automatically logged in to the application upon subsequent visits to the site.

The Yii authentication framework defines a separate entity to house the actual authentication logic. This is called an identity class, and in its most general form is a class that implements the IUserIdentity interface. One of the primary roles of this class is to encapsulate the authentication logic to easily allow for different implementations. Depending on the application requirements, we may need to validate a username and password against values stored in a database, or allow users to log in with their OpenID credentials, or integrate with an existing LDAP approach. Separating the logic that is specific to the authentication approach from the rest of the application login process allows us to easily switch between such implementations. The identity class provides this separation.

When we initially created our application, the identity class file protected/components/UserIdentity.php was generated for us. It extends the Yii Framework class, CUserIdentity, which is a base class for authentication implementations that use a username and password. Let's take a closer look at the code that was generated for this class:

```php
<?php
/**
 * UserIdentity represents the data needed to identity a user.
 * It contains the authentication method that checks if the provided
 * data can identify the user.
 */
class UserIdentity extends CUserIdentity
{
  /**
   * Authenticates a user.
   * The example implementation makes sure if the username and
password
   * are both 'demo'.
   * In practical applications, this should be changed to authenticate
   * against some persistent user identity storage (e.g. database).
   * @return boolean whether authentication succeeds.
   */
  public function authenticate()
```

```
    {
      $users=array(
        // username => password
        'demo'=>'demo',
        'admin'=>'admin',
      );
      if(!isset($users[$this->username]))
        $this->errorCode=self::ERROR_USERNAME_INVALID;
      else if($users[$this->username]!==$this->password)
        $this->errorCode=self::ERROR_PASSWORD_INVALID;
      else
        $this->errorCode=self::ERROR_NONE;
      return !$this->errorCode;
    }
  }
```

The bulk of the work in defining an identity class is the implementation of the `authenticate()` method. This is where we place the code that is specific to the authentication approach. This implementation simply uses the hard-coded username/password values of **demo/demo** and **admin/admin**. It checks these values against the username and password class properties (properties defined in the parent class, `CUserIdentity`) and if they don't match, it will set and return an appropriate error code.

In order to better understand how these pieces fit into the entire end-to-end authentication process, let's walk through the logic starting with the login form. If we navigate to the login page: `http://localhost/trackstar/index.php?r=site/login`, we see a simple form allowing the input of a username, a password and an optional checkbox for the **Remember Me Next Time** functionality that we discussed before. Submitting this form invokes the logic contained in the `SiteController::actionLogin()` method. The following sequence diagram depicts the class interaction that occurs during a successful login from the moment the form is submitted.

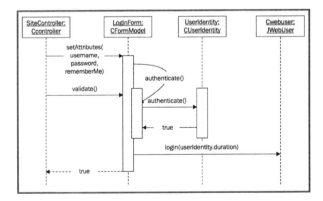

The process starts with setting the class attributes on the form model class, `LoginForm`, to the form values submitted. The `LoginForm->validate()` method is then called, which validates these attribute values based on the rules defined in the `rules()` method. This method is defined as follows:

```
public function rules()
{
   return array(
      // username and password are required
      array('username, password', 'required'),
      // rememberMe needs to be a boolean
      array('rememberMe', 'boolean'),
      // password needs to be authenticated
      array('password', 'authenticate'),
   );
}
```

The last of these rules stipulates that the password attribute be validated using the custom method `authenticate()`, which is also defined in the `LoginForm` class as follows:

```
/**
 * Authenticates the password.
 * This is the 'authenticate' validator as declared in rules().
 */
public function authenticate($attribute,$params)
{
   $this->_identity=new UserIdentity($this->username,$this-
>password);
   if(!$this->_identity->authenticate())
      $this->addError('password','Incorrect username or password.');
}
```

Continuing to follow the sequence diagram, the password validation within `LoginForm` calls the `authenticate()` method within the same class. This method creates a new instance of the authentication identity class being used, in this case it is `/protected/components/UserIdentity.php`, and then calls its `authenticate()` method. This method, `UserIdentity::authenticate()` is as follows:

```
/**
 * Authenticates the password.
 * This is the 'authenticate' validator as declared in rules().
 */
public function authenticate($attribute,$params)
{
   if(!$this->hasErrors())  // we only want to authenticate when no
```

```
input errors
  {
    $identity=new UserIdentity($this->username,$this->password);
    $identity->authenticate();
    switch($identity->errorCode)
    {
      case UserIdentity::ERROR_NONE:
        $duration=$this->rememberMe ? 3600*24*30 : 0; // 30 days
        Yii::app()->user->login($identity,$duration);
        break;
      case UserIdentity::ERROR_USERNAME_INVALID:
        $this->addError('username','Username is incorrect.');
        break;
      default: // UserIdentity::ERROR_PASSWORD_INVALID
        $this->addError('password','Password is incorrect.');
        break;
    }
  }
}
```

This is implemented to use the username and password to perform its authentication. In this implementation, as long as the username/password combination is either **demo/demo** or **admin/admin**, this method will return true. As we are walking through a successful login, the authentication succeeds and the login() method on the user application component is called.

As mentioned, by default the web application is configured to use the Yii Framework class, CWebuser as the user application component. Its login() method takes in an identity class and an optional duration parameter used to set the time to live on the browser cookie. In the above code, we see that this is set to 30 days if the **Remember Me** checkbox was checked when the form was submitted. If you do not pass it a duration, it is set to 0. A value of zero will result in no cookie being created.

The login method takes the information contained in the identity class and saves it in persistent storage for the duration of the user session. By default, this storage is the PHP session storage.

After all of this completes, the validate() method on LoginForm that was initially called by our controller class returns true, which indicates a successful login. The controller class then redirects to the URL value in Yii::app()->user->returnUrl. You can set this on certain pages throughout the application if you want to ensure the user be redirected back to their previous page, that is, wherever they were in the application before they decided (or were forced) to log in. This value defaults to the application entry URL.

Changing the authenticate implementation

Now that we understand the entire authentication process, we can easily see where we need to make the change to use our `tbl_user` table to validate the username and password credentials supplied in the login form. We can simply alter the `authenticate()` method in the user identity class to verify the existence of a matching row with the supplied username and password values. Since, at the moment, there is nothing else in our `UserIdentity.php` class except the authenticate method, let's completely replace the contents of this file with the following code:

```php
<?php
/**
 * UserIdentity represents the data needed to identity a user.
 * It contains the authentication method that checks if the provided
 * data can identify the user.
 */
class UserIdentity extends CUserIdentity
{
    private $_id;

    /**
     * Authenticates a user using the User data model.
     * @return boolean whether authentication succeeds.
     */
    public function authenticate()
    {
        $user=User::model()->findByAttributes(array('username'=>$this->username));
        if($user===null)
        {
            $this->errorCode=self::ERROR_USERNAME_INVALID;
        }
        else
        {
            if($user->password!==$user->encrypt($this->password))
            {
                $this->errorCode=self::ERROR_PASSWORD_INVALID;
            }
            else
            {
                $this->_id = $user->id;
                if(null===$user->last_login_time)
                {
                    $lastLogin = time();
                }
```

```
        else
        {
      $lastLogin = strtotime($user->last_login_time);
        }
        $this->setState('lastLoginTime', $lastLogin); $this-
>errorCode=self::ERROR_NONE;
      }
    }
    return !$this->errorCode;
  }

  public function getId()
  {
    return $this->_id;
  }
}
```

There are a few things going on with this new code that should be pointed out. First, it is now attempting to retrieve a row from the `tbl_user` table, by way of creating a new User model AR class instance, where the username is the same as the `UserIdentity` class attribute value (remember that this is set to be the value from the login form). As we enforced the uniqueness of the username when creating a new user, this should find at most one matching row. If it does not find a matching row, an error message is sent to indicate that the username is incorrect. If a matching row is found, it compares the passwords. As we are encrypting our passwords, it has to use the encryption method, `User::encrypt()`, that we added to the `User` class previously. If these do not match, it sets an error message to indicate an incorrect password.

If the authentication is successful, a couple other things happen before the method returns. First, we have set a new attribute on the `UserIdentity` class for the user ID. The default implementation in the parent class is to return the username for the ID. As we are using a database, and have numeric Primary Keys as our unique user identifier, we want to make sure this numeric ID is what is set and returned throughout the application when the user ID is requested. That is, when the code: `Yii::app()->user->id` is executed, we want to make sure that the unique ID from the database is returned, not the username.

Extending application user attributes

The second thing happening here is the setting of an attribute on the user identity to be the last login time returned from the database. The user application component, `CWebUser`, derives its user attributes from the explicit ID and name attributes defined in the identity class, and then from `name=>value` pairs set in array called the *identity states.* These are the extra user values that should be persisted throughout a user's session. As an example of this, we are setting the attribute named `lastLoginTime` to be the value of the `last_login_time` field in the database. This way, at any place in the application, this attribute can be accessed via:

```
Yii::app()->user->lastLoginTime;
```

As the initial user rows go into the table with null values for the last login time, there is a quick check for null so that we can store an appropriate time when the user logs in for the very first time. We have also taken the time to format the date for better readability.

The reason we take a different approach when storing the last login time versus the ID is that *id* just happens to be an explicitly defined property on the `CUserIdentity` class. So, other than *name* and *id*, all other user attributes that need to be persisted throughout the session can be set in a similar manner.

> When cookie-based authentication is enabled (by setting `CWebUser::allowAutoLogin` to be `true`), these user identity states will be stored in cookie. Therefore, you should not store sensitive information (for example, password) in the same manner as we have stored the user's last login time.

With these changes in place, you will now need to provide a correct username and password combination for a user defined in the `tbl_user` table in the database. Using **demo/demo** or **admin/admin** will, of course, no longer work. Give it a try. You should be able to log in as any one of the users you created earlier in this chapter. If you followed along and have the same user data as we do, the following credentials should work:

Username: Test_User_One

Password: test1

> Now that we have altered the login process to authenticate against the database, we won't be able to access the delete functionality for any of our project, issue or user entities. The reason for this is that there are authorization checks in place to ensure that the user is an admin prior to allowing access. Currently, none of our database users have been configured to be admins. Don't worry, authorization is the focus of the next iteration, so we will be able to access that functionality again soon.

Updating the user last login time

As we mentioned earlier in this chapter, we removed the last login time as an input field on the user creation form, but we still need to add the logic to properly update this field. As we are tracking the last login time in the tbl_user database table, we need to update this field accordingly after a successful login. As the actual login happens in the LoginForm::login() method in the form model class, let's update this value there. Add the following highlighted line to the LoginForm::login() method:

```
/**
 * Logs in the user using the given username and password in the
model.
 * @return boolean whether login is successful
 */
public function login()
{
  if($this->_identity===null)
  {
    $this->_identity=new UserIdentity($this->username,$this-
>password);
    $this->_identity->authenticate();
  }
  if($this->_identity->errorCode===UserIdentity::ERROR_NONE)
  {
    $duration=$this->rememberMe ? 3600*24*30 : 0; // 30 days
    Yii::app()->user->login($this->_identity,$duration);
    User::model()->updateByPk($this->_identity->id, array('last_
login_time'=>new CDbExpression('NOW()')));
    return true;
  }
  else
    return false;
}
```

Here we are calling its updateByPk() method as an efficient approach to simply update the User record, specifying the Primary Key as well as an array of name=>value pairs for the columns we want to update.

Displaying the last login time on the home page

Now that we are updating the last login time in the db, and saving it to persistent session storage when logging in, let's go ahead and display this time on our welcome screen that a user sees after a successful login. This will also help make us feel better because we know that all of this is working as expected.

Open up the default `view` file that is responsible for displaying our homepage: `protected/views/site/index.php`. Add the following highlighted lines of code just below the welcome statement:

```
<h1>Welcome to <i><?php echo CHtml::encode(Yii::app()->name); ?></i></h1>

<?php if(!Yii::app()->user->isGuest):?>
<p>
    You last logged in on <?php echo date( 'l, F d, Y, g:i a',
Yii::app()->user->lastLoginTime ); ?>.
</p>
<?php endif;?>
```

And as we are in there, let's go ahead and remove all of the other autogenerated help text, which is everything below these lines we just added. Once you save your changes and log in again, you should see something similar to the screenshot below, which displays the welcome message following by a formatted time indicating your last successful login:

Summary

This iteration was the first of two iterations focused on user management, authentication and authorization. We created the ability to manage CRUD operations for application users, making many adjustments to the new user creation process along the way. We added a new base class for all of our Active Record classes, so that we can easily manage our audit history table columns that are present on all of our tables. We also updated our code to properly manage the user's last login time, which we are storing in the database. In doing so, we learned about tapping into the CActiveRecord validation workflow to allow for pre and post-validation processing.

We then focused on understanding the Yii authentication model in order to enhance it to meet our application's requirements: that the user credentials be validated against the values stored in the database.

Now that we have covered authentication, we can turn focus to second part of Yii's auth-and-auth framework, *authorization*. This will be the focus of the next iteration.

8

Iteration 5: User Access Control

User based web applications, like our TrackStar application, typically need to control access to certain functionality based on who is making the request. When we speak of *user access control*, we are referring, at a high-level, to some questions the application needs to ask when requests are being made such as:

- Who is making the request?
- Does that user have the appropriate permission to access the requested functionality?

The answers to these questions help the application respond appropriately.

The work completed in the last iteration provides the application with the ability to answer the first question. Our implementation of basic user management extended the application user authentication process to use the database. The application now allows users to establish their own authentication credentials and validates the username and password against the database stored values upon user login. After a successful login, the application now knows exactly who is making subsequent requests.

This iteration is going to focus on helping the application answer the second question. Once the user has provided appropriate identification, the application needs a way to determine if they also have the permission to perform the requested action. We'll extend our basic authorization model by taking advantage of Yii's user access control features. Yii provides both a simple access control filter as well as a more sophisticated **role-based access control (RBAC)** implementation as means to help us address our user authorization requirements. We'll be taking a closer look at both of these as we work to implement the user access requirements for the TrackStar application.

Iteration planning

When we first introduced our TrackStar application back in *Chapter 3, The TrackStar Application*, we mentioned that the application has two high-level user types: anonymous and authenticated. This is simply making a distinction between a user that has successfully logged in, and one who has not. We have also introduced the idea of authenticated users having different roles within a project. We established that, within a project, a user can be in one of three roles:

- A project owner (is granted all administrative access to the project)
- A project member (is granted more limited access to project features and functionality)
- A project reader (only has access to read the content associated with a project, not change it in any way)

The focus of this iteration is to implement an approach to managing the access control granted to application users. We need a way to create and manage our roles and permissions, assign them to users, and enforce the access control rules we want for each user role.

In order to achieve this goal, we need to identify all the more granular items we will work on within this iteration. The following is a list of these items:

- Implement a strategy to force the user to log in before gaining access to any project or issue related functionality
- Create user roles and associate those roles with a specific functionality permission structure
- Implement the ability to assign users to roles (and their associated permissions)
- Ensure our role and permission structure exists on a per project basis (that is, allow users to have different permissions within different projects)
- Implement the ability to associate users to projects and, at the same time, to roles within that project
- Implement the necessary authorization access checking throughout the application to appropriately grant or deny access to the application user based on their permissions

Luckily, Yii comes with a lot of built-in functionality to help us implement these requirements. So, let's get started.

Running our existing test suite

As always, we should kick things off by running all of our existing unit tests to ensure that the tests pass:

```
% cd WebRoot/protected/tests/
% phpunit unit/
PHPUnit 3.4.12 by Sebastian Bergmann.

. . . . . . . . . . . . . . .

Time: 3 seconds
OK (10 tests, 27 assertions)
```

Everything looks good, so we can start making changes.

accessControl filter

We introduced filters back in *Chapter 6, Iteration 3: Adding Tasks* when we added one to help us verify the project context when dealing with our Issue related CRUD operations. The Yii Framework provides a filter called accessControl. This filter can be directly used in controller classes to provide an authorization scheme to verify whether or not a user can access a specific controller action. In fact, the astute reader will remember that when we were implementing our filterProjectContext filter back in *Chapter 6*, we noticed that access control filter was already included in the filters list for both our IssueController and ProjectController classes, as follows:

```
/**
 * @return array action filters
 */
public function filters()
{
    return array(
        'accessControl',
// perform access control for CRUD operations
    );
}
```

This was included in the autogenerated code produced by using the Gii code generator to create our skeleton CRUD operations on the Issue and Project AR classes.

The default implementation is set up to allow anyone to view a list of existing issues and projects. However, it restricts access of creating and updating to authenticated users, and further restricts the Delete action to a special *admin* user. You might remember that when we first implemented CRUD operations on projects, we had to log in before we were able to create new ones. The same was true when dealing with issues and again with users. The mechanism controlling this authorization and access is exactly this accessControl filter. Let's take a closer look at this implementation within the ProjectController.php class file.

There are two methods relevant to access control in this file, ProjectController::filters() and ProjectController::accessRules(). The code for the first method is listed as follows:

```
/**
 * @return array action filters
 */
public function filters()
{
    return array(
        'accessControl', // perform access control for CRUD operations
    );
}
```

The following code is used for the second method:

```
/**
 * Specifies the access control rules.
 * This method is used by the 'accessControl' filter.
 * @return array access control rules
 */
public function accessRules()
{
    return array(
        array('allow',  // allow all users to perform 'index' and
'view' actions
            'actions'=>array('index','view'),
            'users'=>array('*'),
        ),
        array('allow', // allow authenticated user to perform
'create' and 'update' actions
            'actions'=>array('create','update'),
            'users'=>array('@'),
        ),
        array('allow', // allow admin user to perform 'admin' and
'delete' actions
```

```
                    'actions'=>array('admin','delete'),
                    'users'=>array('admin'),
            ),
            array('deny',   // deny all users
                    'users'=>array('*'),
            ),
        );
    }
```

The `filters()` method is already familiar to us. It is where we specify all the filters to be used in the `controller` class. In this case, we have only one, `accessControl`, which refers to a filter provided by the Yii Framework. This filter uses the other method, `accessRules()`, which defines the rules that drive the access restrictions.

In the `accessRules()` method mentioned previously, there are four rules specified. Each rule is represented as an array. The first element of the array is either `allow` or `deny`. These indicate the granting or denying of access respectively. The rest of the array consists of `name=>value` pairs specifying the remaining parameters of the rule.

Let's look at the first rule defined previously:

```
array('allow',   // allow all users to perform 'index' and 'view'
actions
            'actions'=>array('index','view'),
            'users'=>array('*'),
),
```

This rule allows the `index` and `view` controller actions to be executed by any user. The asterisk `'*'` special character is a way to specify any user (anonymous, authenticated, or otherwise).

The second rule is as follows:

```
array('allow', // allow authenticated user to perform 'create' and
'update' actions
        'actions'=>array('create','update'),
        'users'=>array('@'),
),
```

It allows for any authenticated user to access the `create` and `update` controller actions. The '@' special character is a way to specify any authenticated user.

The third rule is as follows:

```
array('allow', // allow admin user to perform 'admin' and 'delete'
actions
        'actions'=>array('admin','delete'),
        'users'=>array('admin'),
),
```

This specifies that a specific user, named admin, is allowed to access the actionAdmin() and actionDelete() controller actions.

The fourth rule is as follows:

```
array('deny',   // deny all users
        'users'=>array('*'),
),
```

It denies access to all controller actions to all users.

Access rules can be defined using a number of context parameters. The previously mentioned rules define actions and users to create the rule context, but there are several others listed as follows:

- **Controllers**: This rule specifies an array of controller IDs to which the rule should apply.
- **Roles**: This rule specifies a list of authorization items (roles, operation, permissions) to which the rule applies. This makes used of the RBAC feature we will be discussing in the next section.
- **Ips:** This rule specifies a list of client IP addresses to which this rule applies.
- **Verbs:** This rule specifies which HTTP request types (GET, POST, and so on) apply to this rule.
- **Expression**: This rule specifies a PHP expression whose value indicates whether or not the rule should be applied.
- **Actions:** This rule specifies the action method, by use of the corresponding action ID, to which the rule should match.
- **Users:** This rule specifies the users to which the rule should apply. The current application user's name attribute is used for matching. Three special characters can also be used here:
    - *: any user
    - ?: anonymous users
    - @: authenticated users

The access rules are evaluated one by one in the order by which they are specified. The first rule that matches the current pattern determines the authorization result. If this rule is an `allow` rule, the action can be executed; if it is a `deny` rule, the action cannot be executed; if none of the rules matches the context, the action can still be executed. It is for this reason that the fourth rule is stipulated. If we did not stipulate a rule that denied all actions to all users at the end of our rules list, then we would not achieve our desired access restrictions. As an example, take the second rule. It specifies that authenticated users are allowed access to the `create` and `update` actions. However, it does not stipulate that anonymous users be denied access. It says nothing about anonymous users. The fourth rule ensures that all other requests that do not match one of the first three specific rules be denied access.

With this already in place, altering our application to deny anonymous users access to all project, issue, and user related functionality is a snap. All we have to do is change the special character '`*`' of the users array value to the '`@`' special character. This will only allow authenticated users to access the `actionIndex()` and `actionView()` controller actions. All other actions are already restricted to authenticated users.

Let's make this change in all of our controllers. Open up all three of the following files: `ProjectController.php`, `IssueController.php`, and `UserController.php` files and alter the first rule in the access control rules to be:

```
array('allow',   // allow only authenticated users to perform 'index'
and 'view' actions
    'actions'=>array('index','view'),
    'users'=>array('@'),
),
```

After making these changes, the application will require a login prior to accessing any of our *project*, *issue*, or *user* functionality. We still allow anonymous user access to the `SiteController` class action methods, which we kept because this is where our login actions are located. We have to be able to access the login page if we are not already logged in.

Role-based access control

Now that we have used the simple `accessControl` filter as a broad stroke to limiting access to authenticated users, we need to turn focus to meeting some more granular access control needs of our application. As we mentioned, users will play certain roles within a project. The project will have users of type `owner`, who can be thought of as project administrators. They will be granted all access to manipulate the project. The project will also have users of type `member`, who will be granted some access to project functionality, but a subset of what owners are able to perform. Finally, the project can have users of type `reader`, who are only able to view project related content and not alter it in any way. To achieve this type of access model based on the role of a user, we turn to the RBAC feature of Yii.

RBAC is an established approach in computer systems security to managing the access permissions of authenticated users. In short, the RBAC approach defines roles within an application. Permissions to perform certain operations are also defined and then associated with roles. Users are then assigned to a role and through the role association, acquire the permissions defined for that role. There is plenty of documentation available for curious readers about the general RBAC concept and approach. One good source of information is Wikipedia: http://en.wikipedia. org/wiki/Role-based_access_control. We'll focus on the specifics of Yii's implementation of RBAC.

Yii's implementation of RBAC is simple, elegant, and powerful. At the foundation of RBAC in Yii is the idea of the **authorization item**. The authorization item is simply a permission to do things in the application. These permissions can be categorized as *roles*, *tasks*, or *operations*, and, as such, form a permission hierarchy. Roles can consist of tasks (or other roles), tasks can consist of operations (or other tasks) and operations are the most granular permission level.

For example, in our TrackStar application, we need a role of type `owner`. So, we would create an authorization item of type role with the name `owner`. This role could then consist of tasks such as a "user management" and "issue management". These tasks could then further consist of the atomic operations that make up these tasks. For example, the user management task could consist of the operations `create new user`, `edit user`, and `delete user`. This hierarchy allows for inheritance of these permissions so that, given this example, if a user is assigned to the `owner` role, they inherit the permission to perform create, edit, and delete user operations.

Typically in RBAC, you assign a user to one or more roles and the user inherits the permissions that have been assigned to those roles. This holds true for RBAC in Yii as well. However, in this model, we can associate users to any authorization item, not just ones of type `role`. This allows us the flexibility to associate a permission to a user at any level of granularity. If we only want to grant the `delete user` operation to a specific user, and not give them all the access that an owner role would have, we can simply associate the user to this atomic operation. This makes RBAC in Yii very flexible.

Configuring the authorization manager

Before we can establish an authorization hierarchy, assign users to roles, and perform access permission checking, we need to configure the authorization manager application component, `authManager`. This component is responsible for storing the permission data and managing the relationships between permissions as well as providing the methods to check whether or not a user does have access to perform a particular operation. Yii provides two types of authorization managers: `CPhpAuthManager` and `CDbAuthManager`. `CPhpAuthManager` uses a PHP script file to store the authorization data. `CDbAuthManager`, as you might have guessed, stores the authorization data in a database. The `authManager` is configured as an application component. Configuring the authorization manager consists simply of specifying which of these two types to use and then setting its initial class property values.

As we are already using a database in the TrackStar application, it makes sense for us to make use of the `CDbAuthManager` implementation. To make this configuration, open up the main `config` file, `protected/config/main.php`, and add the following to the application components array:

```
'authManager'=>array(
    'class'=>'CDbAuthManager',
    'connectionID'=>'db',
),
```

This establishes a new application component named `authManager`, specifies the class type to be `CDbAuthManager`, and sets the `connectionID` class property to be our database connection component. Now we can access this anywhere in our application using `Yii::app()->authManager`.

Creating the RBAC database tables

As mentioned, the CDbAuthManager class uses database tables to store the permission data. It expects a specific schema. That schema is identified in the framework file YiiRoot/framework/web/auth/schema.sql. It is a simple, yet elegant, schema consisting of three tables, AuthItem, AuthItemChild, and AuthAssignment. The AuthItem table holds the information defining the authorization item, that is the role, task or operation. The AuthItemChild table houses the parent/child relationships that form our hierarchy of authorization items. Finally, the AuthAssignment table is an association table that holds the association between a user and an authorization item. The basic DDL statements for the tables are the following:

```
create table AuthItem
(
    name                varchar(64) not null,
    type                integer not null,
    description         text,
    bizrule             text,
    data                text,
    primary key (name)
);

create table AuthItemChild
(
    parent              varchar(64) not null,
    child               varchar(64) not null,
    primary key (parent,child),
    foreign key (parent) references AuthItem (name) on delete cascade
on update cascade,
    foreign key (child) references AuthItem (name) on delete cascade on
update cascade
);

create table AuthAssignment
(
    itemname            varchar(64) not null,
    userid              varchar(64) not null,
    bizrule             text,
    data                text,
    primary key (itemname,userid),
    foreign key (itemname) references AuthItem (name) on delete cascade
on update cascade
);
```

This schema is taken directly from the Yii Framework file /framework/web/auth/schema.sql and does not exactly adhere to our table naming conventions that we use for our other tables. These are the default table names expected by CDbAuthManager class. However, you can configure this class to use different table names. For simplicity, we use the schema exactly as defined in the framework.

Creating the RBAC authorization hierarchy

After adding the previously mentioned tables to our _dev and _test databases, we need to populate them with our roles and permissions. We will do this using the API provided by the authManager. To keep things simple, we are going to only define roles and basic operations. We will not set up any formal RBAC tasks for now. The following figure displays the basic hierarchy we wish to define:

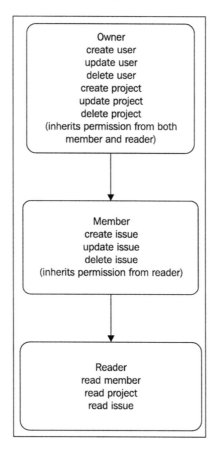

The diagram shows inheritance from the top down. So, **Owners** have all the permissions listed, plus they inherit all the permissions from both the **Member** and **Reader** roles. Likewise, member inherits permissions from the **Reader**. What we now need to do is establish this permission hierarchy in the application. As previously mentioned, the best way to do this is to write code to utilize the `authManager` API. As an example, the following code creates a new role and a new operation and then adds the relationship between the role and the permission:

```
$auth=Yii::app()->authManager;
$role=$auth->createRole('owner');
$auth->createOperation('createProject','create a new project');
$role->addChild('createProject');
```

In the preceding code, we first get an instance of the `authManager`. We then use its `createRole()`, `createOperation()`, and `addChild()` API methods to create a new `owner` role, and a new operation named `createProject`. We then add the permission to the `owner` role. This only demonstrates the creation of a small part of our needed hierarchy, all of the remaining relationships we outlined in the previous figure need to be created in a similar manner.

To accomplish the building of our needed permission hierarchy, we are going to write a simple `shell` command, which is to be executed at the command line. This will extend the command options of the `yiic` command-line tool we used to create our initial application.

Writing a console application command

We introduced the `yiic` command-line tool back in *Chapter 2*, when we created a new *HelloWorld!* application, and again in *Chapter 4* when we used it to initially create the structure of our TrackStar Web application. The `yiic` tool is a console application in Yii that executes tasks in the form of commands. We have used the `webapp` command to create a new applications, and back in *Chapter 2*, we also used the `yiic shell` command to create a new controller class. We have been using the newer Gii code generator tool when initially creating our model classes and our CRUD scaffolding code. However, there are commands available with the `yiic` tool for creating these as well. As a reminder, the `yiic shell` command allows you to interact with a web application on the command line. You can execute it from the folder that contains the entry script for the application. Then, within the context of the specific application, it provides tools to automatically generate new controllers, views and data models.

Console applications in Yii are easily extended by writing custom commands, and this is exactly what we are going to do. We are going to extend the `yiic shell` command tool set by writing a new command-line tool to allow us to build our RBAC authorization hierarchy in a consistent and repeatable manner.

Writing a new command for a console application is quite simple. It is simply a class that extends from `CConsoleCommand` which, at a minimum, implements the needed `run()` method that will be executed when the command is called. The name of the class should be exactly the same as the desired command name, followed by `Command`. In our case, our command will simply be `rbac`, so we'll name our class `RbacCommand`. Lastly, in order to make this command available to the `yiic` console application, we need to save our class into the `/protected/commands/shell/` folder.

So, create a new file called `RbacCommand.php`, and add the following PHP code:

```php
<?php
class RbacCommand extends CConsoleCommand
{

    private $_authManager;

    public function getHelp()
    {
        return <<<EOD
USAGE
  rbac


DESCRIPTION
  This command generates an initial RBAC authorization hierarchy.

EOD;
    }



    /**
     * Execute the action.
     * @param array command line parameters specific for this command
     */
    public function run($args)
    {
        //ensure that an authManager is defined as this is mandatory
for creating an auth heirarchy
        if(($this->_authManager=Yii::app()->authManager)===null)
        {
```

```
                echo "Error: an authorization manager, named 'authManager'
must be configured to use this command.\n";
                echo "If you already added 'authManager' component in
application configuration,\n";
                echo "please quit and re-enter the yiic shell.\n";
                return;
            }


//provide the oportunity for the use to abort the request
        echo "This command will create three roles: Owner, Member, and
Reader and the following premissions:\n";
        echo "create, read, update and delete user\n";
        echo "create, read, update and delete project\n";
        echo "create, read, update and delete issue\n";
        echo "Would you like to continue? [Yes|No] ";

//check the input from the user and continue if they indicated yes to
the above question
        if(!strncasecmp(trim(fgets(STDIN)),'y',1))
        {
//first we need to remove all operations, roles, child relationship
and assignments
            $this->_authManager->clearAll();

//create the lowest level operations for users
            $this->_authManager->createOperation("createUser","create
a new user");
            $this->_authManager->createOperation("readUser","read
user profile information");
            $this->_authManager->createOperation("updateUser","update
a users information");
            $this->_authManager->createOperation("deleteUser","remove
a user from a project");

//create the lowest level operations for projects
            $this->_authManager->createOperation("createProject","cre
ate a new project");
            $this->_authManager->createOperation("readProject","read
project information");
             $this->_authManager->createOperation("updateProject","up
date project information");
            $this->_authManager->createOperation("deleteProject","del
ete a project");

//create the lowest level operations for issues
```

```
            $this->_authManager->createOperation("createIssue","crea
te a new issue");
            $this->_authManager->createOperation("readIssue","read
issue information");
            $this->_authManager->createOperation("updateIssue","upda
te issue information");
            $this->_authManager->createOperation("deleteIssue","dele
te an issue from a project");

//create the reader role and add the appropriate permissions as
children to this role
            $role=$this->_authManager->createRole("reader");
            $role->addChild("readUser");
            $role->addChild("readProject");
            $role->addChild("readIssue");

//create the member role, and add the appropriate permissions, as well
as the reader role itself, as children
            $role=$this->_authManager->createRole("member");
            $role->addChild("reader");
            $role->addChild("createIssue");
            $role->addChild("updateIssue");
            $role->addChild("deleteIssue");

//create the owner role, and add the appropriate permissions, as well
as both the reader and member roles as children
            $role=$this->_authManager->createRole("owner");
            $role->addChild("reader");
            $role->addChild("member");
            $role->addChild("createUser");
            $role->addChild("updateUser");
            $role->addChild("deleteUser");
            $role->addChild("createProject");
            $role->addChild("updateProject");
            $role->addChild("deleteProject");

            //provide a message indicating success
            echo "Authorization hierarchy successfully generated.";
        }
    }
}
```

The comments in the previous code should help tell the story of what is happening here. We provide a simple `getHelp()` method so that our new command can be quickly understood by other users. This is also consistent with the other commands offered by `yiic`. All of the real action happens in the `run()` method. It ensures the application has a vaild `authManager` application component defined. It then allows the user to have a last chance to cancel the request before proceeding. If the user of this command indicates they want to continue, it will proceed to clear all previously entered data in the RBAC tables and then create a new authorization hierarchy. The hierarchy that is created here is exactly the one we discussed previously.

We can see that, even based on our fairly simple hierarchy, there is still a significant amount of code needed. Typically, one would need to develop a more intuitive UI wrapped around these authorization manager APIs to provide an easy interface to manage roles, tasks, and operations. For the purposes of our TrackStar application, we can simply set up the needed database tables, execute this logic once to establish the initial relationships, and then hope we don't have to make too many changes to it. This is a great solution for establishing a quick RBAC permission structure, but not ideal for the long-term maintenance of a permission structure that might change significantly.

In a real-world application, you will most likely need a different, more interactive tool to help maintain the RBAC relationships. The Yii extension library (http://www.yiiframework.com/extensions/) provides some packaged solutions for this.

Let's try out this new command. Navigate to the root of your application and execute the `shell` command (Remember `YiiRoot` stands for where you have installed the Yii Framework):

```
% YiiRoot/framework/yiic shell

Yii Interactive Tool v1.1 (based on Yii v1.1.2)

Please type 'help' for help. Type 'exit' to quit.

>>
```

Now type `help` to see a list of available commands:

```
>> help
At the prompt, you may enter a PHP statement or one of the following
commands:
 - controller
 - crud
 - form
 - help
```

```
- model

- module

- rbac
```

```
Type 'help <command-name>' for details about a command.
```

We see that our `rbac` command has now been added to the list. Let's attempt to learn more by typing `help rbac`:

```
>> help rbac
```

```
USAGE
```

```
  rbac
```

```
DESCRIPTION
```

```
  This command generates an initial RBAC authorization hierarchy.
```

This is exactly what we wrote in the `getHelp()` method of our command class. You can certainly be more verbose, and add more detail as desired.

Now let's run the command to establish the required hierarchy:

```
>> rbac
```

```
This command will create three roles: Owner, Member, and Reader and the
following premissions:
```

```
create, read, update and delete user
```

```
create, read, update and delete project
```

```
create, read, update and delete issue
```

```
Would you like to continue? [Yes|No] Yes
```

```
Authorization hierarchy successfully generated.
```

Then go ahead and `exit` the shell:

```
>> exit
```

Assuming you typed `Yes` when prompted to continue, all of the authorization hierarchy was created.

As you may recall, we have setup a separate database to run our tests against, namely `trackstar_test`. As we will need this authorization hierarchy in our test database as well, we need to run the `yiic shell` command under the context of the TrackStar application pointed to the test database. As our test database connection string is defined in our `test` config file, `/protected/config/test.php`, we need to bootstrap the `yiic shell` with this `config` file rather than `main.php`. This is easy to do, as the `yiic shell` command allows you to explicitly specify a `config` file to load. So, let's once again start the `yiic shell`, but let's specify our test configuration when starting up so that the interactive web application shell is configured to use our test database:

```
% YiiRoot/framework/yiic shell protected/config/test.php

Yii Interactive Tool v1.1 (based on Yii v1.1.2)

Please type 'help' for help. Type 'exit' to quit.

>> rbac

This command will create three roles: Owner, Member, and Reader and the
following premissions:

create, read, update and delete user

create, read, update and delete project

create, read, update and delete issue

Would you like to continue? [Yes|No] Yes

Authorization hierarchy successfully generated.

>> exit
```

Now we have our RBAC authorization hierarchy available in our test database as well.

Assigning users to roles

Everything we have done thus far does establish an authorization hierarchy, but it does not yet assign permissions to users. We accomplish this by assigning users to one of the three roles we created: `owner`, `member`, or `reader`. For example, if we wanted to associate the user whose unique user ID is 1 with the member role, we would execute the following:

```
$auth=Yii::app()->authManager;
$auth->assign('member',1);
```

Once these relationships are established, checking a user's access permission is a simple matter. We simply ask the application user component whether or not the current user has the permission. For example, if we wanted to check whether or not the current user is allowed to create a new issue, we could do so with the following syntax:

```
If( Yii::app()->user->checkAccess('createIssue'))
{
    //perform needed logic
}
```

In this example, we assigned user ID 1 to the role of member, and as in our authorization hierarchy the member role inherits the createIssue permission, the previously mentioned if statement would evaluate to true, assuming we were logged in to the application as user 1.

We will be adding this authorization assignment logic as part of the business logic executed when adding a new member to a project. We'll be adding a new form that allows us to add users to projects, and the ability to choose a role as part of the process. But first we need to address one other aspect of how user roles need to be implemented within this application, namely that they need to apply on a per project basis.

Adding RBAC roles to projects

We now have a basic RBAC authorization model in place, but these relationships apply to the application as a whole. Our needs for the TrackStar application are slightly more complex. We need to define roles within the context of projects, not just globally across the application. We need to allow users to be in different roles, depending on the project. For example, a user may be in the reader role of one project, a member of a second project, and an owner of some third project. Users can be associated with many projects, and the role they are assigned needs to be specific to the project.

The RBAC framework in Yii does not have anything built-in that we can take advantage of to meet this requirement. The RBAC model is only intended to establish relationships between roles and permissions. It does not know (nor should it) anything about our TrackStar projects. In order to achieve this extra dimension to our authorization hierarchy, we will create a separate database table to maintain the relationship between a user, a role and a project. The DDL statement for this table is as follows:

```
create table tbl_project_user_role
(
    project_id INTEGER NOT NULL,
    user_id INTEGER NOT NULL,
    role VARCHAR(64) NOT NULL,
    primary key (projectId,userId,role),
    foreign key (project_id) references tbl_project (id),
    foreign key (user_id) references tbl_user (id),
    foreign key (role) references AuthItem (name)
);
```

So, open your favorite database editor and ensure this table is part of both the main and test database models.

Adding RBAC business rules

Although the previous database table will hold the basic information to answer the question as to whether a user is assigned to a role within the context of a particular project, we still need our RBAC authorization hierarchy to answer questions concerning whether or not a user has permission to perform certain functionality. Although the RBAC model in Yii does not know about our TrackStar projects, it does have a very powerful feature that we can take advantage of. When you create authorization items or assign an item to a user, you can associate a snippet of PHP code that will be executed during the `Yii::app()->user->checkAccess()` call. When defined, this bit of code must return `true` before the user would be granted that permission.

One example of the usefulness of this feature is in the context of applications that allow users to maintain personal profile information. Often in this case, the application would like to ensure that a user have the permission to update only their own profile information and no one else's. In this case we could create an authorization item called `updateProfile`, and then associate a business rule that checks if the current user's ID is the same as the user ID associated with the profile information.

In our case, we are going to associate a business rule with the role assignment. When we assign a user to a specific role, we will also associate a business rule that will check the relationship within the context of the project. The checkAccess() method also allows us to pass in an array of additional parameters for the business rule to use to perform its logic. We'll use this to pass in the current project context so that the business rule can call a method on the Project AR class to determine whether or not the user is assigned to that role within that project.

The business rule we'll create will be slightly different for each role assignment. For example, the one we'll use when assigning a user to the owner role will look like the following:

```
$bizRule='return isset($params["project"]) && $params["project"]-
>isUserInRole('owner');';
```

The ones for member and reader will be the similar.

We will also have to pass in the project context when we call the checkAccess() method. So now when checking if a user has access to, for example, the createIssue operation, the code would look like:

```
$params=array('project'=>$project);
if(Yii::app()->user->checkAccess('createIssue',$params))
{
    //proceed with issue creation logic
}
```

Here, the $project variable is the Project AR class instance associated with the current project context (remember that almost all functionality in our application occurs within the context of a project).

Implementing the new Project AR methods

Now that we have added a new database table to house the relationship between user, role and project, we need to implement the required logic to manage and verify the data in this table. We will be adding public methods to the Project AR class to handle adding and removing data from this table, as well as verifying the existence of rows. As you may have guessed, we will start by writing a test.

First, let's add the ability to create a new association between a user, project and role. Open up the unit test file `protected/tests/unit/ProjectTest.php`, and add the following test:

```
public function testUserRoleAssignment()
{
        $project = $this->projects('project1');
        $this->assertEquals(1,$project->associateUserToRole());
}
```

and then run the following test:

```
% cd /Webroot/protected/tests/
% phpunit unit/ProjectTest.php
PHPUnit 3.4.12 by Sebastian Bergmann.
.....E
Time: 0 seconds
There was 1 error:
1) ProjectTest::testUserRoleAssignment
CException: Project does not have a method named "associateUserToRole".
...
FAILURES!
Tests: 6, Assertions: 13, Errors: 1.
```

We have our test failing, and for obvious reasons. We need to add the `public` method to the `Project` AR class that will take in a role name and a user ID and create the association between role, user and project. Open up the `protected/models/Project.php` file and add the following method with just enough logic to get the test to pass:

```
/**
 * creates an association between the project, the user and the
user's role within the project
 */
public function associateUserToRole()
{
        return 1;
}
```

Running the test again will result in success, as we have simply returned exactly what test is looking to compare:

```
% phpunit unit/ProjectTest.php
PHPUnit 3.4.12 by Sebastian Bergmann.

......

Time: 0 seconds

OK (6 tests, 14 assertions)
```

Now let's alter the test to pass in the role name and the user ID to the method on the `project` class:

```
public function testUserRoleAssignment()
{
    $project = $this->projects('project1');
    $user = $this->users('user1');
    $this->assertEquals(1,$project->associateUserToRole('owner',
$user->id));
}
```

Then alter the `Project::associateUserToRole()` method to take in these parameters, and actually insert a row into our `tbl_project_user_role` table:

```
public function associateUserToRole($role, $userId)
{
    $sql = "INSERT INTO tbl_project_user_role (project_id, user_id,
role) VALUES (:projectId, :userId, :role)";
    $command = Yii::app()->db->createCommand($sql);
    $command->bindValue(":projectId", $this->id, PDO::PARAM_INT);
    $command->bindValue(":userId", $userId, PDO::PARAM_INT);
    $command->bindValue(":role", $role, PDO::PARAM_STR);
    return $command->execute;
}
```

Here we are using the Yii Framework `CDbCommand` class to execute an SQL statement against the database. An instance of `CDbCommand` is what is returned from calling the `createCommand()` method on our database connection. We are also using binding our parameter values using the `bindValue()` method on the `CDbCommand`. This is a good practice which can reduce the risk of SQL injection attacks as well as help improve the performance of SQL statements that are executed multiple times.

The `CDbCommand::execute()` method used previously returns the number of rows affected by the executed SQL `insert` statement. A successful `insert` will affect one row, so the integer value 1, will be returned. The test compares the return value of this execution to the integer 1. If you are following along, you should verify that the test does pass. However, if you run it a second time, it will fail with a database integrity constraint violation, as it will be trying to insert the same Primary key again. We should take a moment to address this issue.

As we are dealing with a database table in our tests, we should really add a fixture for this table to be able to run our tests in a repeatable and consistent manner.

Add a new file called `tbl_project_user_role.php` to the `fixtures` folder, `protected/tests/fixtures/`, and have it simply return a blank array:

```php
<?php
return array(
);
```

Next, alter the `fixtures` array at the top of the `protected/tests/unit/Project-Test.php` file to include this new fixture:

```php
public $fixtures=array(
        'projects'=>'Project',
        'users'=>'User',
        'projUsrAssign'=>':tbl_project_user_assignment',
        'projUserRole'=>':tbl_project_user_role',
        );
```

Even though we did not add any explicit `fixture` data to our fixture, the fixture manager will truncate our `tbl_project_user_role` table, thereby removing all previously inserted rows before each test. We can now run our tests multiple times without incurring any database constraint errors.

When we change a user's role within a project, or remove a user from a project, we will need to remove this association. So, let's also add a method to do that. We can keep working with the same test method.

Let's alter our test and add a call to remove the association, just after we add it:

```php
public function testUserRoleAssignment()
{
        $project = $this->projects('project1');
        $user = $this->users('user1');
        $this->assertEquals(1,$project->associateUserToRole('owner',
$user->id));
        $this->assertEquals(1,$project->removeUserFromRole('owner',
$user->id));
}
```

Run the test again and, of course, it will fail. We need to implement this new method on the `Project` AR class. Add the following method at the bottom of that class:

```
/**
     * removes an association between the project, the user and the
user's role within the project
     */
    public function removeUserFromRole($role, $userId)
    {
        $sql = "DELETE FROM tbl_project_user_role WHERE project_
id=:projectId AND user_id=:userId AND role=:role";
        $command = Yii::app()->db->createCommand($sql);
        $command->bindValue(":projectId", $this->id, PDO::PARAM_INT);
        $command->bindValue(":userId", $userId, PDO::PARAM_INT);
        $command->bindValue(":role", $role, PDO::PARAM_STR);
        return $command->execute();
    }
```

This simply deletes the row from the table that houses the association between the role, user and the project. It will return the number of rows affected, which, if it successfully deleted a row, should be 1. So far, our test adds a new association and then removes it. We should run it again to make sure everything passes:

```
% phpunit unit/ProjectTest.php
PHPUnit 3.4.12 by Sebastian Bergmann.

......

Time: 1 second

OK (6 tests, 15 assertions)
```

We now have implemented the methods for adding and removing our associations. We now need to add functionality to determine whether or not a given user is associated with a role within the project. We will also add this as a `public` method to our `Project` AR class.

So, starting with a test, add the following test method to `ProjectTest.php`:

```
    public function testIsInRole()
    {
        $project = $this->projects('project1');
        $this->assertTrue($project->isUserInRole('member'));
    }
```

This is designed to test the implementation of the `Project::isUserInRole()` method. As we have not implemented this method yet, our test will certainly fail. Let's ensure it does:

```
% phpunit unit/ProjectTest.php
PHPUnit 3.4.12 by Sebastian Bergmann.
......E
Time: 0 seconds
There was 1 error:


1) ProjectTest::testIsInRole
CException: Project does not have a method named "isUserInRole".
...
FAILURES!
Tests: 7, Assertions: 15, Errors: 1.
```

To get it to pass, add the following method to the bottom of the `Project` AR model class:

```
/**
    * @return boolean whether or not the current user is in the
specified role within the context of this project
    */
    public function isUserInRole($role)
    {
            return true;
    }
```

This should be enough to get our test to pass:

```
% phpunit unit/ProjectTest.php
...
OK (7 tests, 16 assertions)
```

Now we need to implement the appropriate logic to see if an association exists. Alter the method in the `Project` AR class to be:

```
public function isUserInRole($role)
    {
        $sql = "SELECT role FROM tbl_project_user_role WHERE project_
id=:projectId AND user_id=:userId AND role=:role";
        $command = Yii::app()->db->createCommand($sql);
        $command->bindValue(":projectId", $this->id, PDO::PARAM_INT);
        $command->bindValue(":userId", Yii::app()->user->getId(),
PDO::PARAM_INT);
        $command->bindValue(":role", $role, PDO::PARAM_STR);
        return $command->execute()==1 ? true : false;
    }
```

This again executes the SQL directly to select from our table. It expects an input role name and uses the current application user, defined by `Yii::app()->user`, to make up the primary key it is searching for. Run the test again:

```
% phpunit unit/ProjectTest.php

...

Time: 1 second, Memory: 14.25Mb

There was 1 failure:

1) ProjectTest::testIsInRole
Failed asserting that <boolean:false> is true.

...

FAILURES!

Tests: 7, Assertions: 16, Failures: 1.
```

Our test is failing again. The test is failing because the `isUserInRole()` method is using `Yii::app()->user->getId()` to get the current user ID, and this is returning nothing. Our test did not explicitly set the current user prior to making this call. Let's add the needed logic to properly set the current user's user ID. Alter the test method to be:

```
public function testIsInRole()
    {
        $user = $this->users('user1');
        Yii::app()->user->setId($user->id);
        $project = $this->projects('project1');
        $this->assertTrue($project->isUserInRole('member'));
    }
```

This sets the current user ID to that of `user1` from our users `fixture` data. Now run the test again:

```
% phpunit unit/ProjectTest.php

...

Time: 1 second, Memory: 14.25Mb

There was 1 failure:

1) ProjectTest::testIsInRole

Failed asserting that <boolean:false> is true.

...

FAILURES!

Tests: 7, Assertions: 16, Failures: 1.
```

Our test is still failing, but now it is failing because the row does not exist in the table, the user ID of `user1` is not associated with the `owner` role for this project. So, let's create that association before we call the `isUserInRole()` method.

We could use the other methods we added and tested earlier to create and remove these associations in order to establish the relationship. However, in an attempt to keep this test as isolated as possible from other tests or `Project AR` methods, we'll lean on `fixture` data to provide the initial conditions.

When we first added the fixture file `tests/fixtures/tbl_project_user_role.php`, we had it simply return an empty array. Let's change that to have it populate a row with a project ID of 2, a user ID of 2, and a role name of `member`:

```
return array(
    'row1'=>array(
        'project_id' => 2,
        'user_id' => 2,
        'role' => 'member',
    ),
);
```

As our previous tests for the adding and removing of associations are using `user1` and `project1` fixture data, we've played it safe to avoid any conflicts by using different IDs to seed this data.

Now we'll use this `fixture` data to set our application user ID as well as to create the
`Project AR` class. Alter the test method to be:

```
public function testIsInRole()
    {
        $row1 = $this->projUserRole['row1'];
        Yii::app()->user->setId($row1['user_id']);
        $project=Project::model()->findByPk($row1['project_id']);
        $this->assertTrue($project->isUserInRole('member'));
    }
```

Here we are using the `fixture` data defined at the top of the class, called
`projUserRole`, to retrieve our seeded row data. We then use this data to set the user
ID, and create the `Project AR` instance by calling `Project::model()->findByPk`.
We then test to ensure the user has, indeed, been associated with the `member` role.
Now if we run our test:

```
% phpunit unit/ProjectTest.php

...

OK (7 tests, 16 assertions)
```

Our test is passing once again.

We have written and tested the methods to add and remove our role associations
within a project, and the method to determine whether or not a given user is
associated with a project role. We are going to write one final test. We are going to
write a test for our end-to-end implementation of how we plan to add this extra
project dimension to Yii's RBAC structure. We talked about achieving this by adding
a business rule to the Yii RBAC auth assignment whenever we associate a user to a
role. Let's write one final method in to test this approach.

Open back up the `ProjectTest.php` unit test file, and add the following
test method:

```
public function testUserAccessBasedOnProjectRole()
    {
        $row1 = $this->projUserRole['row1'];
        Yii::app()->user->setId($row1['user_id']);
        $project=Project::model()->findByPk($row1['project_id']);
        $auth = Yii::app()->authManager;
        $bizRule='return isset($params["project"]) &&
$params["project"]->isUserInRole("member");';
        $auth->assign('member',$row1['user_id'], $bizRule);
        $params=array('project'=>$project);
        $this->assertTrue(Yii::app()->user->checkAccess('updateIssue'
,$params));
```

```
        $this->assertTrue(Yii::app()->user->checkAccess('readIssue',$
params));
        $this->assertFalse(Yii::app()->user->checkAccess('updateProje
ct',$params));
    }
```

This final test method uses other existing, and already tested, API methods to achieve the test, so there is no need to go through our normal TDD steps. In some ways it could be argued that this is more of a functional test than a unit test, but we think it still belongs in this unit test class.

We will take the same approach (as we did with the previous test) to setup our user ID, and establish the `project` AR instance by using the data from the `tbl_project_user_role.php` fixture file. We then create an instance of the auth manager class that we use to establish the assignment of the user to the role `owner`. However, before we make that assignment, we create the business rule. The business rule uses the `$params` array by first checking the existence of a `project` element in the array, and then calls the `isUserInRole()` method on the `Project` AR class, which it assumes is the value of that array element. We explicitly pass in the name, `owner`, to this method, as that is the role we are going to be assigning. Finally, we make the call to the Yii RBAC related method `Yii::app()->user->checkAccess()` to see if the current user, who has now been assigned to the role `owner` in our RBAC auth hierarchy as well as is associated with this role within the project.

We are checking whether or not the user has the permission to update an issue, which we know anyone in the `member` role should have. We expect this to return `true`. We are also making a couple of other assertions to test (and demonstrate) the permission inheritance. We expect a user in the `member` role to inherit permissions from `reader`. So we also test that the user has access to the `readIssue` permission, which we know is a child of the `reader` role in our auth hierarchy. Finally, we should expect to be denied access to operations exclusive to the `owner` role. So we test to ensure false is returned when we check access to the `updateProject` operation.

Running the tests again:

```
% phpunit unit/ProjectTest.php

...

OK (8 tests, 19 assertions)
```

All the project tests are passing. It seems as if this approach will do the trick.

As we are explicitly using the code:

```
$auth->assign('member',$row1['user_id'], $bizRule);
```

to insert a row in the `AuthAssignment` table, we will get a database integrity violation if we attempt to run this test again. Basically, it will be try to re-insert the same row, and this will violate a data integrity constraint we have defined on this table. To avoid this, we need to allow the fixture manager to also manage this table. We have seen this before. Simply add a new file to the fixtures folder `protected/tests/fixtures/AuthAssignment.php`, and have it return an empty array. Then, alter the `fixtures` array defined at the top of the `ProjectTest.php` file to include this in the fixtures definition:

```
public $fixtures=array(
        'projects'=>'Project',
        'users'=>'User',
        'projUsrAssign'=>':tbl_project_user_assignment',
        'projUserRole'=>':tbl_project_user_role',
        'authAssign'=>':AuthAssignment',
    );
```

Now our `AuthAssignment` table will be reset to a consistent state before each test is run.

Before we leave this test, let's add a little more to ensure that if we pass in a project to which the user is not assigned, they have no access. As we explicitly set up the association to be with project id #2, let's just check the user's access using project id #1. Add the following at the end of the `testUserAccessBasedOnProjectRole()` method:

```
//now ensure the user does not have any access to a project they are
not associated with
    $project=Project::model()->findByPk(1);
    $params=array('project'=>$project);
    $this->assertFalse(Yii::app()->user->checkAccess('updateIssue',$p
arams));
    $this->assertFalse(Yii::app()->user->checkAccess('readIssue',$par
ams));
    $this->assertFalse(Yii::app()->user->checkAccess('updateProject',
$params));
```

Here we are creating a new project instance based on `project_id` = 1. We know the user is not associated with this project at all, so all of the `checkAccess()` calls should return false.

Adding Users To Projects

In the previous iteration, we added the ability to create new users of the application. However, we do not yet have a way to assign users to specific projects, and further, assign them to roles within these projects. Now that we have our RBAC approach in place, we need to build out this new functionality.

The implementation of this needed functionality involves several coding changes. However, we have provided similar examples of the types of changes needed, and have covered all of the related concepts when implementing functionality from previous iterations. Consequently, we will move pretty quickly through this, and pause only briefly to highlight just a few things we have not yet seen. At this point, the reader should be able to make all of these changes without much help, and is encouraged to do so as a hands-on exercise. To further encourage this exercise, we'll first list everything we are going to do fulfill this new feature requirement. You can then close the book and try some of these out yourself before looking further down at our implementation.

To achieve this goal we will perform the following:

- Using a test-first approach, add a `public static` method called `getUserRoleOptions()` to the `Project` model class that returns a valid list of role options using the auth manager's `getRoles()` method. We will use this to populate a roles selection drop-down field in the form for adding a new user to a project.

- Using a test-first approach, add a new `public` method called `associateUserToProject($user)` to the `Project` model class to associate a user to a project. This can insert directly into the `tbl_project_use_ assignment` table to make an association between the user and the project.

- Using a test-first approach, add a new `public` method called `isUserInProject($user)` to the `Project` model class to determine if a user is already associated with a project. We will use this in our validation rules upon form submission so that we don't attempt to add a duplicate user to a project.

- Add a new form model class called `ProjectUserForm`, extending from `CFormModel` for a new input form model. Add to this form model class three attributes: `$username`, `$role`, and `$project`. Also add validation rules to ensure that both the username and the role are required input fields and that the username should further be validated through a custom `verify()` class method. This `verify()` method should:
    ◦ Attempt to create a new `User` AR class instance by finding a user by matching the input username.

- ○ If the attempt was successful, it should continue to associate the user to a project using the new method, `associateUserToProject($user)`, added previously as well as associate the user to the role in the RBAC approach discussed earlier in this chapter. If no user was found matching the username, it needs to set and return an error. (If needed, review the `LoginForm::authenticate()` method as an example of a custom validation rule method.)

- Add a new `view` file under `views/project` called `adduser.php` to display our new form for adding users to projects. This form only needs two input fields: *username* and *role*, which is a dropdown choice listing.

- Add a new controller action method called `actionAdduser()` to the `ProjectController` class, and alter its `accessRules()` method to ensure it is accessible by authenticated members. This new action method is responsible for rendering the new view to display the form and handling the post back when the form is submitted.

Again, we encourage the reader to attempt these changes on their own first. We list our code changes in the following sections.

Altering the Project model class

To the `Project` class, we added three new `public` methods, one of them `static` so it can be called without the need for a specific instance:

```
/**
 * Returns an array of available roles in which a user can be
placed when being added to a project
 */
public static function getUserRoleOptions()
{
return CHtml::listData(Yii::app()->authManager->getRoles(),
'name', 'name');
}

/**
 * Makes an association between a user and a the project
 */
public function associateUserToProject($user)
{
    $sql = "INSERT INTO tbl_project_user_assignment (project_id,
user_id) VALUES (:projectId, :userId)";
    $command = Yii::app()->db->createCommand($sql);
```

```
        $command->bindValue(":projectId", $this->id, PDO::PARAM_INT);
        $command->bindValue(":userId", $user->id, PDO::PARAM_INT);
        return $command->execute();
    }
    /*
     * Determines whether or not a user is already part of a project
     */
    public function isUserInProject($user)
    {
        $sql = "SELECT user_id FROM tbl_project_user_assignment WHERE
project_id=:projectId AND user_id=:userId";
        $command = Yii::app()->db->createCommand($sql);
        $command->bindValue(":projectId", $this->id, PDO::PARAM_INT);
        $command->bindValue(":userId", $user->id, PDO::PARAM_INT);
        return $command->execute()==1 ? true : false;
    }
```

There is nothing special to further describe in the preceding code. As these were all
`public` methods on the `Project` model class, we ended up with the following two
test methods within the `ProjectTest` unit test class:

```
    public function testGetUserRoleOptions()
    {
        $options = Project::getUserRoleOptions();
        $this->assertEquals(count($options),3);
        $this->assertTrue(isset($options['reader']));
        $this->assertTrue(isset($options['member']));
        $this->assertTrue(isset($options['owner']));
    }


    public function testUserProjectAssignment()
    {
        //since our fixture data already has the two users assigned
to project 1, we'll assign user 1 to project 2
        $this->projects('project2')->associateUserToProject($this-
>users('user1'));
        $this->assertTrue($this->projects('project1')-
>isUserInProject($this->users('user1')));
    }
```

Adding the new form model class

Just as was used in the approach for the login form, we are going to create a new form model class as a central place to house our form input parameters and to centralize the validation. This is a fairly simple class that extends from the Yii class CFormModel and has attributes that map to our form input fields, as well as one to hold the valid project context. We need the project context to be able to add users to projects. The entire class is listed as follows:

```php
<?php
/**
 * ProjectUserForm class.
 * ProjectUserForm is the data structure for keeping
 * the form data related to adding an existing user to a project. It
is used by the 'Adduser' action of 'ProjectController'.
 */
class ProjectUserForm extends CFormModel
{
    /**
     * @var string username of the user being added to the project
     */
    public $username;

    /**
     * @var string the role to which the user will be associated
within the project
     */
    public $role;

    /**
     * @var object an instance of the Project AR model class
     */
    public $project;

    /**
     * Declares the validation rules.
     * The rules state that username and password are required,
     * and password needs to be authenticated using the verify()
method
     */
    public function rules()
    {
        return array(
            // username and password are required
            array('username, role', 'required'),
```

```
            // password needs to be authenticated
            //array('username', 'verify'),
            array('username', 'exist', 'className'=>'User'),
            array('username', 'verify'),
        );
    }



    /**
     * Authenticates the existence of the user in the system.
     * If valid, it will also make the association between the user,
role and project
     * This is the 'verify' validator as declared in rules().
     */
    public function verify($attribute,$params)
    {
        if(!$this->hasErrors())  // we only want to authenticate when
no other input errors are present
        {
            $user = User::model()->findByAttributes(array('username'=>
$this->username));
            if($this->project->isUserInProject($user))
            {
                $this->addError('username','This user has already been
added to the project.');
            }
            else
            {
                $this->project->associateUserToProject($user);
                $this->project->associateUserToRole($this->role,
$user->id);
                $auth = Yii::app()->authManager;
                $bizRule='return isset($params["project"]) &&
$params["project"]->isUserInRole("'.$this->role.'");';
                $auth->assign($this->role,$user->id, $bizRule);
            }
        }
    }
}
```

Adding the new action method to the project controller

We need a controller action to handle the initial request to display the form for adding a new user to a project. We placed this in the ProjectController class and named it actionAdduser(). The code for this is as follows:

```
public function actionAdduser()
    {
        $form=new ProjectUserForm;
        $project = $this->loadModel();
        // collect user input data
        if(isset($_POST['ProjectUserForm']))
        {
            $form->attributes=$_POST['ProjectUserForm'];
            $form->project = $project;
            // validate user input and set a sucessfull flassh message
if valid
            if($form->validate())
            {
                Yii::app()->user->setFlash('success',$form->username .
" has been added to the project." );
                $form=new ProjectUserForm;
            }
        }
        // display the add user form
        $users = User::model()->findAll();
        $usernames=array();
        foreach($users as $user)
        {
            $usernames[]=$user->username;
        }
        $form->project = $project;
        $this->render('adduser',array('model'=>$form,
'usernames'=>$usernames));
    }
```

This is all pretty familiar to us at this point. It handles both the initial GET request to display the form as well as the POST request after the form is submitted. It follows very much the same approach as our actionLogin() method in our site controller. The preceding highlighted code is, however, something we have not seen before. If the submitted form request is successful, it sets what is called a **flash message**. A flash message is a temporary message stored briefly in the session. It is only available in the current and the next requests. Here we are using the setFlash() method of our CWebUser application user component to store a temporary message that the request was successful. When we talk about the view next, we will see how to access this message, and display it to the user.

Also, in the previous code, we created an array of available usernames from the system. We will use this array to populate the data of one of Yii's UI widgets, CAutoComplete, which we will use for the username input form element. As its name suggests, as we type in the input form field, it will provide choice suggestions based on the elements in this array.

One other change we had to make to the ProjectController class, was to add in this new action method to the basic access rules list so that a logged in user is allowed to access this action:

```php
public function accessRules()
    {
        return array(
            array('allow',   // allow all users to perform 'index' and
'view' actions
                'actions'=>array('index','view', 'adduser'),
                'users'=>array('@'),
            ),
            ...
```

Adding the new view file to display the form

Our new action method is calling ->render('adduser') to render a view file, so we need to get that created. A full listing of our implementation for protected/views/project/adduser.php is as follows:

```php
<?php
$this->pageTitle=Yii::app()->name . ' - Add User To Project';
$this->breadcrumbs=array(
    $model->project->name=>array('view','id'=>$model->project->id),
    'Add User',
);
```

```php
$this->menu=array(
    array('label'=>'Back To Project',
'url'=>array('view','id'=>$model->project->id)),
);
?>

<h1>Add User To <?php echo $model->project->name; ?></h1>

<?php if(Yii::app()->user->hasFlash('success')):?>
    <div class="successMessage">
        <?php echo Yii::app()->user->getFlash('success'); ?>
    </div>
<?php endif; ?>

<div class="form">
<?php $form=$this->beginWidget('CActiveForm'); ?>

    <p class="note">Fields with <span class="required">*</span> are
required.</p>

    <div class="row">
        <?php echo $form->labelEx($model,'username'); ?>
        <?php $this->widget('CAutoComplete', array(
            'model'=>$model,
            'attribute'=>'username',
            'data'=>$usernames,
            'multiple'=>false,
            'htmlOptions'=>array('size'=>25),
        )); ?>
        <?php echo $form->error($model,'username'); ?>
    </div>

    <div class="row">
        <?php echo $form->labelEx($model,'role'); ?>
        <?php echo $form->dropDownList($model,'role',
Project::getUserRoleOptions()); ?>
        <?php echo $form->error($model,'role'); ?>
    </div>

    <div class="row buttons">
        <?php echo CHtml::submitButton('Add User'); ?>
    </div>

<?php $this->endWidget(); ?>
</div>
```

Most of this we have seen before. We are defining active labels and active form elements that tie directly to our `ProjectUserForm` form model class. We populate our dropdown using the `static` method we implemented earlier on the project model class. We also added a simple link to the menu op to take us back to the project details page.

The highlighted code above is new to us. This is an example of using the flash message that we introduced and used in the `actionAdduser()` method. We access the message we set using `setFlash()` by asking the same user component if it has a flash message, using `hasFlash('succcess')`. We feed the `hasFlash()` method the exact name we gave it when we set the message. This is a nice way to present the user with some simple feedback about their previous request.

One other small change we made as to add a simple link from the project details page so we could access this form form the application. The following line was added to the project `show.php` view file's list of link options:

```
[<?php echo CHtml::link('Add User To Project',array('adduser','id'=>$m
odel->projectId)); ?>]
```

This gives us access to the new form.

Putting it all together

With all of these changes in place, we can navigate to our new form by viewing one of the project details pages. For example, viewing project id #1 through the URL: `http://localhost/trackstar/index.php?r=project/view&id=1`. In the right column menu of operations is a hyperlink **Add User To Project** and clicking on that link should display the following page:

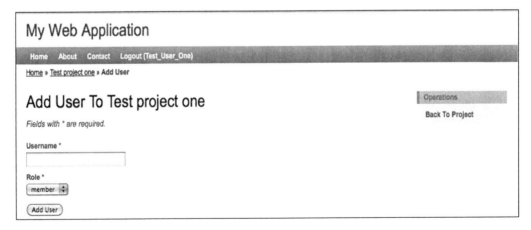

You can use the forms we have previously built to create new projects and users to ensure you have a few added to the application. Then you can play around with adding users to projects. As you type in the **Username** field, you will see suggestions for auto-completion. If you attempt to add a user that is not in the user database table, you should see an error telling you so. If you attempt to enter a user that has already been added to the project, you will see an error message. On successful additions, you will see a short flash message indicating success.

Checking authorization level

The last thing we need to do in this iteration is to add the authorization checks for the different functionality that we have implemented. Earlier in this chapter we outlined and then implemented the RBAC authorization hierarchy for the different roles we have. Everything is in place to allow or deny access to functionality based on the permissions that have been granted to users within projects, with one exception. We have not yet implemented the necessary access checking when attempting to request functionality. The application is still using the simple access filter that is defined on each of our project, issue and user controllers. We'll do this for one of our permissions and then leave the remaining implementation as an exercise for the reader.

We can notice from looking back at our authorization hierarchy that only project owners should be able to add new users to a project. So, let's start with that. What we will do is not even display the link on the project details page unless the current user is in the `owner` role for that project (you might want to make sure you have added at least one `owner` and one `member` or `reader` to a project so you can test it when complete). Open up the `protected/views/project/view.php` view file where we placed the link on the menu items for adding a new user. Remove that `array` element from the menu array items, and then push it on the end of the array only if the `checkAccess()` method returns `true`. The following code shows how the menu items should be defined:

```
$this->menu=array(
    array('label'=>'List Project', 'url'=>array('index')),
    array('label'=>'Create Project', 'url'=>array('create')),
    array('label'=>'Update Project', 'url'=>array('update',
'id'=>$model->id)),
    array('label'=>'Delete Project', 'url'=>'#', 'linkOptions'=>array
('submit'=>array('delete','id'=>$model->id),'confirm'=>'Are you sure
you want to delete this item?')),
    array('label'=>'Manage Project', 'url'=>array('admin')),
    array('label'=>'Create Issue', 'url'=>array('issue/create',
'pid'=>$model->id)),
```

```
);
if(Yii::app()->user->checkAccess('createUser',array('project'=>$mod
el)))
{
    $this->menu[] = array('label'=>'Add User To Project',
'url'=>array('adduser', 'id'=>$model->id));
}
```

This implements the same approach we had discussed earlier in the chapter. We call checkAccess() on the current user, and send in the name of the permission we want to check. Also, as our roles are within the context of projects, we send in the project model instance as an array input. This will allow the business rule to execute what has been defined in the authorization assignment. Now if we log in as a project owner for a particular project and navigate to that project details page, we'll see the menu option for adding a new user to the project. Conversely, if you log in in as a user in the member or reader role of that same project, and again navigate to the details page, this link will not display.

This, of course, will not prevent a savvy user from gaining access to this functionality by navigating using the URL directly. For example, even while logged in to the application as a user in the reader role for, say, project id #2, if I navigate directly to the URL: http://hostname/tasctrak/index.php?r=project/adduser&id=2 I can still access the form.

To prevent this, we need to add our access check directly to the action method itself. So, in the actionAdduser() method in the project controller class, we can add the check:

```
public function actionAdduser()
    {
        $project = $this->loadModel();
        if(!Yii::app()->user->checkAccess('createUser',
array('project'=>$project)))
            {
            throw new CHttpException(403,'You are not authorized to
per-form this action.');
            }
        $form=new ProjectUserForm;
        // collect user input data
        ...
```

Now when we attempt to access this URL directly, we will be denied access unless we in the project owner role for the project.

We won't go through implementing the access checks for all of the other functionality. Each would be implemented in a similar manner.

Summary

We have covered a lot in this iteration. First we were introduced to the basic access control filter that Yii provides as one method to allow and deny access to specific controller action methods. We used this approach to ensure that users be logged into that application before gaining access to any of the main functionality. We then took a detailed walk through Yii's RBAC model which allows for much more sophisticated approach to access control. We built an entire user authorization hierarchy based on application roles. In the process, we were introduced to writing console applications in Yii, and to some of the benefits of this wonderful feature. We then built in new functionality to allow the addition of users to projects and being able to assign them to appropriate roles within those projects. Finally, we discovered how to implement the needed access checks throughout the application to utilize the RBAC hierarchy to appropriately grant/deny access to feature functionality.

9
Iteration 6: Adding User Comments

With the implementation of user management in the past two iterations, our Trackstar application is really starting to take shape. The bulk of our primary application feature functionality is now behind us. We can now start to focus on some of the nice-to-have features. The first of these features that we will tackle is the ability for users to leave comments on project issues.

The ability for users to engage in a dialogue about project issues is an important part of what any issue tracking tool should provide. One way to achieve this is to allow users to leave comments directly on the issues. The comments will form a conversation about the issue and provide an immediate, as well as historical context to help track the full lifespan of any issue. We will also use comments to demonstrate using Yii widgets and establishing a portlet model for delivering content to the user (for more information on **Portlets**, visit `http://en.wikipedia.org/wiki/Portlet`).

Iteration planning

The goal of this iteration is to implement feature functionality in the Trackstar application to allow users to leave and read comments on issues. When a user is viewing the details of any project issue, they should be able to read all comments previously added as well as create a new comment on the issue. We also want to add a small fragment of content, or portlet, to the project-listing page that displays a list of recent comments left on all of the issues. This will be a nice way to provide a window into recent user activity and allow easy access to the latest issues that have active conversations.

The following is a list of high-level tasks that we will need to complete in order to achieve these goals:

- Design and create a new database table to support comments
- Create the Yii AR class associated with our new comments table
- Add a form directly to the issue details page to allow users to submit comments
- Display a list of all comments associated with an issue directly on the issues details page
- Take advantage of Yii *widgets* to display a list of the most recent comments on the projects listing page

Creating the model

As always, we should run our existing test suite at the start of our iteration to ensure all of our previously written tests are still passing as expected. By this time, you should be familiar with how to do that, so we will leave it to the reader to ensure that all the unit tests are passing before proceeding.

We first need to create a new table to house our comments. Below is the basic DDL definition for the table that we will be using:

```
CREATE TABLE tbl_comment
(
    `id` INTEGER NOT NULL PRIMARY KEY AUTO_INCREMENT,
    `content` TEXT NOT NULL,
    `issue_id` INTEGER,
    `create_time` DATETIME,
    `create_user_id` INTEGER,
    `update_time` DATETIME,
    `update_user_id` INTEGER
)
```

As each comment belongs to a specific issue, identified by the issue_id, and is written by a specific user, indicated by the create_user_id identifier, we also need to define the following foreign key relationships:

```
ALTER TABLE `tbl_comment` ADD CONSTRAINT `FK_comment_issue` FOREIGN
KEY (`issue_id`) REFERENCES `tbl_issue` (`id`);

ALTER TABLE `tbl_comment` ADD CONSTRAINT `FK_comment_author` FOREIGN
KEY (`create_user_id`) REFERENCES `tbl_user` (`id`);
```

If you are following along, please ensure this table is created in both the
`trackstar_dev` and `trackstar_test` databases.

Once a database table is in place, creating the associated AR class is a snap. We have
seen this many times in previous iterations. We know exactly how to do this. We
simply use the Gii code creation tool's `Model Generator` command and create an
AR class called `Comment`. If needed, refer back to *Chapters 5 and 6* for all the details
on using this tool to create model classes.

Since we have already created the model class for issues, we will need to explicitly add
the relations to to the Issue model class for comments. We will also add a relationship
as a statistical query to easily retrieve the number of comments associated with a given
issue (just as we did in the Project AR class for issues). Alter the `Issue::relations()`
method as such:

```php
public function relations()
{
  return array(
    'requester' => array(self::BELONGS_TO, 'User', 'requester_id'),
    'owner' => array(self::BELONGS_TO, 'User', 'owner_id'),
    'project' => array(self::BELONGS_TO, 'Project', 'project_id'),
    'comments' => array(self::HAS_MANY, 'Comment', 'issue_id'),
    'commentCount' => array(self::STAT, 'Comment', 'issue_id'),
  );
}
```

Also, we need to change our newly created `Comment` AR class to extend our custom
`TrackStarActiveRecord` base class, so that it benefits from the logic we placed in
the `beforeValidate()` method. Simply alter the beginning of the class definition
as such:

```php
<?php
    /**
 * This is the model class for table "tbl_comment".
 */
class Comment extends TrackStarActiveRecord
{
```

We'll make one last small change to the definitions in the `Comment::relations()` method. The relational attributes were named for us when the class was created. Let's change the one named `createUser` to be `author`, as this related user does represent the author of the comment. This is just a semantic change, but will help to make our code easier to read and understand. Change the method as such:

```
    /**
     * @return array relational rules.
     */
    public function relations()
    {
        // NOTE: you may need to adjust the relation name and the related
        // class name for the relations automatically generated below.
        return array(
            'author' => array(self::BELONGS_TO, 'User', 'create_user_id'),
            'issue' => array(self::BELONGS_TO, 'Issue', 'issue_id'),
        );
    }
```

Creating the Comment CRUD

Once we have an AR class in place, creating the CRUD scaffolding for managing the related entity is equally as easy. Again, use the Gii code generation tool's `Crud Generator` command with the AR class name, `Comment`, as the argument. Again, we have seen this many times in previous iterations, so we will leave this as an exercise for the reader. Again, if needed, refer back to *Chapters 5 and 6* for all the details on using this tool to create CRUD scaffolding code. Although we will not immediately implement full CRUD operations for our comments, it is nice to have the scaffolding for the other operations in place.

As long as we are logged in, we should now be able to view the autogenerated comment submission form via the following URL:

```
http://localhost/trackstar/index.php?r=comment/create
```

Altering the scaffolding to meet requirements

As we have seen many times before, we often have to make adjustments to the autogenerated scaffolding code in order to meet the specific requirements of the application. For one, our autogenerated form for creating a new comment has an input field for every single column defined in the `tbl_comment` database table.

We don't actually want all of these fields to be part of the form. In fact, we want to greatly simplify this form to have only a single input field for the comment content. What's more, we don't want the user to access the form via the above URL, but rather only by visiting an issue details page. The user will add comments on the same page where they are viewing the details of the issue. We want to build towards something similar to what is depicted in the following screenshot:

In order to achieve this, we are going to alter our `Issue` controller class to handle the post of the comment form as well as alter the issue details view to display the existing comments and new comment creation form. Also, as comments should only be created within the context of an issue, we'll add a new method to the `Issue` model class to create new comments.

Adding a comment

Let's start by writing a test for this new public method on the `Issue` model class. Open up the `IssueTest.php` file and add the following test method:

```
public function testAddComment()
{
  $comment = new Comment;
  $comment->content = "this is a test comment";
  $this->assertTrue($this->issues('issueBug')->addComment($comment));
}
```

This, of course, will fail until we add the method to our Issue AR class. Add the following method to the Issue AR class:

```
/**
 * Adds a comment to this issue
 */
public function addComment($comment)
{
  $comment->issue_id=$this->id;
  return $comment->save();
}
```

This method ensures the proper setting of the comment issue ID before saving the new comment. Run the test again to ensure it now passes.

With this method in place, we can now turn focus to the issue controller class. As we want the comment creation form to display from and post its data back to the `IssueController::actionView()` method, we will need to alter that method. We will also add a new protected method to handle the form POST request. First, alter the `actionView()` method to be the following:

```
public function actionView()
{
    $issue=$this->loadModel();
    $comment=$this->createComment($issue);

    $this->render('view',array(
      'model'=>$issue,
      'comment'=>$comment,
    ));
}
```

Then add the following `protected` method to create a new comment and handle the form `post` request for creating a new comment for this issue:

```php
protected function createComment($issue)
{
    $comment=new Comment;
    if(isset($_POST['Comment']))
    {
        $comment->attributes=$_POST['Comment'];
        if($issue->addComment($comment))
        {
            Yii::app()->user->setFlash('commentSubmitted',"Your comment has
been added." );
            $this->refresh();
        }
    }
    return $comment;
}
```

Our new protected method, `createComment()` is responsible for handling the POST request for creating a new comment based on the user input. If the comment is successfully created, the page will be refreshed displaying the newly created comment. The changes made to `IssueController::actionView()` are responsible for calling this new method and also feeding the new comment instance to the view.

Displaying the form

Now we need to alter our view. First we are going to create a new view file to render the display of our comments and the comment input form. As we'll render this as a partial view, we'll stick with the naming conventions and begin the filename with a leading underscore. Create a new file called `_comments.php` under the `protected/views/issue/` folder and add the following code to that file:

```php
<?php foreach($comments as $comment): ?>
<div class="comment">
        <div class="author">
      <?php echo $comment->author->username; ?>:
    </div>

    <div class="time">
        on <?php echo date('F j, Y \a\t h:i a',strtotime($comment->create_
time)); ?>
    </div>

    <div class="content">
```

```php
<?php echo nl2br(CHtml::encode($comment->content)); ?>
    </div>
        <hr>
</div><!-- comment -->
<?php endforeach; ?>
```

This file expects as an input parameter an array of comment instances and displays them one by one. We now need to alter the `view` file for the issue detail to use this new file. We do this by opening `protected/views/issue/view.php` and adding the following to the end of the file:

```php
<div id="comments">
  <?php if($model->commentCount>=1): ?>
    <h3>
       <?php echo $model->commentCount>1 ? $model->commentCount . '
comments' : 'One comment'; ?>
    </h3>

    <?php $this->renderPartial('_comments',array(
      'comments'=>$model->comments,
    )); ?>
  <?php endif; ?>

  <h3>Leave a Comment</h3>

  <?php if(Yii::app()->user->hasFlash('commentSubmitted')): ?>
    <div class="flash-success">
      <?php echo Yii::app()->user->getFlash('commentSubmitted'); ?>
    </div>
  <?php else: ?>
    <?php $this->renderPartial('/comment/_form',array(
      'model'=>$comment,
    )); ?>
  <?php endif; ?>

</div>
```

Here we are taking advantage of the statistical query property, `commentCount`, we added earlier to our Issue AR model class. This allows us to quickly determine if there are any comments available for the specific issue. If there are comments, it proceeds to render them using our `_comments.php` display view file. It then displays the input form that was created for us when we used the Gii Crud Generator functionality. It will also display the simple flash message set upon a successfully saved comment.

One last change we need to make is to the comment input form itself. As we have seen many times in the past, the form created for us has an input field for every column defined in the underlying `tbl_comment` table. This is not what we want to display to the user. We want to make this a simple input form where the user only needs to submit the comment content. So, open up the `view` file that houses the input form, that is, `protected/views/comment/_form.php` and edit it to be simply:

```
<div class="form">
<?php $form=$this->beginWidget('CActiveForm', array(
  'id'=>'comment-form',
  'enableAjaxValidation'=>false,
)); ?>
    <p class="note">Fields with <span class="required">*</span> are
required.</p>
    <?php echo $form->errorSummary($model); ?>
    <div class="row">
  <?php echo $form->labelEx($model,'content'); ?>
  <?php echo $form->textArea($model,'content',array('rows'=>6,
'cols'=>50)); ?>
    <?php echo $form->error($model,'content'); ?>
  </div>

  <div class="row buttons">
    <?php echo CHtml::submitButton($model->isNewRecord ? 'Create' :
'Save'); ?>
  </div>

<?php $this->endWidget(); ?>

</div>
```

With all of this in place, we can visit an issue listing page, for example `http://hostname/trackstar/index.php?r=issue/view&id=1`

And we see the following comment input form at the bottom of the page:

If we attempt to submit the comment without specifying any content, we see an error as depicted in the following screenshot:

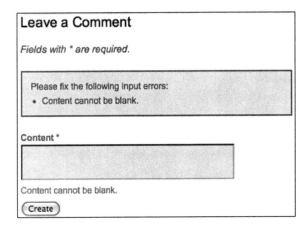

And then, if we are logged in as **Test User One** and we submit the comment **My first test comment**, we are presented with the following display:

Creating a recent comments widget

Now that we have the ability to leave comments on issues, we are going to turn our focus to the second primary goal of this iteration. We want to display to the user a list of all of the recent comments that have been left on various issues across all of the projects. This will provide a nice snapshot of user communication activity within the application. We also want to build this small block of content in a manner that will allow it to be re-used in various different locations throughout the site. This is very much in the style of web portal applications such as news forums, weather reporting applications and sites such as Yahoo and iGoogle. These small snippets of content are often referred to as *portlets,* and this is why we referred to building a portlet architecture at the beginning of this iteration. Again, you can refer to http://en.wikipedia.org/wiki/Portlet for more information on this topic.

Introducing CWidget

Lucky for us, Yii is readymade to help us achieve this architecture. Yii provides a component class, called `CWidget`, which is intended for exactly this purpose. A Yii *widget* is an instance of this class (or its child class), and is a presentational component typically embedded in a `view` file to display self-contained, reusable user interface features. We are going to use a Yii widget to build a recent comments portlet and display it on the main project details page so we can see comment activity across all issues related to the project. To demonstrate the ease of re-use, we'll take it one step further and also display a list of project-specific comments on the project details page.

To begin creating our widget, we are going to first add a new `public` method on our `Comment` AR model class to return the most recently added comments. As expected, we will begin by writing a test.

But before we write the `test` method, let's update our comment fixtures data so that we have a couple of comments to use throughout our testing. Create a new file called `tbl_comment.php` within the `protected/tests/fixtures` folder. Open that file and add the following content:

```php
<?php

return array(
  'comment1'=>array(
    'content' => 'Test comment 1 on issue bug number 1',
    'issue_id' => 1,
    'create_time' => '',
    'create_user_id' => 1,
    'update_time' => '',
    'update_user_id' => '',
  ),
  'comment2'=>array(
    'content' => 'Test comment 2 on issue bug number 1',
    'issue_id' => 1,
    'create_time' => '',
    'create_user_id' => 1,
    'update_time' => '',
    'update_user_id' => '',
  ),
);
```

Now we have consistent, predictable, and repeatable comment data to work with.

Create a new unit test file, `protected/tests/unit/CommentTest.php` and add the following content:

```php
<?php
class CommentTest extends CDbTestCase
{
    public $fixtures=array(
        'comments'=>'Comment',
    );
    public function testRecentComments()
    {
        $recentComments=Comment::findRecentComments();
            $this->assertTrue(is_array($recentComments));
    }
}
```

This test will of course fail, as we have not yet added the `Comment::findRecentComments()` method to the Comment model class. So, let's add that now. We'll go ahead and add the full method we need, rather than adding just enough to get the test to pass. But if you are following along, feel free to move at your own TDD pace. Open `Comment.php` and add the following `public static` method:

```php
public static function findRecentComments($limit=10, $projectId=null)
{
    if($projectId != null)
    {
        return self::model()->with(array(
            'issue'=>array('condition'=>'project_id='.$projectId)))-
>findAll(array(
            'order'=>'t.create_time DESC',
            'limit'=>$limit,
        ));
    }
    else
    {
        //get all comments across all projects
        return self::model()->with('issue')->findAll(array(
            'order'=>'t.create_time DESC',
            'limit'=>$limit,
        ));
    }
}
```

Our new method takes in two optional parameters, one to limit the number of returned comments, the other to specify a specific project ID to which all of the comments should belong. The second parameter will allow us to use our new widget to display all comments for a project on the project details page. So, if the input project id was specified, it restricts the returned results to only those comments associated with the project, otherwise, all comments across all projects are returned.

More on relational AR queries in Yii

The above two relational AR queries are a little new to us. We have not been using many of these options in our previous queries. Previously we have been using the simplest approach to executing relational queries:

1. Load the AR instance.
2. Access the relational properties defined in the `relations()` method.

For example if we wanted to query for all of the issues associated with, say, project id #1, we would execute the following two lines of code:

```
// retrieve the project whose ID is 1
$project=Project::model()->findByPk(1);

// retrieve the project's issues: a relational query is actually being
performed behind the scenes here
$issues=$project->issues;
```

This familiar approach uses what is referred to as a **Lazy Loading**. When we first create the project instance, the query does not return all of the associated issues. It only retrieves the associated issues upon an initial, explicit request for them, that is, when `$project->issues` is executed. This is referred to as *lazy* because it waits to load the issues.

This approach is convenient and can also be very efficient, especially in those cases where the associated issues may not be required. However, in other circumstances, this approach can be somewhat inefficient. For example, if we wanted to retrieve the issue information across **N** projects, then using this lazy approach would involve executing **N** join queries. Depending on how large **N** is, this could be very inefficient. In these situations, we have another option. We can use what is called **Eager Loading**.

The Eager Loading approach retrieves the related AR instances at the same time as the main AR instances are requested. This is accomplished by using the `with()` method in concert with either the `find()` or `findAll()` methods for AR query. Sticking with our project example, we could use Eager Loading to retrieve all issues for all projects by executing the following single line of code:

```
//retrieve all project AR instances along with their associated issue
AR instances
$projects = Project::model()->with('issues')->findAll();
```

Now, in this case, every project AR instance in the `$projects` array already has its associated issues property populated with an array of issues AR instances. This result has been achieved by using just a single join query.

We are using this approach in both of the relational queries executed in our `findRecentComments()` method. The one we are using to restrict the comments to a specific project is slightly more complex. As you can see, we are specifying a query condition on the eagerly loaded issue property for the comments. Let's look at the following line:

```
Comment::model()->with(array('issue'=>array('condition'=>'project_
id='.$projectId)))->findAll();
```

This query specifies a single join between the `tbl_comment` and the `tbl_issue` tables. Sticking with project id #1 for this example, the previous relational AR query would basically execute something similar to the following SQL statement:

```
SELECT tbl_comment.*, tbl_issue.* FROM tbl_comment LEFT OUTER JOIN
tbl_issue ON (tbl_comment.issue_id=tbl_issue.id) WHERE (tbl_issue.
project_id=1)
```

The added array we specify in the `findAll()` method simply sets an `order by` clause and a `limit` clause to the executed SQL statement.

One last thing to note about the two queries we are using is how the column names that are common to both tables are disambiguated. Obviously when the two tables that are being joined have columns with the same name, we have to make a distinction between the two in our query. In our case, both tables have the `create_time` column defined. We are trying to order by this column in the `tbl_comment` table and not the one defined in the `issue` table. In a relational AR query in Yii, the alias name for the primary table is fixed as `t`, while the alias name for a relational table, by default, is the same as the corresponding relation name. So, in our two queries, we specify `t.create_time` to indicate we want to use the primary table's column. If we wanted to instead order by the issue `create_time` column, we would alter, the second query for example, as such:

```
return Comment::model()->with('issue')->findAll(array(
    'order'=>'issue.create_time DESC',
    'limit'=>$limit,
));
```

Completing the test

Okay, now that we fully understand what our new method is doing, we need to complete testing of it. In order to fully test our new method, we need to make a few changes to our fixture data. Open each of the fixture data files: `tbl_project.php`, `tbl_issue.php`, and `tbl_comment.php` and ensure each of these entries is in place:

Add the following code in `tbl_project`:

```
'project3'=>array(
    'name' => 'Test Project 3',
    'description' => 'This is test project 3',
    'create_time' => '',
    'create_user_id' => '',
    'update_time' => '',
    'update_user_id' => '',
),
```

In `tbl_issue`, add the following code:

```
'issueFeature2'=>array(
    'name' => 'Test Feature For Project 3',
    'description' => 'This is a test feature issue associated with
project # 3 that is completed',
    'project_id' => 3,
    'type_id' => 1,
    'status_id' => 2,
    'owner_id' => 1,
    'requester_id' => 1,
    'create_time' => '',
    'create_user_id' => '',
    'update_time' => '',
    'update_user_id' => '',
),
```

Finally, add the following code in `tbl_comment`:

```
'comment3'=>array(
    'content' => 'The first test comment on the first feature issue
associated with Project #3',
    'issue_id' => 3,
    'create_time' => '',
    'create_user_id' => '',
    'update_time' => '',
    'update_user_id' => '',
),
```

We now have a total of three comments in our test database. Two of them associated with project #1 and one associated with project #3.

Now we can alter our test method to test:

- Requesting all comments
- Limiting the number of returned comments to just two
- Restricting the returned comments to only those associated with project #3

The following method tests all three scenarios:

```
public function testRecentComments()
{
        //retrieve all the comments for all projects
    $recentComments = Comment::findRecentComments();
        $this->assertTrue(is_array($recentComments));
        $this->assertEquals(count($recentComments),3);

        //make sure the limit is working
        $recentComments = Comment::findRecentComments(2);
        $this->assertTrue(is_array($recentComments));
        $this->assertEquals(count($recentComments),2);

        //test retrieving comments only for a specific project
        $recentComments = Comment::findRecentComments(5, 3);
        $this->assertTrue(is_array($recentComments));
        $this->assertEquals(count($recentComments),1);
}
```

We also need to ensure that our `CommentTest` class is using the fixture data for `comments`, `issues`, and `projects`. Make sure the following fixtures are defined at the top of our `CommentTest` class:

```php
<?php
class CommentTest extends CDbTestCase
{
  public $fixtures=array(
     'comments'=>'Comment',
     'projects'=>'Project',
     'issues'=>'Issue',
  );
```

Now, if we run this test again, we should have all six assertions passing:

```
>>phpunit unit/CommentTest.php
PHPUnit 3.4.12 by Sebastian Bergmann.

.

Time: 0 seconds

OK (1 test, 6 assertions)
```

Armed with the knowledge of the benefits of Lazy Loading versus Eager Loading in Yii, we should make an adjustment to how the `Issue` model is loaded within the `IssueController::actionView()` method. Since we have altered the issues detail view to display our comments, including the author of the comment, we know it will be more efficient to use the Eager Loading approach to load our comments along with their respective authors when we make the call to `loadModel()` in this method. To do this, we can add a simple input flag to this `loadModel()` method to indicate whether or not we want to load the comments as well.

Alter the `IssueController::loadModel()` method as shown below:

```php
public function loadModel($withComments=false)
  {
    if($this->_model===null)
    {
      if(isset($_GET['id']))
      {
        if($withComments)
        {
          $this->_model=Issue::model()->with(array(
          'comments'=>array('with'=>'author')))
                                ->findbyPk($_GET['id']);
        }
        else
```

```
            {
                $this->_model=Issue::model()->findbyPk($_GET['id']);
            }
        }
        if($this->_model===null)
        throw new CHttpException(404,'The requested page does not
                                    exist.');
    }
    return $this->_model;
}
```

Now we can change the call to this method in `IssueController::actionView()`, as such:

```
public function actionView()
    {
        $issue=$this->loadModel(true);
```

With this in place, we will load all of our comments, along with their respective author information, with just one database call.

Creating the widget

Now we are ready to create our new widget to use our new method to display our recent comments.

As we previously mentioned a widget in Yii is a class that extend from the framework class `CWidget` or one of its child classes. We'll add our new widget to the `protected/components/` directly, as the contents of this folder are already specified in the main configuration file to be auto-loaded within the application. This way we won't have to explicitly import the class every time we wish to use it. We'll name our widget `RecentComments`, so we need to add a php file of the same name to this directly. Add the following class definition to this newly created `RecentComment`.php file:

```
<?php
/**
 * RecentComments is a Yii widget used to display a list of recent
comments
 */
class RecentComments extends CWidget
{
    private $_comments;
    public $displayLimit = 5;
    public $projectId = null;
    public function init()
```

```
    {
        $this->_comments = Comment::model()
        ->findRecentComments($this->displayLimit,
        $this->projectId);
    }
    public function getRecentComments()
    {
        return $this->_comments;
    }
    public function run()
    {
        // this method is called by CController::endWidget()
        $this->render('recentComments');
    }
}
```

The primary work involved when creating a new widget is to override the init()
and run() methods of the base class. The init() method initializes the widget and
is called after its properties have been initialized. The run() method executes the
widget. In this case, we simply initialize the widget by requesting recent comments
based on the $displayLimit and $projectId properties. The execution of the widget
itself simply renders its associated view file, which we have yet to create. view files,
by convention, are placed in views/ directly within the same folder where the widget
resides, and have the same name as the widget, but start with a lowercase letter.
Sticking with convention, create a new file whose fully qualified path is protected/
components/views/renderComments.php. Once created, add the following markup
to that file:

```
<ul>
  <?php foreach($this->getRecentComments() as $comment): ?>
    <div class="author">
      <?php echo $comment->author->username; ?> added a comment.
    </div>
    <div class="issue">
      <?php echo CHtml::link(CHtml::encode($comment->issue->name),
array('issue/view', 'id'=>$comment->issue->id)); ?>
    </div>
  <?php endforeach; ?>
</ul>
```

This calls the RenderComments widget's getRecentComments() method, which
returns an array of comments. It then iterates over each of them displaying who
added the comment and the associated issue on which the comment was left.

In order to see the results, we need to embed this widget into an existing controller view file. As previously mentioned, we want to use this widget on the projects listing page, to display all recent comments across all projects, and also on a specific project details page, to display the recent comments for just that specific project.

Let's start with the project listing page. The `view` file responsible for displaying that content is `protected/views/project/index.php`. Open up that file and add the following at the bottom:

```php
<?php $this->widget('RecentComments'); ?>
```

Now if we view the projects listing page `http://localhost/trackstar/index.php?r=project`, we see something similar to the following screenshot:

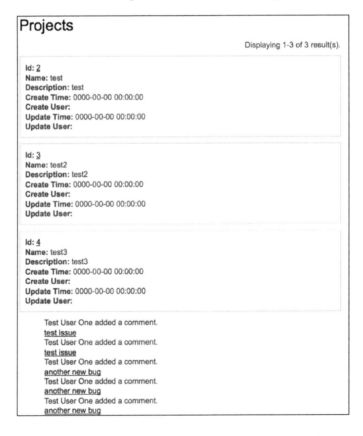

We have now embedded our new recent comments data within the page simply by calling the widget. This is nice, but we can take our little widget one step further to have it display in a consistent manner with all other potential portlets in the application. We can do this by taking advantage of another class provided to us by Yii, `CPortlet`.

Introducing CPortlet

CPortlet is part of zii, the official extension class library that comes packaged with Yii. It provides a nice base class for all portlet-style widgets. It will allow us to render a nice title as well as consistent HTML markup, so that all portlets across the application can be easily styled in a similar manner. Once we have a widget that renders content (like our RecentComments widget), we can simply use the rendered content of our widget as the content for CPortlet, which itself is a widget, as it also extends from CWidget. We can do this by placing our call to the RecentComments widget between a beginWidget() and an endWiget() call for CPortlet, as such:

```php
<?php $this->beginWidget('zii.widgets.CPortlet', array(
  'title'=>'Recent Comments',
));

$this->widget('RecentComments');

$this->endWidget(); ?>
```

Since CPortlet provides a title property, we set it to be something meaningful for our portlet. We then use the rendered content of the RecentComments widget to drive the content for the porlet widget. The end result of this is depicted in the following screenshot:

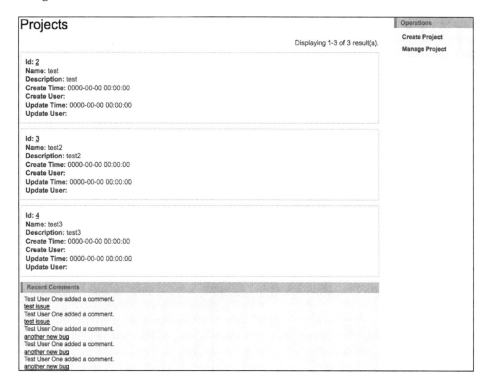

This is not a huge change from what we had previously, but we have now placed our content into a consistent container that is already being used throughout the site. Notice the similarity between the right column menu content block and our newly created recent comments content block. I am sure it will come as no surprise to you that this right column menu block is also displayed within a `CPortlet` container. Taking a peek in `protected/views/layouts/column2.php`, which is a file that the `yiic webapp` command autogenerated for us when we initially created the application, reveals the following code:

```php
<?php
  $this->beginWidget('zii.widgets.CPortlet', array(
    'title'=>'Operations',
  ));
  $this->widget('zii.widgets.CMenu', array(
    'items'=>$this->menu,
    'htmlOptions'=>array('class'=>'operations'),
  ));
  $this->endWidget();
?>
```

So it seems that the application has been taking advantage of portlets all along.

Adding our widget to another page

Let's also add our portlet to the project details page, and restrict the comments to just those associated with the specific project.

Add the following to the bottom of the `protected/views/project/view.php` file:

```php
<?php $this->beginWidget('zii.widgets.CPortlet', array(
    'title'=>'Recent Project Comments',
));

$this->widget('RecentComments', array('projectId'=>$model->id));

$this->endWidget(); ?>
```

This is basically the same thing we added to the project listings page, except we are initializing the `RecentComments` widget's $projectId property by adding an array of *name=>value* pairs to the call.

Now if we visit a specific project details page, we should see something similar to the following screenshot:

This screenshot shows the details page for project #3, which has one associated issue with just one comment on that issue, as depicted in the picture. You may need to add a few issues and comments on those issues in order to generate a similar display. We now have a way to display recent comments with a few different configurable parameters anywhere throughout the site in a consistent and easily maintainable manner.

Summary

With this iteration, we have started to flesh out our Trackstar application with functionality that has come to be expected of most user-based web applications today. The ability for users to communicate with each other within the application is an essential part of a successful issue management system.

As we created this essential feature, we were able to deeper look into how to write relational AR queries. We were also introduced to content components called widgets and portlets. This introduced us to an approach to developing small content blocks and being able to use them anywhere throughout the site. This approach greatly increases reuse, consistency, and ease of maintenance.

In the next iteration, we'll build upon the recent comments widget created here, and expose the content generated by our widget as an RSS feed to allow users to track application or project activity without having to visit the application.

10
Iteration 7: Adding an RSS Web Feed

In the previous iteration, we added the ability for the user to leave comments on issues and to display a list of these comments utilizing a portlet architecture to allow us to easily and consistently display that listing anywhere throughout the application. In this iteration, we are going to build upon this feature and expose this list of comments as an RSS data feed. Furthermore, we are going to use the existing feed functionality available in another open source framework, the Zend Framework, to demonstrate just how easy it is for a Yii application to integrate with other third-party tools.

Iteration planning

The goal of this iteration is to create an RSS feed using the content created from our user generated comments. We should allow users to subscribe to a comment feed that spans all projects as well as subscribe to individual project feeds. Luckily, the widget functionality we built previously has the capability to return a list of recent comments across all projects, as well as restrict the data to one specific project. So, we have already coded the appropriate methods to access the needed data. The bulk of this iteration will focus on putting that data in the correct format to be published as an RSS feed, and adding links to our application to allow users to subscribe to these feeds.

The following is a list of high-level tasks we will need to complete in order to achieve these goals:

- Download and install Zend Framework into the Yii application
- Create a new action in a controller class to respond to the feed request and return the appropriate data in an RSS format

- Alter our URL structure for ease of use
- Add our newly created feed to both the projects listings page, as well as to each individual project details page

As always, be sure to run the full suite of unit tests prior to making any changes to ensure everything that is still working as expected.

A little background: Content Syndication, RSS, and Zend Framework

Web Content Syndication has been around for many years, but has recently gained enormous popularity. The term Web Content Syndication refers to publishing information in a standardized format so that it can easily be used by other websites and easily consumed by reader applications. Many news sites have long been electronically syndicating their content, but the massive explosion of web logs (also known as blogs) across the Internet has turned Content Syndication (also known as known as feeds) into an expected feature of almost every website. Our TrackStar application will be no exception.

RSS is an acronym that stands for **Really Simple Syndication**. It is an XML format specification that provides a standard for Web Content Syndication. There are other formats that could be used, but due to the overwhelming popularity of RSS among most websites, we will focus on delivering our feed in this format.

Zend is known as "The PHP Company". Their founders are key contributors to the core PHP language and the company focuses on creating products to help improve the entire PHP application development life-cycle experience. They provide products and services to help with configuration and installation, development, deployment and with production application administration and maintenance. One of the products they offer to assist in application development is the Zend Framework. The framework can be used as a whole to provide an entire application foundation, much in the same way we are using Yii for our TrackStar application, or piece-meal by utilizing single feature components of the framework's library. Yii is flexible enough to allow us to use pieces of other frameworks. We will be using just one component of the Zend framework library, called `Zend_Feed`, so that we don't have to write all of the underlying "plumbing" code to generate our RSS formatted web feeds. For more on `Zend_Feed`, visit `http://www.zendframework.com/manual/en/zend.feed.html`

Installing Zend Framework

As we are using the Zend Framework to help support our RSS needs, we first need to download and install the framework. To get the latest version, visit `http://framework.zend.com/download/latest`. We will only be utilizing a single component of this framework, `Zend_Feed`, so the minimal version of the framework will suffice.

When you expand the downloaded framework file, you should see the following high-level folder and file structure:

```
INSTALL.txt

LICENSE.txt

README.txt

bin/

library/
```

In order to use this framework within our Yii application, we need to move some of the files within our application's folder structure. Let's create a new folder under the `/protected` folder within our application called `vendors/`. Then, move the Zend Framework folder `/library/Zend` underneath this newly created folder. After everything is in place, ensure that `protected/vendors/Zend/Feed.php` exists in the TrackStar application.

Using Zend_Feed

`Zend_Feed` is a small component of the Zend Framework that encapsulates all of the complexities of creating web feeds behind a simple, easy-to-use interface. It will help us get a working, tested, RSS compliant data feed in place in very little time. All we will need to do is format our comment data in a manner expected by `Zend_Feed`, and it does the rest.

We need a place to house the code to handle the requests for our feed. We could create a new controller for this, but to keep things simple, we'll just add a new action method to our main `CommentController.php` file to handle the requests. Rather than add to the method a little at a time, we'll list the entire method here, and then talk through what it is doing.

Open up `CommentController.php` and add the following `public` method:

```php
public function actionFeed()
{
    if(isset($_GET['pid'])) $projectId = intval($_GET['pid']);
    else $projectId = null;

    $comments = Comment::model()->findRecentComments(20, $projectId);

    //convert from an array of comment AR class instances to an
    name=>value array for Zend
    $entries=array();

    foreach($comments as $comment)
    {

        $entries[]=array(
                'title'=>$comment->issue->name,
                'link'=>CHtml::encode($this->createAbsoluteUrl('issue/
view',array('id'=>$comment->issue->id))),
                'description'=> $comment->author->username . '
says:<br>' . $comment->content,
                'lastUpdate'=>strtotime($comment->create_time),
                'author'=>$comment->author->username,
            );
    }

    //now use the Zend Feed class to generate the Feed
    // generate and render RSS feed
    $feed=Zend_Feed::importArray(array(
            'title'   => 'Trackstar Project Comments Feed',
            'link'    => $this->createUrl(''),
            'charset' => 'UTF-8',
            'entries' => $entries,
        ), 'rss');

    $feed->send();

}
```

This is all fairly simple. First we check the input request querystring for the existence of a `pid` parameter, which we take to indicate a specific project ID. Remember that we want to optionally allow the data feed to restrict the content to comments associated with a single project. Next we use the same method that we used in the previous iteration to populate our widget to retrieve a list of up to 20 recent comments, either across all projects, or if the project ID is specified, specific to that project.

You may remember that this method returns an array of Comment AR class instances. We iterate over this returned array and convert the data into the format expected by the Zend_Feed component. Zend_Feed expects a simple array containing elements which are themselves arrays containing the data for each comment entry. Each individual entry is a simple associative array of name=>value pairs. To comply with the specific RSS format, each of our individual entries must minimally contain a title, a link, and a description. We have also added two optional fields, one called *lastUpdate*, which Zend_Feed translates to the RSS field, *pubDate,* and one to specify the author.

There are a few extra helper methods we take advantage of in order to get the data in the correct format. For one, we use the controller's createAbsoluteUrl() method, rather than just the createUrl() method in order to generate a fully qualified URL. Using createAbsoluteUrl() will generate a link like the following

http://localhost/trackstar/index.php?r=issue/view &id=5 as opposed to just /index.php?r=issue/view&id=5.

Also, to avoid errors such as "unterminated entity reference" being generated from PHP's DOMDocument::createElement(), which is used by Zend_Feed to generate the RSS XML, we need to convert all applicable characters to HTML entities by using our handy helper function, CHTML::encode. So, we encode the link such that a URL that looks like:

http://localhost/trackstar/index.php?r=issue/view&id=5

will be converted to:

http://localhost/trackstar/index.php?r=issue/view&id=5

Once all of our entries have been properly populated and formatted, we use Zend_ Feed's importArray() method which expects an array to construct the RSS feed. Finally, once the Zend feed class is built from the input array of entries and returned, we call the send() method on that class. This returns the properly formatted RSS XML and appropriate headers to the client.

We need to make a couple of configuration changes to the CommentController.php file and class before this will work. First, we need to import the /vendors/Zend/ Feed.php file as well as the Rss.php file under the Feed/ folder. Add the following statements to the top of CommentController.php:

```
Yii::import('application.vendors.*');
require_once('Zend/Feed.php');
require_once('Zend/Feed/Rss.php');
```

Then, alter the `CommentController::accessRules()` method to allow any user to access our newly added `actionFeed()` method:

```
public function accessRules()
    {
        return array(
                array('allow',  // allow all users to perform 'index'
and 'view' actions
                        'actions'=>array('index','view', 'feed'),
                        'users'=>array('*'),
                ),
                ...
```

This is really all there is to it. If we now navigate to `http://localhost/trackstar/index.php?r=comment/feed`, we can view the results of our effort. As browsers handle the display of RSS feeds differently, what you see might differ from the following screenshot. The following screenshot is what you should see you are if viewing the feed in the Firefox browser:

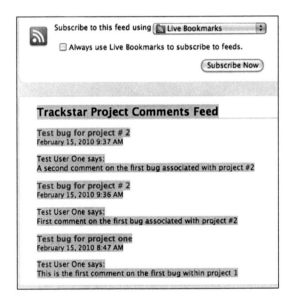

Creating user friendly URLs

So far, throughout the development process, we have been using the default format of our Yii application URL structure. This format, discussed back in *Chapter 2*, uses a querystring approach. We have the main parameter, 'r', which stands for *route*, followed by a `controllerID/actionID` pair, and then optional querystring parameters as needed by the specific action methods being called. The URL we created for our new feed is no exception. It is a long, cumbersome and dare we say ugly URL. There has got to be a better way! Well, in fact, there is.

We could make the above URL look cleaner and more self-explanatory by using the so-called *path* format, which eliminates the query string and puts the GET parameters into the path info part of URL:

Taking our comment feed URL as an example, instead of:

```
http://localhost/trackstar/index.php?r=comment/feed
```

we would have:

```
http://localhost/trackstar/index.php/comment/feed/
```

What's more, we don't even need to always specify the entry script for each request. We can also take advantage of Yii's request routing configuration options to remove the need to specify the `controllerID/actionID` pair as well. Our request could then look like:

```
http://localhost/trackstar/commentfeed
```

Also, it is common, especially with feed URL, to have the .xml extension specified at the end. So, it would be nice if we could alter our URL to look like:

```
http://localhost/trackstar/commentfeed.xml
```

This greatly simplifies the URL for users and is also an excellent format for URLs to be properly indexed into major search engines (often referred to as "search engine friendly URLs"). Let's see how we can use Yii's URL management features to alter our URL to match the desired format.

Using the URL manager

The built-in URL manager in Yii is an application component that can be configured in the `protected/config/main.php` file. Let's open up that file and add a new URL manager component declaration to the components array:

```
'urlManager'=>array(
    'urlFormat'=>'path',
),
```

As long as we stick with the default and name it `urlManager`, we do not need to specify the class of the component because it is pre-declared to be `CUrlManager.php` in the `CWebApplication.php` framework class.

With this one simple addition, our URL structure has changed to the 'path' format throughout the site. For example, previously if we wanted to view, say, a specific issue whose ID is 1, we would make the request using the following URL:

```
http://localhost/trackstar/index.php?r=issue/view&id=1
```

but with these changes in place, our URL now looks like:

```
http://localhost/trackstar/index.php/issue/view/id/1
```

You'll notice the changes we have made have affected all the URLs generated throughout the application. To see this, visit our feed again by going to `http://localhost/trackstar/index.php/comment/feed/`. We notice that all of our issue links have been reformatted to this new structure for us. This is all thanks to our consistent use of the controller methods and other helper methods to generate our URLs. We can alter the URL format in just one single configuration file, and the changes will automatically propagate throughout the application.

Our URLs are looking better, but we still have the entry script, `index.php`, specified and we are not yet able to append the `.xml` suffix on the end of our feed URL. So, we'll hide the `index.php` as part of the URL, and also setup the request routing to understand that a request for `commentfeed.xml` actually means a request for the `actionFeed()` method within the `CommentController.php` class. Let's actually tackle the latter, first.

Configuring routing rules

Yii's URL manager allows us to specify rules that define how URLs are parsed and created. A rule consists of defining a *route* and a *pattern*. The pattern is used to match on the path information part of the URL to determine which rule is used for parsing or creating URLs. The pattern may contain named parameters using the syntax `ParamName:RegExp`. When parsing a URL, a matching rule will extract these named parameters from the path info and put them into the `$_GET` variable. When a URL is being created by the application, a matching rule will extract the named parameters from `$_GET` and put them into the path info part of the created URL. If a pattern ends with '/*', it means additional GET parameters may be appended to the path info part of the URL.

To specify URL rules, set the set the `CUrlManager`'s `rules` property as an array of rules in the format `pattern=>route`.

As an example, let's look at the following two rules:

```
'urlManager'=>array(
    'urlFormat'=>'path',
'rules'=>array(
```

```
'issues'=>'issue/index',
'issue/<id:\d+>/*'=>'issue/view',
)
```

There are two rules specified in the above code. The first rule says that if the user requests the URL `http://localhost/trackstar/index.php/issues`, it should be treated as `http://localhost/trackstar/index.php/issue/index` and the same applies when constructing such a URL.

The second rule contains a named parameter `id` which is specified using the `<ParamName:RegExp>` syntax. It says that, for example, if the user requests the URL `http://localhost/trackstar /index.php/issue/1`, it should be treated as `http://localhost/trackstar/index.php/issue/view?id=1`. The same also applies when constructing such a URL.

The route can also be specified as an array itself to allow the setting of other attributes such as the URL suffix and whether or not the route should be considered as case sensitive. We'll take advantage of these as we specify the rule for our comment feed.

Let's add the following rule to our `urlManager` application component configuration:

```
'urlManager'=>array(
                'urlFormat'=>'path',
                'rules'=>array(    'commentfeed'=>array('comment/feed',
 'urlSuffix'=>'.xml', 'caseSensitive'=>false),
                    ),
    ),
```

Here, we have used the `urlSuffix` attribute to specify our desired URL `.xml` suffix.

Now we can access our feed by using the following URL:

`http://localhost/trackstar/index.php/commentFeed.xml`

Removing the entry script from the URL

Now we just need to remove the `index.php` from the URL. This is done in two steps:

1. Alter the web server configuration to re-route all requests that don't correspond to existing files or directories to `index.php`.

2. Set the `UrlManager`'s `showScriptName` property to false.

The first takes care of the how the application routes the requests, the second takes care of how URLs will be created throughout the application.

As we are using Apache HTTP Server, we can perform the first step by by creating a .htaccess file in the application root folder and adding the following directives to that file:

```
Options +FollowSymLinks
IndexIgnore */*
RewriteEngine on

# if a directory or a file exists, use it directly
RewriteCond %{REQUEST_FILENAME} !-f
RewriteCond %{REQUEST_FILENAME} !-d

# otherwise forward it to index.php
RewriteRule . index.php
```

Note: This approach is only for use with the Apache HTTP Server. You will need to consult your web server's re-write rules documentation if you are using a different web server. Also note that this information could be placed in the Apache configuration file as an alternative to using the .htaccess file approach.

With the .htaccess file in place, we can now visit our feed by navigating to

http://localhost/trackstar/commentfeed.xml (or http://localhost/trackstar/commentFeed.xml as we set the case-sensitivity to false)

However, even with this in place, if we use one of the controller methods or one of our CHTML helper methods in our application to create our URL, say by executing the following in a controller class:

```
$this->createAbsoluteUrl('comment/feed');
```

it will generate the following URL, with index.php still in the URL:

http://localhost/trackstar/index.php/commentfeed.xml

In order to instruct it to not use the entry script name when generating URLs, we need to set that property on the urlManager component. We do this again in the main.php config file as such:

```
'urlManager'=>array(
    'urlFormat'=>'path',
    'rules'=>array(
```

```
            'commentfeed'=>array('site/commentFeed', 'urlSuffix'=>'.xml',
'caseSensitive'=>false),
        ),
      'showScriptName'=>false,
    ),
```

In order to handle the addition of the project ID in the URL, which we need to restrict the comment feed data to comments associated with specific projects, we need to add one other rule:

```
'urlManager'=>array(
                'urlFormat'=>'path',
                'rules'=>array(
                    '<pid:\d+>/commentfeed'=>array('site/
   commentFeed', 'urlSuffix'=>'.xml', 'caseSensitive'=>false),
Comment/Feed          'commentfeed'=>array('site/commentFeed',
   'urlSuffix'=>'.xml', 'caseSensitive'=>false),   comment/feed
                ),
                'showScriptName'=>false,
    ),
```

This rule also uses the `<Parameter:RegEx>` syntax to specify a pattern to allow for a project ID to be specified before the `commentfeed.xml` part of the URL. With this rule in place, we can restrict our RSS feed to comments specific to a project. For example, if we just want the comments associated with project # 2, the URL format would be:

```
http://localhost/trackstar/2/commentfeed.xml
```

Adding the feed links

Now that we have created our feed and altered the URL structure to make it more user and search engine friendly, we need to add the ability for users to subscribe to the feed. One way to do this is to add the following code before rendering the pages in which we want to add the RSS feed link. Let's do this for both the project listing page as well as a specific project details page. We'll start with the project listings page. This page is rendered by the `ProjectController::actionIndex()` method. Alter that method as such:

```
public function actionIndex()
{
            $dataProvider=new CActiveDataProvider('Project');


            Yii::app()->clientScript->registerLinkTag(
```

```
            'alternate',
            'application/rss+xml',
            $this->createUrl('comment/feed'));


        $this->render('index',array(
                'dataProvider'=>$dataProvider,

        ));

}
```

The above highlighted code adds the following to the `<head>` tag of the rendered HTML:

```
<link rel="alternate" type="application/rss+xml" href="/commentfeed.
xml" />
```

In many browsers, this will automatically generate a little RSS feed icon in the address bar. The following screenshot depicts what this icon looks like in the Firefox 3.6 address bar:

We make a similar change to add this link to a specific project details page. The rendering of these pages is handled by the `ProjectController::actionView()` method. Alter that method to be the following:

```
public function actionView()
    {
        $issueDataProvider=new CActiveDataProvider('Issue', array(
            'criteria'=>array(
                'condition'=>'project_id=:projectId',
                'params'=>array(':projectId'=>$this-
>loadModel()->id),
                ),
                'pagination'=>array(
                    'pageSize'=>1,
                ),
            ));

        Yii::app()->clientScript->registerLinkTag(
            'alternate',
            'application/rss+xml',
            $this->createUrl('comment/feed',array('pid'=>$this-
>loadModel()->id)));
```

```
$this->render('view',array(
        'model'=>$this->loadModel(),
        'issueDataProvider'=>$issueDataProvider,
    ));
}
```

This is almost the same as what we added to the index method, except that we are specifying the project ID so that our comment entries are restricted to just those associated with that project. A similar icon will now display in the address bar on our project details page. Clicking on one of these icons allow the user to subscribe to these comment feeds.

Summary

This iteration demonstrated just how easy it is to integrate Yii with other external frameworks. We specifically used the popular Zend Framework to demonstrate this and were able to quickly add an RSS compliant web feed to our application. Though we specifically used Zend_Feed, we really demonstrated how to integrate any of the Zend Framework components into the application. This further extends the already extensive feature offering of Yii, making Yii applications incredibly feature rich.

We also learned about the URL Management features within Yii and altered our URL format throughout the application to be more user and search engine friendly. This is a first step in improving upon the look and feel of our application. Something we have very much neglected up to this point. Turning our focus to styles, themes, and generally making things pretty is the focus of the next iteration.

11
Iteration 8: Making it Pretty - Design, Layout, Themes, and Internationalization(i18n)

In the previous iteration, we started to add a little beauty to our application by making our URLs more attractive to both, the user and to search engine bots that crawl the site. In this iteration, we are going to turn more focus to the look and feel of our application by covering the topics of page layouts and themes in Yii. Though we will live up to the title of this chapter by changing the look of our application to something we believe is slightly better looking, we will be focused on the approach one takes and the tools available to help design the front-end of a Yii application rather than design itself. So this iteration will focus more on *how* you can make your applications pretty, rather than spending a lot of time specifically designing our TrackStar application.

Iteration planning

This iteration aims to focus on the frontend. We want to create a new look for our site that is reusable and able to be implemented dynamically. We also want to accomplish without overwriting or otherwise removing our current design. Also, we are going to dig into the internationalization features of Yii, so we need to clearly understand how to accommodate application users from different geographic regions.

The following is a list of high-level tasks that we will need to complete in order to achieve our goals:

- Create a new theme for our application by creating new layout, CSS and other asset files for providing the application with a new front-end design

- Use the internationalization and localization features of Yii to help translate a portion of our application to a new language

Designing with layouts

One thing that you may have noticed is that we have added a lot of functionality to our application without adding any explicit navigation to access this functionality. Our home page has not yet changed from the default application we built. We still have the same navigation items as we did when we first created our new application. We need to change our basic navigation to better reflect the underlying functionality present in the application.

Thus far, we have not fully covered how our application is using all of the view files responsible for displaying the content. We know that our view files are responsible for our data display and housing the HTML sent back for each page request. When we create new controller actions, we also often create new views to handle the display of the returned content from these action methods. Most of these views are very specific to the action methods they support and not used across multiple pages. However, there are some things, like the main menu navigation, that are used across multiple pages throughout the site. These types of UI components are better suited to reside in what are called **layout files**.

A layout in Yii, is a special view file used to decorate other view files. Layouts typically contain markup or other user interface components that are common across multiple view files. When using a layout to render a view file, Yii embeds the view file into the layout.

Specifying a layout

There are two main places where a layout can be specified. One is the property called $layout of the CWebApplication itself. This defaults to protected/views/layouts/main.php if not otherwise explicitly specified. As is the case with all application settings, this can be overridden in the main config file, protected/config/main.php. For example, if we created a new layout file, protected/views/layouts/newlayout.php, and wanted to use this new file as our application-wide layout file, we could alter our main config file to set the layout property as such:

```
return array(
  'layout'=>'newlayout',
```

The filename is specified without the .php extension and is relative to the $layoutPath property of CWebApplication, which defaults to Webroot/protected/views/layouts (which itself could be overridden in a similar manner if this location does not suit your application's needs).

The other place to specify the layout is by setting the $layout property of the controller class. This allows for more granular control of the layout on a controller-by-controller basis. This is the way it was specified when we generated the initial application. Using the yiic tool to create our initial application automatically created a controller base class, Webroot/protected/components/Controller.php, from which all of our other controller classes extend. Opening up this file reveals that the $layout property has been set to "column1". Setting the layout file at the more granular controller level will override the setting in the CWebApplication class.

Applying and using a layout

The use of a layout file is implicit in the call to the CController::render() method. That is, when you make the call to the render() method to render a view file, Yii will embed the contents of the view file into the layout file specified in either the controller class, or the one specified at the application level. You can avoid applying any layout decoration of the rendered view file by calling the CController::renderPartial() method instead.

As previously mentioned, a layout file is typically used to decorate other view files. One example use of a layout is to provide a consistent header and footer layout to each and every page. When the render() method is called, what happens behind the scenes is first a call to renderPartial() on the specified view file. The output of this is stored in a variable called $content, which is then made available to the layout file. So, a simple layout file might look like the following:

```
<!DOCTYPE html PUBLIC "-//W3C//DTD XHTML 1.0 Transitional//EN"
"http://www.w3.org/TR/xhtml1/DTD/xhtml1-transitional.dtd">
```

```html
<html xmlns="http://www.w3.org/1999/xhtml" xml:lang="en" lang="en">
<head>
  <meta http-equiv="Content-Type" content="text/html; charset=utf-8"
/>
  <meta name="language" content="en" />
</head>
<body>
  <div id="header">
    Some Header Content Here
  </div>
  <?php echo $content; ?>

  <div id="footer">
      Some Footer Content Here
  </div>
</body>
</html>
```

In fact, let's try this out. Create a new file called `newlayout.php` and place it in the default folder for layout files, `/protected/views/layouts/`. Add the above HTML content to this file and save it. Now we'll put this to use by altering our site controller to use this new layout. Open up `SiteController.php` and override the layout property set in the base class by explicitly adding it to this class, as such:

```php
class SiteController extends Controller
{
  public $layout='newlayout';
```

This will set the layout file to `newlayout.php`, but only for this controller. Now, every time we make the call to the `render()` method within `SiteController`, the `newlayout.php` layout file will be used.

One page that `SiteController` is responsible for rendering is the login page. Let's take a look at that page to verify these changes. If we navigate to `http://localhost/trackstar/site/login` (assuming we are not already logged in), we will see something similar to the following screenshot:

Some Header Content Here

Login

Please fill out the following form with your login credentials:

Fields with * are required.

Username * [_____]
Password * [_____]

Hint: You may login with `demo/demo` or `admin/admin`.

☐ Remember me next time
(Login)
Some Footer Content Here

If we simply comment out the `$layout` attribute we just added, and refresh the login page again, we are back to using the original `main.php` layout and our page is now back to what it looked like before.

Deconstructing the main.php layout file

So far, all of our application pages have been using the `main.php` layout file to provide the primary layout markup. Before we go making changes to our page layout and design, it would serve us well to take a closer look at this main layout file. The following is a listing of the entire contents of that file:

```
<!DOCTYPE html PUBLIC "-//W3C//DTD XHTML 1.0 Transitional//EN"
"http://www.w3.org/TR/xhtml1/DTD/xhtml1-transitional.dtd">
<html xmlns="http://www.w3.org/1999/xhtml" xml:lang="en" lang="en">
<head>
  <meta http-equiv="Content-Type" content="text/html; charset=utf-8"
/>
  <meta name="language" content="en" />

  <!-- blueprint CSS framework -->
  <link rel="stylesheet" type="text/css" href="<?php echo Yii::app()-
>request->baseUrl; ?>/css/screen.css" media="screen, projection" />
  <link rel="stylesheet" type="text/css" href="<?php echo Yii::app()-
>request->baseUrl; ?>/css/print.css" media="print" />
  <!--[if lt IE 8]>
  <link rel="stylesheet" type="text/css" href="<?php echo Yii::app()-
>request->baseUrl; ?>/css/ie.css" media="screen, projection" />
```

```
   <![endif]-->

   <link rel="stylesheet" type="text/css" href="<?php echo Yii::app()-
>request->baseUrl; ?>/css/main.css" />
   <link rel="stylesheet" type="text/css" href="<?php echo Yii::app()-
>request->baseUrl; ?>/css/form.css" />

   <title><?php echo CHtml::encode($this->pageTitle); ?></title>
</head>

<body>

<div class="container" id="page">

   <div id="header">
     <div id="logo"><?php echo CHtml::encode(Yii::app()->name); ?></
div>
   </div><!-- header -->

   <div id="mainmenu">
     <?php $this->widget('zii.widgets.CMenu',array(
       'items'=>array(
         array('label'=>'Home', 'url'=>array('/site/index')),
         array('label'=>'About', 'url'=>array('/site/page',
'view'=>'about')),
         array('label'=>'Contact', 'url'=>array('/site/contact')),
         array('label'=>'Login', 'url'=>array('/site/login'),
'visible'=>Yii::app()->user->isGuest),
         array('label'=>'Logout ('.Yii::app()->user->name.')',
'url'=>array('/site/logout'), 'visible'=>!Yii::app()->user->isGuest)
       ),
     )); ?>
   </div><!-- mainmenu -->

   <?php $this->widget('zii.widgets.CBreadcrumbs', array(
     'links'=>$this->breadcrumbs,
   )); ?><!-- breadcrumbs -->

   <?php echo $content; ?>

   <div id="footer">
     Copyright &copy; <?php echo date('Y'); ?> by My Company.<br/>
     All Rights Reserved.<br/>
     <?php echo Yii::powered(); ?>
   </div><!-- footer -->

</div><!-- page -->

</body>
</html>
```

We'll walk through this starting at the top. The first five lines probably look somewhat familiar to you.

```
<!DOCTYPE html PUBLIC "-//W3C//DTD XHTML 1.0 Transitional//EN"
"http://www.w3.org/TR/xhtml1/DTD/xhtml1-transitional.dtd">
<html xmlns="http://www.w3.org/1999/xhtml" xml:lang="en" lang="en">
<head>
  <meta http-equiv="Content-Type" content="text/html; charset=utf-8"
/>
  <meta name="language" content="en" />
```

These lines define a standard HTML document type declaration, followed by a starting `<html>` element, then the start of our `<head>` element. Within the `<head>` tag, we first have a meta tag to declare the standard, and very important, XHTML-compliant UTF-8 character encoding, followed by another `<meta>` tag that specifies English as the primary language in which the website is written.

Introducing the Blueprint CSS framework

The next several lines, beginning with the comment `<!–blueprint CSS framework -->` may be less familiar to you. Another great thing about Yii is that it utilizes other best-in-breed frameworks, when appropriate, and the **Blueprint CSS framework** is one such example.

The Blueprint CSS framework was included in the application as a by-product of using the `yiic` tool when we initially created our application. It is included to help standardize the CSS development. Blueprint is a CSS Grid framework. It helps standardize your CSS, provides cross-browser compatibility, and provides consistency in HTML element placement helping reduce CSS errors. It comes with many screen and print-friendly layout definitions and helps jumpstart your design by providing much of the css you need to get something that looks good and in place quickly. For more on the Blueprint framework, visit `http://www.blueprintcss.org/`.

So, the following lines of code are required by and specific to the Blueprint CSS framework:

```
<!-- blueprint CSS framework -->
<link rel="stylesheet" type="text/css" href="<?php echo Yii::app()-
>request->baseUrl; ?>/css/screen.css" media="screen, projection" />
<link rel="stylesheet" type="text/css" href="<?php echo Yii::app()-
>request->baseUrl; ?>/css/print.css" media="print" />
<!--[if lt IE 8]>
<link rel="stylesheet" type="text/css" href="<?php echo Yii::app()-
>request->baseUrl; ?>/css/ie.css" media="screen, projection" />
<![endif]-->
```

Understanding the Blueprint installation

Yii by no means requires the use of Blueprint. However, as the default application generated does include the framework, understanding its installation and use will be beneficial.

The typical installation of Blueprint involves first downloading the framework files, and then placing three of its `.css` files into the Yii application's main CSS folder. If we take a peek under the main `Webroot/css` folder within our TrackStar application, we already see the inclusion of these three files:

- `ie.css`
- `print.css`
- `screen.css`

So, luckily for us, the basic installation has already been completed as a consequence of our using the `yiic webapp` command to generate our application. In order to take advantage of the framework, the above `<link>` tags needs to be placed under the `<head>` tag for each web page. This is why these declarations are made in the layout file.

The next two `<link>` tags:

```
<link rel="stylesheet" type="text/css" href="<?php echo Yii::app()-
>request->baseUrl; ?>/css/main.css" />
<link rel="stylesheet" type="text/css" href="<?php echo Yii::app()-
>request->baseUrl; ?>/css/form.css" />
```

define some custom css definitions used to provide some layout declarations in addition to the ones specified in the Blueprint files. You should always place any custom ones below the ones provide by Blueprint, so that your custom declarations take precedence.

Setting the page title

Setting a specific and meaningful page title on a per page basis is important to properly indexing your website pages in search engines and helpful to users who want to bookmark specific pages of your site. The next line in our main layout file specifies the page title in the browser:

```
<title><?php echo CHtml::encode($this->pageTitle); ?></title>
```

Remember that $this in a view file refers to the controller class that initially rendered the view. The $pageTitle attribute is defined down in the Yii's CController base class and will default to the action name followed by the controller name. This is easily customized in the specific controller class, or even within each specific view file.

Defining a page header

It is often the case that websites are designed to have consistent header content repeated across many pages. The next few lines in our main layout file define the area for a page header:

```
<body>
<div class="container" id="page">

  <div id="header">
    <div id="logo"><?php echo CHtml::encode(Yii::app()->name); ?></div>
  </div><!-- header -->
```

The first <div> tag with a class of "container" is required by the Blueprint framework in order to display the content as a grid.

 Again, using the Blueprint CSS Grid framework, or any other CSS framework is not at all a requirement of Yii. It is just there to help you jumpstart your design layout if desired.

The next three lines layout the first of the main content we see on these pages. It displays the name of the application in large letters. So far, this has been displaying the text 'My Web Application'. I am sure that has been driving some of you crazy. Although we may change this later to use a logo image, let's go ahead and change this to the real name of our application, 'TrackStar'.

We could hardcode this name right here in the HTML. However, if we alter our application configuration to reflect our new name, the changes will propagate everywhere throughout the site wherever Yii::app()->name is being used. I am sure you could make this simple change in your sleep at this point. Simply open up the main configuration file where our application configuration settings are defined, /protected/config/main.php and change the value of the 'name' property from:

```
'name'=>'My Web Application',
```

To:

```
'name'=>'TrackStar'
```

Save the file, refresh your browser and the header on the home page should now look something similar to the following screen:

One thing we immediately notice in the above image is that the change has been made in two places. It just so happens that the `view` file responsible for our home page content, `/protected/views/site/index.php`, also uses the application name property. As we made the change in the application configuration file, it is reflected in both places.

Displaying menu navigation items

The main site navigation controls are often repeated across multiple pages in a web application, and housing this in a layout makes it easy to reuse. The next block of markup and code in our main layout file defines the top-level menu items:

```
<div id="mainmenu">
  <?php $this->widget('zii.widgets.CMenu',array(
    'items'=>array(
      array('label'=>'Home', 'url'=>array('/site/index')),
      array('label'=>'About', 'url'=>array('/site/page',
'view'=>'about')),
      array('label'=>'Contact', 'url'=>array('/site/contact')),
      array('label'=>'Login', 'url'=>array('/site/login'),
'visible'=>Yii::app()->user->isGuest),
      array('label'=>'Logout ('.Yii::app()->user->name.')',
'url'=>array('/site/logout'), 'visible'=>!Yii::app()->user->isGuest)
      ),
    )); ?>
</div><!-- mainmenu -->
```

Here we see that one of the official Zii extensions, called CMenu, is being used. We introduced Zii back in *Chapter 9*. To jog your memory, the Zii extension library is a set of extensions developed by the Yii developer team. This library comes packaged with the download of the Yii Framework. Any of these extensions are easily used within a Yii application by simply referring to the desired extension class file using a path alias in the form of zii.path.to.ClassName. The root alias, zii, is predefined by the application, and the rest of the path is relative to this framework folder. So, as this Zii menu extension resides on your filesystem at Path-to-your-Yii-Framework/zii/widgets/CMenu.php, we can simply use zii.widgets.CMenu when referring to this in our application code.

Without having to know too much about the specifics of CMenu, we can see it that it takes in an array of associative arrays that provide the menu item label, a URL to which that item should link, and an optional third value, *visible*, that can be set to a boolean value indicating whether or not that menu item should display. This is used here when defining the 'login' and 'logout' menu items. Obviously, we only want the 'login' menu item to display as a clickable link if the user is not already logged in. And, conversely, we would only want the "Logout" menu link to display if the user is already logged-in. The use of the visible element in the array that defines these menu items allows you to display these links dynamically based on whether the user is logged in or not. The use of Yii::app()->user->isGuest is used for this. This returns true if the user is not logged in (that is, they are a guest of the application) or false if the user is logged in. I am sure that you have already noticed that the 'login' option turns into a 'logout' option in our application's main menu whenever you are logged in, and vice versa.

Let's update our menu to provide a way to navigate to our specific TrackStar functionality. First off, we don't want anonymous users to be able to access any real functionality except the login. So we want to make sure that the login page is more or less the home page for anonymous users. Also, the main home page for logged-in users should just be a listing of their projects. We'll achieve this by making the following changes:

1. Change our default home URL for the application to be the project listing page, rather than just site/index as it is now.

2. Change the default action within our default controller, SiteController, to be the login action. This way, any anonymous user that visits the top-level URL, http://localhost/trackstar/, will be redirected to the login page.

3. Alter our actionLogin() method to redirect the user to the project listing page if they are already logged in.

4. Change the 'home' menu item to read 'project', and change the URL to be the project listing page.

These are actually very simple changes to make. Starting at the top, we can change the 'homeUrl' application property in our main application configuration file. Open up protected/config/main.php and add the following name=>value pair to the returned array:

```
'homeUrl'=>'/trackstar/project',
```

This is all that is needed to make that change.

For the next change, open up protected/controllers/SiteController.php and add the following to the top of the controller class:

```
public $defaultAction = 'login';
```

This sets the default action to be 'login'. Now if you visit your top-level URL for the application, http://localhost/trackstar/, you should be taken to the login page. The only issue with this is that you will continue to be taken to the login page from this top-level URL regardless of whether you are already logged in or not. Let's fix this by implementing step 3 above. Change the actionLogin() method within SiteController to include the following code at the beginning of the method:

```
public function actionLogin()
{
    if(!Yii::app()->user->isGuest)
    {
        $this->redirect(Yii::app()->homeUrl);
    }
```

This will redirect all logged-in users to the application homeUrl that we just previously set to be the project listing page.

Finally, let's alter the input array to our CMenu widget to change the specification for the "Home" menu item. Alter that block of code in the main.php layout file and replace:

```
array('label'=>'Home', 'url'=>array('/site/index')),
```

with:

```
array('label'=>'Projects', 'url'=>array('/project')),
```

With this replacement, all of our previously outlined changes are in place. If we now visit the TrackStar application as an anonymous user, we are directed to the login page. If we click on the **Projects** link, we are still directed to the login page. We can still access the **About** and **Contact** pages, which is fine for an anonymous user. If we log in we are directed to the project listing page. Now if we click the **Projects** link, we are allowed to see the project listings.

Creating a breadcrumb navigation

Turning back to our `main.php` layout file, the three lines of code that follow our menu widget define another Zii extension widget called `CBreadcrumbs`:

```php
<?php $this->widget('zii.widgets.CBreadcrumbs', array(
   'links'=>$this->breadcrumbs,
)); ?><!-- breadcrumbs -->
```

This widget is used to display a list of links indicating the position of the current page, relative to other pages, in the whole website. For example, a linked navigation list of the format:

Projects >> Project 1 > > Edit

indicates the user is viewing an **Edit** page for **Project 1**. This is helpful for the user to find their way back to where they started, which is a listing of all the projects, as well as easily see where they are in the website page hierarchy. This is why it is referred to as a breadcrumb. Many websites implement this type of UI navigational component in their design.

To use this widget, we need to configure its `links` property, which specifies the links to be displayed. The expected value for this property is an array that defines the breadcrumb path from a starting point, down to the specific page being viewed. Using our previous example, we could specify the links array as such:

```php
array(
   'Projects'=>array('project/index'),
   'Project 1'=>array('project/view','id'=>1),
   'Edit',
   )
```

The breadcrumbs widget, by default, adds in the very top level "Home" link automatically, based on the application configuration setting `homeUrl`. So, what would be generated from the above would be a breadcrumb like:

Home >> Projects >> Project 1 >> Edit

As we explicitly set our application $homeUrl property to be the project listings page, our first two links are the same in this case. The code in the layout file sets the link property to be the $breadcrumbs property of the controller class that is rendering the view. You can see this explicitly being set in several of the view files that were autogenerated for us when we created our controller files using the Gii code generation tool. For example, if you take a look at protected/views/project/update.php, you see at the very top of that file the following:

```php
<?php
$this->breadcrumbs=array(
    'Projects'=>array('index'),
    $model->name=>array('view','id'=>$model->id),
    'Update',
);
```

And if we navigate to that page in the site, we see the following navigational breadcrumb generated, just below the main navigation:

Home » Projects » Test project one » Update

Specifying the content being decorated by the layout

The next line in the layout file is where the content of the view file that is being decorated by this layout file is placed:

```php
<?php echo $content; ?>
```

As was discussed earlier in this chapter, when you use $this->render() in a controller class to display a certain view file, the use of a layout file is implied. Part of what this method does is to place all of the content in the specific view file being rendered into a special variable called $content, which is then made available to the layout file. So, if we again take our project update view file as an example, the contents of $content would be the rendered content contained in the file protected/views/project/update.php.

Defining the footer

Just as with the header area, it is often the case that websites are designed to have consistent footer content repeated across many pages The final few lines of our `main.php` layout file define a consistent footer for very page:

```
<div id="footer">
    Copyright &copy; <?php echo date('Y'); ?> by My Company.<br/>
    All Rights Reserved.<br/>
    <?php echo Yii::powered(); ?>
</div><!-- footer -->
```

There is nothing special going on here but we should go ahead and update it to reflect our specific site. We can leave the **Powered by Yii Framework** line in there to help promote this great framework. So, just change the "My Company" in the above code to "TrackStar", and we're done. Refreshing the pages in the site now displays a consistent footer as depicted in the following figure:

Copyright © 2010 by TrackStar.
All Rights Reserved.
Powered by Yii Framework.

Nesting the layouts

Though it is true that the original layout we have been seeing on our pages is utilizing the file `protected/layouts/main.php`, that is not the whole story. When our initial application was created, all of the controllers were created to extend from the base controller located at `protected/components/Controller.php`. If we take a peek into this file, we see that there is a layout property explicitly defined. But it does not specify the main layout file. It specifies "column1" as the default layout file for all child classes. You may have already noticed that when the new application was created, there were a few layout files generated for us as well, all in the `protected/views/layouts/` folder:

- `column1.php`
- `column2.php`
- `main.php`

So, unless this is being explicitly overridden in a child class, our controllers are defining `column1.php` as the primary layout file, not `main.php`.

So, why did we spend all that time going through `main.php`, you ask? Well, it turns out that the `column1.php` layout file is itself decorated by the `main.php` layout file. So, not only can normal view files be decorated by layout files, but layout files themselves can be decorated by other layout files, forming a hierarchy of nested layout files. This allows for great flexibility in design and also greatly minimizes the need for any repeated markup in view files. Let's take a closer look at `column1.php` to see how this is achieved.

The contents of that file are as follows:

```php
<?php $this->beginContent('/layouts/main'); ?>
<div class="container">
  <div id="content">
    <?php echo $content; ?>
  </div><!-- content -->
</div>
<?php $this->endContent(); ?>
```

Here we see the use of a couple of methods we have not seen before. The use of the base controller methods `beginContent()` and `endContent()` are being used to decorate the enclosed content with the specified view. The view being specified here is our main layout page `'layouts/main'`. The `beginContent()` method actually makes use of the built-in Yii widget, `CContentDecorator`, whose primary purpose is to allow for nested layouts. So, whatever content is between the calls to `beginContent()` and `endContent()` will be decorated with the view specified in the call to `beginContent()`. If nothing is specified, it will use the default layout specified either at the controller level, or if not specified at the controller level, at the application level.

The rest works just as a normal layout file. All of the markup in the specific view file will be contained in the variable `$content` when this `column1.php` layout file is rendered, and then the other markup contained in this layout file will be contained again in the variable `$content` made available to the final rendering of the main parent layout file, `main.php`.

Let's walk through an example. If we take the rendering of the login view as an example, i.e. the following code in the `SiteController::actionLogin()` method:

```php
$this->render('login');
```

Behind the scenes, the following steps are taken:

1. Render all of the content in the specific view file `/protected/views/site/login.php` and make that content available via the variable `$content` to the layout file specified in the controller, which in this case is `column1.php`.

2. As `column1.php` is itself being decorated by the layout `main.php`, the content between the `beingContent()` and `endContent()` calls is again rendered and made available to the `main.php` file, also again via the `$content` variable

3. The layout file `main.php` is rendered and returned to the user, incorporating both the content from the specific view file for the login page, as well as the *nested* layout file, `column1.php`.

Another layout file that was autogenerated for us and being used in the application is `column2.php`. You probably won't be surprised to discover that this file lays out a two-column design. We can see this used in the project pages, where we have a little sub-menu **Operations** widget display along the right hand side. The contents of this layout are as follows, and we can see the same approach is being used to achieve the nested layout:

```php
<?php $this->beginContent('/layouts/main'); ?>
<div class="container">
  <div class="span-19">
    <div id="content">
      <?php echo $content; ?>
    </div><!-- content -->
  </div>
  <div class="span-5 last">
    <div id="sidebar">
    <?php
      $this->beginWidget('zii.widgets.CPortlet', array(
        'title'=>'Operations',
      ));
      $this->widget('zii.widgets.CMenu', array(
        'items'=>$this->menu,
        'htmlOptions'=>array('class'=>'operations'),
      ));
      $this->endWidget();
    ?>
    </div><!-- sidebar -->
  </div>
</div>
<?php $this->endContent(); ?>
```

Creating themes

Themes provide a systematic way of customizing the design layout of a web application. One of the many benefits of an MVC architecture is the separation of the presentation tier from both the rest of the *back-end* stuff. Themes make great use of this separation by allowing you to easily and dramatically change the overall look and feel of a web application during runtime. Yii allows for an extremely easy application of themes to provide great flexibility in your web application design.

Building themes in Yii

In Yii, each theme is represented as a folder consisting of view files, layout files, and relevant resource files such as images, CSS files, JavaScript files, and so on. The name of a theme is the same as its folder name. By default, all themes reside under the same folder `WebRoot/themes`. Of course, as is the case with all other application settings, this default folder can be configured to be a different one. To do so, simply alter the `basePath` and the `baseUrl` properties of the `themeManager` application component.

Contents under a theme folder should be organized in the same way as those under the application base path. For example, all view files must be located under `views/`, layout view files under `views/layouts/`, and system view files under `views/system/`. For example, if we have created a new theme, called `custom`, and we want to replace the update view of our `ProjectController` with a new view under this theme, we need to create a new `update.php` view file and save it in our application project as `themes/custom/views/project/update.php`.

Creating a Yii theme

Let's take this for a spin to give our TrackStar application a little facelift. We need to name our new theme and create a folder under the `Webroot/themes` folder with this same name. We'll exercise our extreme creativity and call our new theme, `new`.

Create a new folder to hold this new theme located at `Webroot/themes/new`. Also under this newly created folder, create two other new folders called `css/` and `views/`. The former is not required by the theming system, but helps us keep our CSS organized. The latter is required if we are going to make any alterations to our default view files, which we are. As we are going to change the `main.php` layout file just a little, we need yet another folder under this newly created `views/` folder called `layouts/` (remember the folder structure needs to mirror that in the default `Webroot/protected/views/` folder).

Now let's make some changes. As our `view` file markup is already referencing CSS class and ID names currently defined in the `Webroot/css/main.css` file, the fastest path to a new face on the application is to use this as a starting point, and make changes to it as needed to implement a new design. Of course, this is not a requirement, as we could re-create every single view file of our application in the new theme. However, to keep things simple, we'll create our new theme by making a few changes to the `main.css` file that was auto-generated for us when we created the application, as well as the primary layout file, `main.php`.

To begin with, let's make a copy of these two files and place them in our new theme folder. Copy `Webroot/css/main.css` to `Webroot/themes/new/css/main.css` and also copy `Webroot/protected/views/layouts/main.php` to `Webroot/themes/new/views/layouts/main.php`.

Now, open the newly copied version of the `main.css` file remove the contents and then add all of the following:

```
body
{
  margin: 0;
  padding: 0;
  color: #555;
  font: normal 10pt Arial,Helvetica,sans-serif;
  background: #d6d6d6 url(background.gif) repeat-y center top;
}

#page
{
  margin-bottom: 20px;
  background: white;
  border: 1px solid #898989;
  border-top:none;
  border-bottom:none;
}

#header
{
  margin: 0;
  padding: 0;
  height:100px;
  background:white url(header.jpg) no-repeat left top;
  border-bottom: 1px solid #898989;
}

#content
{
    padding: 20px;
}

#sidebar
```

```
{
  padding: 20px 20px 20px 0;
}

#footer
{
  padding: 10px;
  margin: 10px 20px;
  font-size: 0.8em;
  text-align: center;
  border-top: 1px solid #C9E0ED;
}

#logo
{
  padding: 10px 20px;
  font-size: 200%;
  /* HIDES LOGO TEXT */
  text-indent:-5000px;
}

#mainmenu
{
  background:white url(bg2.gif) repeat-x left top;
  border-top:1px solid #CCC;
  border-bottom: 1px solid #7d7d7d;
}

#mainmenu ul
{
  padding:6px 20px 5px 20px;
  margin:0px;
}

#mainmenu ul li
{
  display: inline;
}

#mainmenu ul li a
{
  color:#333;
  background-color:transparent;
  font-size:12px;
  font-weight:bold;
  text-decoration:none;
  padding:5px 8px;
}

#mainmenu ul li a:hover, #mainmenu ul li a.active
{
  color: #d1e1e;
```

```
    background-color:#ccc;
    text-decoration:none;
}

div.flash-error, div.flash-notice, div.flash-success
{
    padding:.8em;
    margin-bottom:1em;
    border:2px solid #ddd;
}

div.flash-error
{
    background:#FBE3E4;
    color:#8a1f11;
    border-color:#FBC2C4;
}

div.flash-notice
{
    background:#FFF6BF;
    color:#514721;
    border-color:#FFD324;
}

div.flash-success
{
    background:#E6EFC2;
    color:#264409;
    border-color:#C6D880;
}

div.flash-error a
{
    color:#8a1f11;
}

div.flash-notice a
{
    color:#514721;
}

div.flash-success a
{
    color:#264409;
}

div.form .rememberMe label
{
    display: inline;
}

div.view

{
```

```
  padding: 10px;
  margin: 10px 0;
  border: 1px solid #C9E0ED;
}

div.breadcrumbs
{
  font-size: 0.9em;
  padding: 10px 20px;
}

div.breadcrumbs span
{
  font-weight: bold;
}

div.search-form
{
  padding: 10px;
  margin: 10px 0;
  background: #eee;
}

.portlet
{

}

.portlet-decoration
{
  padding: 3px 8px;
  background:white url(bg2.gif) repeat-x left top;
}

.portlet-title
{
  font-size: 12px;
  font-weight: bold;
  padding: 0;
  margin: 0;
  color: #fff;
}

.portlet-content
{
  font-size:0.9em;
  margin: 0 0 15px 0;
  padding: 5px 8px;
  background:#ccc;
}

.operations li a

{
```

```css
  font: bold 12px Arial;
  color: #d11e1e;
  display: block;
  padding: 2px 0 2px 8px;
  line-height: 15px;
  text-decoration: none;
}

.portlet-content ul
{
  list-style-image:none;
  list-style-position:outside;
  list-style-type:none;
  margin: 0;

  padding: 0;
}

.portlet-content li
{
  padding: 2px 0 4px 0px;
}

.operations
{
  list-style-type: none;
  margin: 0;
  padding: 0;
}

.operations li
{
  padding-bottom: 2px;
}

.operations li a
{
  font: bold 12px Arial;
  color: #0066A4;
  display: block;
  padding: 2px 0 2px 8px;
  line-height: 15px;
  text-decoration: none;
}

.operations li a:visited
{
  color: #d11e1e;
}

.operations li a:hover
{
  background: #fff;
}
```

You may have noticed that some of these changes are referencing image files that do not yet exist in our project. We have added a `background.gif` image reference in the body declaration, a new `bg2.gif` image referenced in the `#mainmenu` ID declaration and a new `header.jpg` image in the `#header` ID declaration. These can be viewed, downloaded and used by viewing the site online or accessing the images directly from `http://www.yippyii.com/trackstar/themes/new/css/background.gif`, `http://www.yippyii.com/trackstar/themes/new/css/bg2.gif`, and `http://www.yippyii.com/trackstar/themes/new/css/header.jpg`.

We need to place these new images into the same CSS folder we are using for this theme, namely `Webroot/themes/new/css/`.

After these changes are in place, we need to make a couple of small adjustments to our `main.php` layout file in this new theme. For one, we need to alter the markup in the `<head>` element to properly reference our new `main.css` file. Currently the `main.css` file is being pulled in via this line:

```
<link rel="stylesheet" type="text/css" href="<?php echo Yii::app()-
>request->baseUrl; ?>/css/main.css" />
```

This is referencing the application request `baseUrl` property to construct the relative path to the CSS file. However, we want to use our new `main.css` file located in our new theme. For this, we can lean on the theme manager application component, defined by default to use the Yii built-in `CThemeManager.php` class. We access the theme manager in the same way as we access other application components. So, rather than use the request base URL, we should use the one defined by the theme manager, which knows what theme the application is using at any given time. So, we need to alter the above line in `/themes/new/views/layouts/main.php` as follows:

```
<link rel="stylesheet" type="text/css" href="<?php echo Yii::app()-
>theme->baseUrl; ?>/css/main.css" />
```

Once we configure our application to use our new theme (something we have not yet done), this `baseUrl` will resolve to a relative path to where our theme folder resides.

The other small change we need to make is to remove the display of the application title from the header. As we altered our CSS to use a new image file to provide our header and logo information, we don't need to display the application name in this section. So, again in `/themes/new/views/layouts/main.php`, we simply need to change this:

```
<div id="header">
   <div id="logo"><?php echo CHtml::encode(Yii::app()->name); ?></div>
</div><!-- header -->
```

To the following:

```
<div id="header"></div><!-- header image is embeded into the #header
declaration in main.css -->
```

We have put in a comment to remind us where our header image is defined.

One final change we need to make is to the other two layout files used in the application that we are not copying over to our new theme folder, namely `protected/views/layouts/column1.php` and `protected/views/layouts/column2.php`. As previously discussed in the section on nesting layouts, these two layout files also use the main layout file via explicit calls to the `beginContent()` and `endContent()`. These files were auto-generated by the Gii code generation tool, and are explicitly referencing the main layout file in `protected/views/layouts/` folder. We need to change the input specified to the `beginContent()` method so that, if available, our new theme layout will be used. Open both the `column1.php` and `column2.php` files and change the following line of code:

```
$this->beginContent('application.views.layouts.main');
```

To be the following:

```
$this->beginContent('/layouts/main');
```

Now, once we configure the application to use our new theme, it will first look for a `main.php` layout in the themes folder and use that file.

Configuring the application to use a theme

Okay, with our new theme now created and in place, we need to tell the application itself to use it. Doing so is easy. We just alter the main application's `theme` property setting by changing the main application configuration file. By now, we are old pros at doing this. Simply add the following `name=>value` pair to the returned array in the `/protected/config/main.php` file:

```
'theme'=>'new',
```

Once this is saved, our application is now using our newly created theme, `new`, and our application has a brand new face. Taking a look at the login page, which is also our default home page if not logged-in, we now see what is depicted in the following figure:

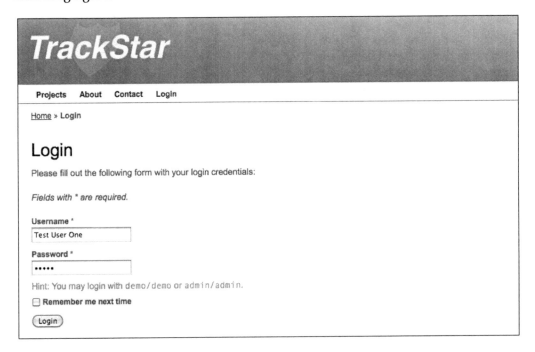

This, of course is not a huge change. We have kept the changes fairly minimal, but it does illustrate the process of creating a new theme. The application will first look for view files in this new theme and use them if they exists, otherwise, it will pull them from the default location. You can see how easy it is to give the application a new look and feel. You could create a new theme for each season, or maybe based on your different moods and then change the application to fit the season or mood quickly and easily as desired.

Translating the site to other languages

Before we leave this iteration, we are going to talk about internationalization (**i18n**) and localization (**L10n**) in Yii. Internationalization refers to the process of designing software applications in such a manner that it can be adapted to various languages without having to make underlying engineering changes. Localization refers to the process of adapting internationalized software applications for a specific geographic location or language by adding locale-dependent formatting and translating text. Yii provides support for these in the following ways:

- It provides the locale data for nearly every language and region
- It provides services to assist in the translation of text message and file
- It provides locale-dependent date and time formatting
- It provides locale-dependent number formatting

Defining locale and language

Locale refers to a set of parameters that define the user's language, country, and any other user interface preferences that may be relevant to a user's location. It is typically identified by a composite ID consisting of a language identifier and a region identifier. For example, a locale ID of en_US stands for the English language and the region of the United States. For consistency, all locale IDs in Yii are standardized to the format of either LanguageID or LanguageID_RegionID in lower case (for example, en or en_us).

In Yii, locale data is represented as an instance of the CLocale class, or a child class thereof. It provides locale-specific information including currency and numeric symbols; currency, number, date, and time formats; date-related names like months, days of week, and so on. Given a locale ID, one can get the corresponding CLocal instance by either using the static method CLocal::getInstance($localeID) or using the application. The following example code creates a new instance based on the en_us local identifier using the application component:

```
Yii::app()->getLocale('en_us');
```

Yii comes with locale data for nearly every language and region. The data comes from the **Common Locale Data Repository (CLDR)** (http://cldr.unicode.org/) and is stored in files that are named according to their respective locale id in the Yii Framework folder framework/i18n/data/. So, in the above example of creating a new CLocale instance, the data used to populate the attributes came from the file framework/i18n/data/en_us.php. If you look under this folder, you will see data files for a great many languages and regions.

So, going back to our example, if we wanted to get, say, the names of the months in English specific to the US region, we could execute the following code:

```
$locale = Yii::app()->getLocale('en_us');
print_r($locale->monthNames);
```

Which would produce the following:

Array ([1] => January [2] => February [3] => March [4] => April [5] => May [6] => June [7] => July [8] => August [9] => September [10] => October [11] => November [12] => December)

Where as if we wanted, say, the same month names for the Italian language, we could do the same, but create a different CLocale instance:

```
$locale = Yii::app()->getLocale('it');
print_r($locale->monthNames);
```

Which would produce the following:

Array ([1] => gennaio [2] => febbraio [3] => marzo [4] => aprile [5] => maggio [6] => giugno [7] => luglio [8] => agosto [9] => settembre [10] => ottobre [11] => novembre [12] => dicembre)

The first instance is based on the data file framework/i18n/data/en_us.php and the latter on framework/i18n/data/it.php. If desired, the application's localeDataPath property can be configured in order to specify a custom folder in which to add your custom locale data files.

Performing language translation

Perhaps the most desired feature of i18n is language translation. As mentioned previously, Yii provides both message translation and view translation. The former translates a single text message to a desired language, and the latter translates an entire file to the desired language.

A translation request consists of the object to be translated (either a string of text or a file), the source language that the object is in and the target language to which the object is to be translated. A Yii application makes a distinction between its target language and its source language. The target language is the language (or locale) that we are targeting for the user, where the source language refers to the language in which the application files are written. So far, our TrackStar application has been written in English and also targeted to English language users. So our target and source languages thus far have been the same. The internationalization features of Yii, which include translation, are applicable only when these two languages are different.

Performing message translation

Message translation is performed by calling the application method:

```
t(string $category, string $message, array $params=array ( ), string
$source=NULL, string $language=NULL)
```

This method translates the message from the source language to the target language.

When translating a message, the category must be specified to allow a message to be translated differently under different categories (contexts). The category *yii* is reserved for messages used by the Yii Framework core code.

Messages can also contain parameter placeholders which will be replaced with the actual parameter values upon calling `Yii::t()`. The following example depicts the translation of an error message. This message translation request would replace the {errorCode} placeholder in the original message with the actual $errorCode value:

```
Yii::t('category', 'The error: "{errorCode}" was encountered during
the last request.',    array('{errorCode}'=>$errorCode));
```

The translated messages are stored in a repository called *message source*. A message source is represented as an instance of `CMessageSource` or its child class. When `Yii::t()` is invoked, it will look for the message in the message source and return its translated version if it is found.

Yii comes with the following types of message sources:

- **CPhpMessageSource**: This is the default message source. The message translations are stored as key-value pairs in a PHP array. The original message is the key and the translated message is the value. Each array represents the translations for a particular category of messages and is stored in a separate PHP script file whose name is the category name. The PHP translation files for the same language are stored under the same folder named as the locale ID. All these folders are located under the folder specified by `basePath`.

- **CGettextMessageSource**: The message translations are stored as GNU `Gettext` files.

- **CDbMessageSource**: The message translations are stored in database tables.

A message source is loaded as an application component. Yii pre-declares an application component named `messages` to store messages that are used in a user application. By default, the type of this message source is `CPhpMessageSource` and the base path for storing the PHP translation files is `protected/messages`.

An example will go a long way to helping bring all of this together. Let's translate the form field labels on our Login form into a fictitious language we'll call **Reversish**. Reversish is written by taking an English word or phrase and writing it in reverse. So, here are the Reversish translations of our login form field labels:

English	Reversish
Username	Emanresu
Password	Drowssap
Remember me next time	Emit txen em rebmemer

We'll use the default CPhpMessageSource implementation to house our message translations. So, the first thing we need to do is create a PHP file containing our translations. We'll make the locale ID be 'rev' and we'll just call the category 'default' for now. So, we need to create a new file under the messages base folder that follows the format /localeID/CategoryName.php. So, for this example, we need to create a new file located at /protected/messages/rev/default.php, and then add the following translation array:

```php
<?php
return array(
    'Username' => 'Emanresu',
    'Password' => 'Drowssap',
    'Remember me next time' => 'Emit txen em rebmemer',
);
```

The next thing we need to do is to set the application target language to be Reversish. We could do this in the application configuration file, so that it would impact the entire site. However, as we only have translations for our login form, we'll just set it down in the SiteController::actionLogin() method, so that it will only apply when rendering the login form for now. So, open that file and set the application target language right at the beginning of that method:

```php
public function actionLogin()
{
    Yii::app()->language = 'rev';
```

Now, the last thing we need to do is to make our calls to Yii::t() so that these form field labels are sent through the translation. These form field labels are defined in the LoginForm:: attributeLabels() method. Replace that entire method with the following:

```php
/**
 * Declares attribute labels.
 */
public function attributeLabels()
{
    return array(
        'rememberMe'=>Yii::t('default','Remember me next time'),
        'username'=>Yii::t('default', 'Username'),
        'password'=>Yii::t('default', 'Password'),
    );
}
```

Now if we visit our login form again, we see a new Reversish version as depicted in the following screenshot:

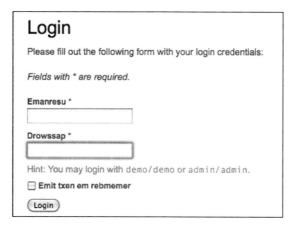

Performing file translation

Yii also provides the ability to use different files based on the target locale ID setting of the application. File translation is accomplished by calling the application method `CApplication::findLocalizedFile()`. This method takes in the path to a file and this method will look for a file with the same name, but under a directory named the same as the target locale ID specified either as explicit input to the method, or what is specified in the application configuration.

Let's try this out. All we really need to do is to create the appropriate translation file. We'll stick with translating the login form. So, create a new view file `/protected/views/site/rev/login.php` and add the following contents that have already been translated to Reversish:

```php
<?php
$this->pageTitle='Nigol';
$this->breadcrumbs=array(
   'Nigol',
);
?>

<h1>Nigol</h1>

<p>Slaitnederc nigol ruoy htiw mrof gniwollof eht tuo llif esaelp:</p>

<div class="form">
<?php $form=$this->beginWidget('CActiveForm', array(
   'id'=>'login-form',
```

```
        'enableAjaxValidation'=>true,
)); ?>

    <p class="note">Deriuqer era <span class="required">*</span> htiw
sdleif.</p>

    <div class="row">
      <?php echo $form->labelEx($model,'username'); ?>
      <?php echo $form->textField($model,'username'); ?>
      <?php echo $form->error($model,'username'); ?>
    </div>

    <div class="row">
      <?php echo $form->labelEx($model,'password'); ?>
      <?php echo $form->passwordField($model,'password'); ?>
      <?php echo $form->error($model,'password'); ?>
      <p class="hint">
        <tt>nimda\nimda</tt> ro <tt>omed\omed</tt> htiw nigol yam uoy
:tnih
      </p>
    </div>

    <div class="row rememberMe">
      <?php echo $form->checkBox($model,'rememberMe'); ?>
      <?php echo $form->label($model,'rememberMe'); ?>
      <?php echo $form->error($model,'rememberMe'); ?>
    </div>

    <div class="row buttons">
      <?php echo CHtml::submitButton('Nigol'); ?>
    </div>

<?php $this->endWidget(); ?>
</div><!-- form -->
```

We are already setting the target language for the application within the
`SiteController::actionLogin()` method, and the call to get the localized file
will be taken care of for us behind the scenes when calling `render('login')`. So,
with this in place, our login form now looks as shown in the following screenshot:

Home » Nigol

Nigol

Slaitnederc nigol ruoy htiw mrof gniwollof eht tuo llif esaelp:

*Deriuqer era * htiw sdleif.*

Emanresu *

Drowssap *

.nimda\nimda ro omed\omed htiw nigol yam uoy :tnih

☐ Emit txen em rebmemer

(Nigol)

Summary

In this iteration, we have seen how a Yii application allows you to quickly and easily polish up the design. We were introduced to the concept of layout files and walked through how to use these in an application to layout content and design that needs to be implemented in a similar manner across many different web pages. This also introduced us to the CMenu and CBreadcrumbs built-in widgets that provide easy to use and implement UI navigational constructs on each page.

We then introduced the idea of a theme within Web applications and how they are specifically implementing within a Yii application. We saw that themes allow you to easily put a new face on an existing Web application and allow you to re-design your application without re-building any of the functionality or backend

Finally, we looked at changing the face of the application through the lens of i18n and language translation. We learned how to set the target locale of the application to enable localization settings and language translations.

We have made a few references in this and past chapters to *modules*, but have yet to dive into what exactly these are within a Yii application. That is going to be the focus of the next chapter.

12

Iteration 9: Modules - Adding Administration

So far we have added a lot of functionality to our TrackStar application. If you recall back in *Chapter 8*, we introduced user access controls to restrict certain functionality based on a user role hierarchy. This was helpful in restricting access to some of the administrative functions on a per-project basis. For example, within a specific project, you may not want to allow all members of the team access to delete the project. We used a role based access control implementation to assign users to specific roles within a project, and then allowed/restricted access to functionality based on those roles.

However, what we have not yet addressed are the administrative needs of the application as a whole. Web applications such as TrackStar often require the ability for very special users to have full access to administer everything. One example is the ability to manage all the CRUD operations for every single user of the system, regardless of the project. A system administrator of our application should be able to log in and remove or update any user, any project, any issues, moderate all comments, and so on. Also, it is often the case that we build extra features that apply to the whole application, like the ability to leave site-wide system messages to all users, manage e-mail campaigns, turn on/off certain application features, manage the roles and permissions hierarchy itself, change the site theme, and so on. As the functionality exposed to the administrator can differ greatly from the functionality exposed to normal users, it is often a good idea to keep these features separate from the rest of the application. We will be accomplishing this separation by building all of our administrative functionality in what is called a *module* in Yii.

Iteration planning

In this iteration, we will focus on the following granular development tasks:

- Creating a new module to house administrative functionality
- Creating the ability for administrators to add system-wide messages for application users to view on the projects listing page
- Applying a new theme to the module
- Creating a new table to hold the system message data
- Generating all CRUD functionality for our system messages
- Limiting access to all functionality within the new module only to admin users
- Displaying new system messages on the projects listing page

Modules

A module is similar to an entire mini-application contained within a larger application. It has a similar structure, containing models, views, controllers, and other supporting components. However, modules cannot be deployed themselves as stand-alone applications, they must reside within an application.

Modules are useful in helping architect your application in a modular fashion. Large applications can often be segmented into discrete application features that could be separately built using modules. Site features such as adding a user forum, user blogs, or site-administrator functionality are some example candidates that could be segmented from the main site features allowing them to be developed separately and easily reused in future projects. We are going to use a module to create a distinct place in our application to house our administrative functionality.

Creating a module

Creating a new module is a snap using our old friend, the Gii code generation tool. With our URL changes in place, the tool is now accessible via `http://localhost/trackstar/gii`. Navigate there, and choose the **Module Generator** option from the left menu. You will be presented with the following screen:

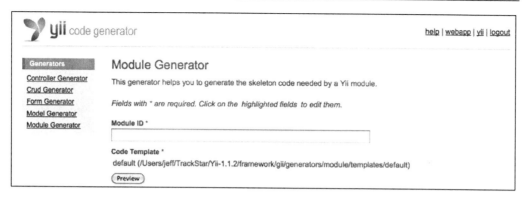

We need to provide a unique name for the module. As we are creating an admin module, we'll be super creative and give it the name *admin*. So type this in for the **Module ID** field, and click on the **Preview** button. As the following screenshot shows, it will present you with all of the files it intends to generate, allowing you to preview each of these files prior to creating them:

Code File	Generate ☐
modules/admin/AdminModule.php	new ☑
modules/admin/components	new ☑
modules/admin/controllers/DefaultController.php	new ☑
modules/admin/messages	new ☑
modules/admin/models	new ☑
modules/admin/views/default/index.php	new ☑
modules/admin/views/layouts	new ☑

Then click the **Generate** button to have it create all of these files. You will need to ensure that your /protected folder is writable by the web server process for it to automatically create the required folders and files. The following screenshot shows a successful module generation:

Let's take a closer look at what the module generator created for us. A module in Yii is organized as a folder, the name of which is the same as the unique name of the module. By default, all module folders reside under protected/modules. The structure of each module folder is very similar to that of our main application. What this command has done for us is to create the skeleton folder structure for the admin module. As this was our first module, the top-level folder protected/modules was created, and then an admin/ folder underneath. The following shows all of the folders and files that were created when we executed the module command:

Name of folder	Use/contents
admin/	
AdminModule.php	the module class file
components/	containing reusable user components
controllers/	containing controller class files

Name of folder	Use/contents
DefaultController.php	the default controller class file
messages/	stores message translations specific to the module
models/	containing model class files
views/	containing controller view and layout files
default/	containing view files for DefaultController
index.php	the index view file
layouts/	containing layout view files

A module must have a module class that extends either directly or from a child of CWebModule. The module class name is created by combining the module ID (that is, the name we supplied when we created the module, *admin*) and the string Module. The first letter of the module ID is also capitalized. So, in our case, our admin module class file is named AdminModule.php. The module class serves as the central place for storing information shared by the module code. For example, we can use the params property of CWebModule to store module specific parameters, and use its components property to share application components at the module level. This module class serves a similar role to the module as the application class does to the entire application. So CWebModule is to our module what CWebApplication is to our application.

Using a module

Just as the successful creation message indicated, before we can use our new module we need to configure the modules property of the main application to include it for use. We did this before when we added the gii module to our application, which allowed us to access the Gii code generation tool. We make this change in the main configuration file, protected/config/main.php. The following highlighted code indicates the required change:

```
'modules'=>array(
    'gii'=>array(
            'class'=>'system.gii.GiiModule',
            'password'=>'iamadmin',
    ),
    'admin',
),
```

After saving this change, our new admin module is wired-up for use. We can take a look at the simple index page that was created for us by visiting `http://localhost/ trackstar/admin/default/index`. The request routing structure to access pages in our module is similar to that for our main application pages, except that we need to include the `moduleID` in the route as well. So our routes will be of the general form `/ moduleID/controllerID/actionID`. Our URL request `/admin/default/index` is requesting the admin module's default controller's index method. When we visit this page, we see something similar to the following screenshot:

---

admin/default/index

This is the view content for action "index". The action belongs to the controller "DefaultController" in the "admin" module.

You may customize this page by editing `/Webroot/trackstar/protected/modules/admin/views/default/index.php`

Theming a module

We immediately notice that there doesn't seem to be any layout applied to this view. One might guess that maybe the controller that is rendering this view is calling `renderPartial()` rather than `render()`. However, upon inspection of our default admin controller file, `/protected/modules/admin/controllers/ DefaultController.php`, we see that it is, in fact, using the `render()` method. Thus, we expect a layout file (if one exists) to be applied.

The issue is that almost everything is separate in a module, including the default path for layout files. The default layout path for web modules is `/protected/ modules/[moduleID]/views/layouts`, where `moduleID` in our case is admin. We can see that there are no files under this folder, so there is no default layout to be applied.

There is slightly more to the story in our case, however. In the previous iteration, we implemented a new theme, called *new*. We can also manage all of our module view files, including the layout view files, within this theme as well. If we were to do that, we need to add to our theme folder structure to accommodate our new module. The folder structure is very much as expected. It is of a general form: `/ themes/[themeName]/views/[moduleID]/layouts/` for layout files and `/themes/ [themeName]/views/[moduleID]/[controllerID]/` for controller view files.

To clarify, let's walk through Yii's decision-making process when it is trying to decide what `view` files to use for our new admin module. Here is what is happening when `$this->render('index')` is issued in the `DefaultController.php` file within our admin module:

1. As `render()` is being called, as opposed to `renderPartial()`, it is going to attempt to decorate the specified `index.php` view file with a layout file. Our application is currently configured to use a theme called new, so it is going to look for layout files under this theme folder. Our new module's `DefaultController` class extends our application component `Controller.php`, which has `column1` specified as its `$layout` property. This property is not overridden so it is also the layout file for `DefaultController`. Finally, as this is all happening within the admin module, Yii first looks for the following layout file: `/themes/new/views/admin/layouts/column1.php`. Notice the inclusion of the `moduleID` in this folder structure.

2. This file does not exist, so it reverts to looking in the default location for the module. As previously mentioned, the default layout folder is specific to each module. So, in this case it will attempt to locate the following layout file: `/protected/modules/admin/views/layouts/column1.php`.

3. This file also does not exist, so it will be unable to apply a layout. It will now simply attempt render the specified `index.php` view file without a layout. However, again as we have specified the specific "new" theme for the application, it first looks for the following view file: `/themes/new/views/admin/default/index.php`.

4. This file also does not exist, so it will look again in the default location for this controller (`DefaultController.php`) within this module (`AdminModule`), namely: `/protected/modules/admin/views/default/index.php`.

This explains why the page `http://localhost/trackstar/admin/default/index` is rendered without any layout. To keep things completely separate and simple for now, let us manage our view files in the default location for our module, rather than under the new theme. Also, let's apply to our admin module the same design as our original application had, that is, how the application looked before we applied the new theme. This way our admin pages will have a different look from our normal application pages, which will help remind us that we are in the special admin section, but we won't have to spend any time coming up with a new design.

Applying a theme

First, let's set a default layout value for our module. We set our module-wide configuration settings in the `init()` method within our module class, `/protected/modules/AdminModule.php`. So open that file and add the following code in bold:

```
class AdminModule extends CWebModule
{
    public function init()
    {
        // this method is called when the module is being created
```

```
        // you may place code here to customize the module or the
   application

        // import the module-level models and components
        $this->setImport(array(
            'admin.models.*',
            'admin.components.*',
        ));

        $this->layout = 'main';


   }
   . . .
```

This way, if we have not specified a layout file at a more granular level, like in a controller class, all of the module views will be decorated by the layout file `main.php` located in the default layout folder for our module, namely `/protected/modules/admin/views/layouts/`.

Now, of course, we need to create this file. Make a copy of the two layout files from the main application: `/protected/views/layouts/main.php` and `/protected/views/layouts/column1.php`, and place them both in the `/protected/modules/admin/views/layouts/` folder. After you have copied those over, we need to make a few changes to both of them.

First let's alter `column1.php`. Remove the explicit reference to `/layouts/main` in the call to `beginContent()` as follows:

```php
<?php $this->beginContent(); ?>
    <div class="container">
        <div id="content">
            <?php echo $content; ?>
        </div><!-- content -->
    </div>
    <?php $this->endContent(); ?>
```

Not specifying an input file when calling `beginContent()` will result in it using the default layout for our module, which we just set to be our newly copied `main.php` file.

Now let's make a few changes to our `main.php` layout file. We are going to add `Admin Console` to our application header text to underscore that we are in a separate part of the application. We will also alter our menu items to have a link to the admin home page, as well as a link to go back to the main site. We can remove the **About** and **Contact** links from this menu, as we don't need to repeat those options in our admin section. The changes to the file are highlighted below:

```
...
<div class="container" id="page">
<div id="header">
    <div id="logo"><?php echo CHtml::encode(Yii::app()->name) . " Ad-
min Console"; ?></div>
    </div><!-- header -->
    <div id="mainmenu">
        <?php $this->widget('zii.widgets.CMenu',array(
            'items'=>array(
            array('label'=>'Back To Main Site', 'url'=>array('/proj-
ect')),
            array('label'=>'Admin', 'url'=>array('/admin/default/in-
dex')),
                array('label'=>'Login', 'url'=>array('/site/login'),
    'visible'=>Yii::app()->user->isGuest),
                array('label'=>'Logout ('.Yii::app()->user->name.')',
    'url'=>array('/site/logout'), 'visible'=>!Yii::app()->user->isGuest)
                ),
            )); ?>
    </div><!-- mainmenu -->
...
```

We can leave the rest of the file unchanged. Now if we visit our admin module page, we see something similar to the following screenshot:

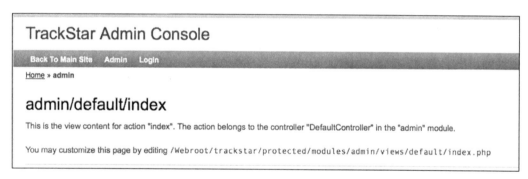

If we click on the **Back To Main Site** link, we see that we are taken back to our newly themed version of our main application.

Restricting admin access

One problem you may have already noticed is that anyone, including guest users, can access our new admin module. We are building this admin module to expose application functionality that should only be accessible to users with administrative access. So, we need to address this issue.

Luckily, we have already implemented an RBAC access model in our application back in *Chapter 8*. All we need to do now is extend it to include a new role for administrators and new permissions available to that role.

If you recall from *chapter 8*, we used a Yii `shell` command to implement our RBAC structure. We need to add to that. So, open up the file containing that `shell` command, `/protected/commands/shell/RbacCommand.php` and add the following:

```
//create a general task-level permission for admins
 $this->_authManager->createTask("adminManagement", "access to the
application administration functionality");
 //create the site admin role, and add the appropriate permissions
$role=$this->_authManager->createRole("admin");
$role->addChild("owner";
$role->addChild("reader");
$role->addChild("member");
$role->addChild("adminManagement");
//ensure we have one admin in the system (force it to be user id #1)
$this->_authManager->assign("admin",1);
```

With these changes in place, we have to rerun our command to update the database with these changes. To do so, just fire-up the `yiic` shell, and execute the `rbac` command:

% cd Webroot/trackstar

% protected/yiic shell

>> rbac

With these changes to our RBAC model in place, we can add an access check to the `AdminModule::beforeControllerAction()` method so that nothing within the admin module will be executed unless the user has the admin role:

```
public function beforeControllerAction($controller, $action)
    {
        if(parent::beforeControllerAction($controller, $action))
        {
            // this method is called before any module controller action
    is performed
            // you may place customized code here
        if( !Yii::app()->authManager->checkAccess("admin", Yii::app()-
>user->id) )
            {
                throw new CHttpException(403,Yii::t('yii','You are not au-
thorized to perform this action.'));
            }
```

```
        else
        {
            return true;
        }
    }
    else
        return false;
}
```

With this in place, if a user who has not been assigned the admin role now attempts to visit any page within the admin module, they will be met with an authorization error page. For example, if you are not logged in and you attempt to visit the admin page, you will be met with the following result:

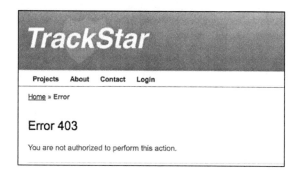

The same holds true for any user that has not been assigned to the admin role.

Now we can conditionally add a link to the admin section of the site to our main application menu. This way, users with administrative access won't have to remember a cumbersome URL to navigate to the admin console. As a reminder, our main application menu is located in our application's theme default application layout file /themes/new/views/layouts/main.php. Open that file and add the following highlighted code to the menu section:

```
<div id="mainmenu">
    <?php $this->widget('zii.widgets.CMenu',array(
        'items'=>array(
            array('label'=>'Projects', 'url'=>array('/project')),
            array('label'=>'About', 'url'=>array('/site/page',
'view'=>'about')),
            array('label'=>'Contact', 'url'=>array('/site/contact')),
        array('label'=>'Admin', 'url'=>array('/admin/default/index'),
'visible'=>Yii::app()->authManager->checkAccess("admin", Yii::app()-
>user->id)),
            array('label'=>'Login', 'url'=>array('/site/login'),
```

```
        'visible'=>Yii::app()->user->isGuest),
                array('label'=>'Logout ('.Yii::app()->user->name.')',
        'url'=>array('/site/logout'), 'visible'=>!Yii::app()->user->isGuest)
            ),
        )); ?>
    </div><!-- mainmenu -->
```

Now, upon logging in to the application as a user with admin access, we will see a new link in our top navigation that will take us to our newly added admin section of the site.

Adding a system-wide message

As a module can really be thought of as a mini-application itself, adding functionality to a module is really the same process as adding functionality to the main application. Let's add some new functionality just for administrators; the ability to manage system-wide messages displayed to users when they first log into the application.

Creating the database table

As is often the case with brand new functionality, we need a place to house our data. We need to create a new table to store our system-wide messages. For our purposes, we can keep this simple. Here is the definition for our table:

```
CREATE TABLE `tbl_sys_message`
(
    `id` INTEGER NOT NULL PRIMARY KEY AUTO_INCREMENT,
    `message` TEXT NOT NULL,
    `create_time` DATETIME,
    `create_user_id` INTEGER,
    `update_time` DATETIME,
    `update_user_id` INTEGER
)
```

Create this new table in both the main `trackstar_dev` and our `trackstar_test` databases.

Creating our model and CRUD scaffolding

With the table in place, our next step is to generate the model class using our favorite tool, the Gii code generator. We'll first use the **Model Generator** option to create the model class, and then the **Crud Generator** to create our basic scaffolding to quickly interact with this model. Go ahead and navigate to the Gii tool form for creating a new model. This time, as we are doing this within the context of a module, we need to explicitly specify the model path. Fill out the form with the values depicted as shown in the following screenshot (though, of course, your **Code Template** path value should be specific to your local setup):

Model Generator

This generator generates a model class for the specified database table.

*Fields with * are required. Click on the highlighted fields to edit them.*

Table Prefix
tbl_

Table Name *
tbl_sys_message

Model Class *
SysMessage

Base Class *
CActiveRecord

Model Path *
application.modules.admin.models

Code Template *
default (/Users/jeff/TrackStar/Yii-1.1.2/framework/gii/generators/model/templates/default)

(Preview)

Now we can create the CRUD scaffolding in the same way. Again, the only real difference between what we have done previously and what we are doing now is our specification that the location of the model class is in the admin module. After choosing the **Crud Generator** option from the Gii tool, fill out the **Model Class** and **Controller ID** form fields as shown in the following screenshot:

*Fields with * are required. Click on the highlighted fields to edit them.*

Model Class *

```
admin.models.SysMessage
```

Controller ID *

```
admin/sysMessage
```

This alerts the tool to the fact that our model class is under the admin module and that our controller class, as well as all other files related to this code generation should be placed within the admin module as well.

Complete the creation by first clicking on the **Preview** button, and then **Generate**. The following is a list of all of the files that are created by this action:

Code File
modules/admin/controllers/SysMessageController.php
modules/admin/views/sysMessage/_form.php
modules/admin/views/sysMessage/_search.php
modules/admin/views/sysMessage/_view.php
modules/admin/views/sysMessage/admin.php
modules/admin/views/sysMessage/create.php
modules/admin/views/sysMessage/index.php
modules/admin/views/sysMessage/update.php
modules/admin/views/sysMessage/view.php

Adding a link to our new functionality

Let's add a new menu item within the main admin navigation that links to our newly created message functionality. Open the file that contains our main menu navigation for our module, `/protected/modules/admin/views/layouts/main.php`, and add the following array item to the menu widget:

```
array('label'=>'System Messages', 'url'=>array('/admin/sysMessage/
index')),
```

As the auto-created controller and view files for our new system message functionality were created to use a 2-column layout file, we can do one of two things. We can alter the controller class to use our existing single column layout file, or we can add a 2 column layout file to our module layout files. The latter is going to be slightly easier and will also look better, as all of the view files are created to have their sub-menu items (that is, the links to all the CRUD functionality) display in a second right-hand column. Here is all we have to do:

1. Copy the 2 column layout from our main application to our module: That is, copy `/protected/views/layouts/column2.php` to `/protected/modules/admin/views/layouts/column2.php`.

2. Remove `/layouts/main` as input to the `beginContent()` method call on the first line in the newly copied `column2.php` file.

3. Alter the `SysMessage` model class to extend `TrackstarActiveRecord` (If you recall, this adds the code to automatically update our `create_time/user` and `update_time/user` properties. Alter the `SysMessageController` controller class to use the new `column2.php` layout file from within the module folder and not the one from the main application. The autogenerated code has specified `$layout='application.views.layouts.column2'`, but we need this to be simply `$layout='column2'`.

4. As we are extending `TrackstarActiveRecord`, we can remove the unnecessary fields from our autogenerated sys messages creation form and remove their associated rules from the model class. Remove the following two rules from the `SysMessage::rules()` method: `array('create_user, update_user', 'numerical', 'integerOnly'=>true)`, and `array('create_time, update_time', 'safe')`.

You don't absolutely have to do this last step, but it is good to get in to the habit of only specifying rules for those fields that the user can input.

One last change we should make is to update our simple access rules to reflect the requirement that only users in the admin role can access our action methods. This is mostly for illustrative purposes as we already took care of the access using our RBAC model approach in the `AdminModule::beforeControlerAction` method itself. We could actually just remove the `accessRules` entirely. However, let's just update them to reflect the requirement so you can see how that would work using the access rule approach. In the `SysMessageController::accessRules()` method, change the entire contents to the following:

```php
public function accessRules()
{
    return array(
        array('allow',  // allow only users in the 'admin' role access
to our actions
            'actions'=>array('index','view', 'create', 'update',
'admin', 'delete'),
            'roles'=>array('admin'),
        ),
        array('deny',  // deny all users
            'users'=>array('*'),
        ),
    );
}
```

Okay, with all of this in place, if we now access our new message input form by visiting `http://localhost/trackstar/admin/sysMessage/create`, we are presented with something similar to the following screenshot:

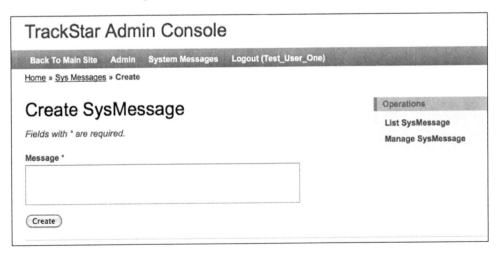

Fill out this form with the message **Hello Users! This is your admin speaking...** and then click **Submit**. The application will redirect you to the details listing page for this newly created message as shown in the following screenshot:

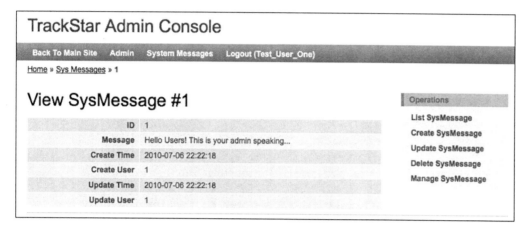

Displaying the message to users

Now that we have a message in our system, let's display it to the user on the application's home page.

Importing the new model class for application-wide access

In order to access the newly created model from anywhere in our application, we need to import it as a part of the application configuration. Alter `protected/config/main.php` to include the new admin module models folder:

```
// autoloading model and component classes
'import'=>array(
    'application.models.*',
    'application.components.*',
  'application.modules.admin.models.*',
),
```

Selecting the most recently updated message

We'll restrict the display to just one message, and we'll choose the most recently updated message, based on the update_time column in the table. As we want to add this to the main projects listing page, we need to alter the ProjectController::act ionIndex() method. Alter that method by adding the following highlighted code:

```
public function actionIndex()
    {
        $dataProvider=new CActiveDataProvider('Project');

        Yii::app()->clientScript->registerLinkTag(
            'alternate',
            'application/rss+xml',
            $this->createUrl('comment/feed'));

        //get the latest system message to display based on the
        update_time column
        $sysMessage = SysMessage::model()->find(array(
            'order'=>'t.update_time DESC',
        ));
        if($sysMessage != null)
            $message = $sysMessage->message;
        else
            $message = null;


        $this->render('index',array(
            'dataProvider'=>$dataProvider,
            'sysMessage'=>$message,
        ));
    }
```

Now we need to alter our view file to display this new bit of content. Add the following to views/project/index.php, just above the <h1>Projects</h1> header text:

```
<?php if($sysMessage != null):?>
    <div class="sys-message">
        <?php echo $sysMessage; ?>
    </div>
<?php endif; ?>
```

Now when we visit our projects listing page (that is, our application's home page) we can see it display as shown in the following screenshot:

Home » Projects

Hello Users, this is your admin speaking....
Projects

Adding a little design tweak

Okay. This does what we wanted it to do, but this message does not really stand out very well to the user. Let's change that by adding a little snippet to our main css file (/themes/new/css/main.css):

```
div.sys-message
{
    padding:.8em;
    margin-bottom:1em;
    border:3px solid #ddd;
    background:#9EEFFF;
    color:#FF330A;
    border-color:#00849E;
}
```

With this in place, our message now really stands out on the page. The following screenshot shows the message with these changes in place:

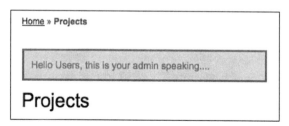

One might argue that this design tweak went a little too far. Users might get a headache if they have to stare at those message colors all day. Rather than toning down the colors, let's use a little JavaScript to fade the message out after five seconds. As we will display the message every time the user visits this home page, it might be nice to prevent them from having to stare at it for too long.

We'll make things easy on ourselves and take advantage of the fact that Yii comes shipped with the powerful JavaScript framework jQuery. jQuery is an open source JavaScript library that simplifies the interaction between the HTML **Document Object Model (DOM)** and JavaScript. It is outside the scope of this book to dive into the details of jQuery, but it is well worth visiting its documentation to become a little acquainted with its features. As Yii comes shipped with jQuery, you can simply register jQuery code in view files and Yii will take care of including the core jQuery library for you.

We'll also use the application helper component CClientScript to register our jQuery JavaScript code for us in the resulting web page. It will make sure it is placed in the appropriate place as well as properly tagged and formatted.

So, let's alter what we previously added to include a snippet of JavaScript that will fade out the message. Replace what we just added to views/project/index.php with the following:

```php
<?php if($sysMessage != null):?>
    <div class="sys-message">
        <?php echo $sysMessage; ?>
    </div>
<?php
    Yii::app()->clientScript->registerScript(
        'fadeAndHideEffect',
        '$(".sys-message").animate({opacity: 1.0}, 5000).
fadeOut("slow");'
    );
endif; ?>
```

Now if we reload our main projects listing page, we see the message fade out after five seconds. For more information on cool jQuery effects you can easily add to your pages, take a look at the JQuery API documentation at: http://api.jquery.com/category/effects/

Finally, to convince yourself everything is working as expected, you can add another system-wide message. As this newer message will have a more recent update_time property, it will be the one to display on the projects listing page.

Summary

In this iteration, we have introduced the concept of a Yii *module* and demonstrated its practicality by using one to create an administrative section of the site. We demonstrated how to create a new module, how to apply a theme, how to add application functionality within the module, and even how to take advantage of an existing RBAC model to apply authorization access controls to a functionality within a module. We also demonstrated how to use jQuery to add a dash of UI flare to our application.

With the addition of this administrative interface, we now have all of the major pieces of the application in place. Though the application is incredibly simple, we feel it is time to get it ready for production. The next iteration will focus on preparing our application for production deployment.

13
Iteration 10: Production Readiness

Even though our application lacks a significant amount of feature functionality, our (albeit imaginary) deadlines are approaching and our (also imaginary) client is getting anxious about getting the application into a production environment. Although it may take some time before our application actually sees the light of day in production it is time to get the application "production ready". In this, our final development iteration, we are going to do just that.

Iteration planning

In order to achieve the goal of preparing our application for a production environment, we are going to focus on the following granular tasks:

- Implement Yii's application logging framework to ensure we are logging information about critical production errors and events

- Implement Yii's application error handling framework to ensure we understand how this works differently in a production environment than in a development environment

- Implement application data caching to help improve performance

Logging

Logging is a topic that should arguably have been covered before this late stage in the application development. Informational, warning, and severe error messages are invaluable when it comes to troubleshooting software applications, most certainly those in a production environment being used by real users.

Yii provides a flexible and extensible logging feature. Messages logged can be classified according to log levels and message categories. Using level and category filters, selected messages can be further routed to different destinations, such as written to files on disc, sent to administrators as e-mails or displayed to browser windows.

Message logging

Our application has actually been logging many informational messages upon each request the entire time. When the initial application was created, it was configured to be in *debug* mode and, while in this mode, the Yii Framework itself logs information messages. We can't actually see these messages because, by default, they are being logged to memory. So, they are around only for the lifetime of the request.

Whether or not the application is in this debug mode is controlled by the following line in the root `index.php` file:

```
defined('YII_DEBUG') or define('YII_DEBUG',true);
```

To see what is being logged, let's whip up a quick little action method in our `SiteController` class to display the messages:

```php
public function actionShowLog()
{
    echo "Logged Messages:<br><br>";
    var_dump(Yii::getLogger()->getLogs());
}
```

If we invoke this action by making the following request at: `http://localhost/trackstar/site/showLog`, we see something similar to the following:

```
Logged Messages:


array
  0 =>
    array
      0 => string 'Loading "log" application component' (length=35)
      1 => string 'trace' (length=5)
      2 => string 'system.web.CModule' (length=18)
      3 => float 1271216483.7354
  1 =>
    array
      0 => string 'Loading "request" application component' (length=39)
      1 => string 'trace' (length=5)
      2 => string 'system.web.CModule' (length=18)
      3 => float 1271216483.7368
  2 =>
    array
      0 => string 'Loading "urlManager" application component' (length=42)
      1 => string 'trace' (length=5)
      2 => string 'system.web.CModule' (length=18)
      3 => float 1271216483.7379
```

If we comment out our global application debug variable, defined in `index.php`, and refresh the page, we'll notice that nothing was logged. This is because this system-level debugging information level logging is accomplished by calling `Yii::trace`, which only logs the message if the application is in this special debug mode.

We can log messages using one of two static application methods:

- `Yii::log($message, $level, $category)`
- `Yii::trace($message, $category)`

As mentioned, the main difference between these two methods is that `Yii::trace` logs the message only when the application is in debug mode.

Categories and levels

When logging a message, we need to specify its category and level. The category is represented by a string in the format of *xxx.yyy.zzz*, which resembles the path alias. For example, if a message is logged in our application's `SiteController` class, we may choose to use the category `application.controllers.SiteController`. The category is there to provide extra context to the message being logged. In addition to specifying the category, when using `Yii::log`, we can also specify a level for the message. The level can be thought of as the severity of the message. You can define your own levels, but typically they take on one of the following values:

- **Trace**: This level is commonly used for tracing the execution flow of the application during development.
- **Info**: This level is for logging general information, and it is the default level if none is specified.
- **Profile**: This level is to be used with the performance profile feature, which is described below.
- **Warning**: This level is for warning messages.
- **Error**: This is level for fatal error messages.

Adding a login message log

As an example, let's add some logging to our user login method. We'll provide some basic debugging information at the beginning of the method to indicate the method is being executed. We'll then log an informational message upon a successful login as well as a warning message if the login fails. Alter our `SiteController::actionLogin()` method as follows:

```
/**
 * Displays the login page
 */
public function actionLogin()
{
    Yii::app()->language = 'rev';

    Yii::trace("The actionLogin() method is being requested",
"application.controllers.SiteController");

        if(!Yii::app()->user->isGuest)
        {
            $this->redirect(Yii::app()->homeUrl);
        }

    $model=new LoginForm;

    // if it is ajax validation request
    if(isset($_POST['ajax']) && $_POST['ajax']==='login-form')
    {
        echo CActiveForm::validate($model);
        Yii::app()->end();
    }

    // collect user input data
    if(isset($_POST['LoginForm']))
    {
        $model->attributes=$_POST['LoginForm'];
        // validate user input and redirect to the previous page
if valid
        if($model->validate() && $model->login())
        {
            Yii::log("Successful login of user: " . Yii::app()->user-
>id, "info", "application.controllers.SiteController");
            $this->redirect(Yii::app()->user->returnUrl);
        }
```

```
        else
        {
                Yii::log("Failed login attempt", "warning", "application.
controllers.SiteController");
        }


        }
        // display the login form
        //public string findLocalizedFile(string $srcFile, string
    $srcLanguage=NULL, string $language=NULL)
        $this->render('login',array('model'=>$model));


    }
```

If we now successfully log in (or perform a failed attempt) and visit our page to view the logs, we don't see them (If you commented out the debug mode declaration, make sure you have put the application back in debug mode for this exercise). Again, the reason is that by default, the logging implementation in Yii simply stores the messages in memory. They disappear when the request completes. This is not terribly useful. We need to route them to a more persistent storage area so we can view them outside of the request in which they are generated.

Message routing

As we mentioned, by default, messages logged using `Yii::log` or `Yii::trace` are kept in memory. Typically, these messages are more useful if they are displayed in browser windows, or saved to some persistent storage such as in a file, or in a database or sent as an e-mail. Yii's *message routing* allows for the log messages to be routed to different destinations.

In Yii, message routing is managed by a `CLogRouter` application component. It allows you to define a list of destinations to which the log messages should be routed.

In order to take advantage of this message routing, we need to configure the `CLogRouter` application component in our `protected/config/main.php` config file. We do this by setting its routes property with the desired log message destinations.

If we open our `config` file, we see that some configuration information has already been provided (again, courtesy of using the `yiic webapp` command to initially create our application). The following is already defined in our configuration:

```
'log'=>array
    'class'=>'CLogRouter',
    'routes'=>array(
```

```
array(
    'class'=>'CFileLogRoute',
    'levels'=>'error, warning',
),
// uncomment the following to show log messages on web pages
/*
array(
    'class'=>'CWebLogRoute',
),
*/
        ),
    ),
```

The **log** application component is configured to use the framework class CLogRouter. You could also certainly create and use a custom child class of this if you have logging requirements not fully met by the base framework implementation, but in our case, this will work just fine.

What follows the class definition in the previous configuration is the definition of the routes property. In this case, there is just one route specified. This one is using the Yii Framework message routing class, CFileLogRoute. The CFileLogRoute message routing class uses the filesystem to save the messages. By default, messages are logged in a file under the application runtime folder, /protected/runtime/ application.log. In fact, if you have been following along with us and have your own application, you can take a peek at this file and will see several messages that have been logged by the framework. The levels specification dictates that only messages whose log level is either **error** or **warning** will be routed to this file. The part of the configuration in the preceding code that is commented out specifies another route, CWebLogRoute. If used, this will route the message to be displayed on the currently requested web page. The following is a list of message routes currently available in version 1.1 of Yii:

- CDbLogRoute: Saves messages in a database table
- CEmailLogRoute: Sends messages to specified e-mail addresses
- CFileLogRoute: Saves messages in a file under the application runtime folder
- CWebLogRoute: Displays messages at the end of the current web page
- CProfileLogRoute: Displays profiling messages at the end of the current web page

The logging that we added to our SiteController::actionLogin() method used Yii::trace for one message and then used Yii::log for two more. When using Yii::trace, the log level is automatically set to **trace**. When using the Yii::log we specified an **info** log level if the login was successful and a **warning** level if the login attempt failed. Let's alter our log routing configuration to write the trace and info level messages to a new, separate file called infoMessages.log in the same folder as our application.log file. Also, let's configure it to write the warning messages to the browser. To do that, we make the following changes to the configuration:

```
'log'=>array(
    'class'=>'CLogRouter',
    'routes'=>array(
        array(
            'class'=>'CFileLogRoute',
            'levels'=>'error',
        ),
        array(
            'class'=>'CFileLogRoute',
            'levels'=>'info, trace',
            'logFile'=>'infoMessages.log',
        ),
    array(
            'class'=>'CWebLogRoute',
            'levels'=>'warning',
        ),
    . . .
```

Now, after saving these changes, let's try out the different scenarios. First, try a successful login. Doing so will write two messages out to our new /protected/runtime/infoMessages.log file, one for the trace and then one logging the successful login. After successfully logging in, viewing that file reveals the following (The full listing was truncated to save a few trees):

...

2010/04/15 00:31:52 [trace] [application.controllers.SiteController] The actionLogin() method is being requested

```
2010/04/15 00:31:52 [trace] [system.web.CModule] Loading "user"
application component
2010/04/15 00:31:52 [trace] [system.web.CModule] Loading "session"
application component
2010/04/15 00:31:52 [trace] [system.web.CModule] Loading "db"
application component
2010/04/15 00:31:52 [trace] [system.db.CDbConnection] Opening DB
connection
```

...

2010/04/15 00:31:52 [info] [application.controllers.SiteController] Successful login of user: 1

...

Wow, there is a lot more in there than just our two messages. But our two did show up; they are bolded in the above listing. Now that we are routing all of trace messages to this new file, all of the framework trace messages are showing up here as well. This is actually very informative and helps you get a picture of the lifecycle of a request as it makes its way through the framework. There is a lot going on under the covers. We would obviously turn off this verbose level of logging when moving this application to production. In non-debug mode, we would only see our single info level message. But this level of detail can be very informative when trying to track down bugs and just figure out what the application is doing. It is comforting to know it is here when/if ever needed.

Now let's try the failed login attempt scenario. If we now log out and try our login again, but this time specify incorrect credentials to force a failed login, we see our **warning** level display along the bottom of the returned web page, just as we configured it to do. The following screenshot shows this warning being displayed:

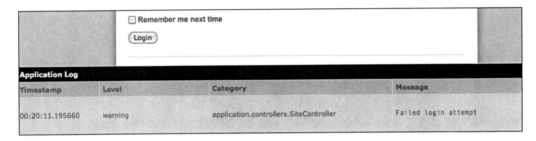

When using the CLogRouter message router, the logfiles are stored under the logPath property and the filename is specified by the logFile. Another great feature of this log router is automatic logfile rotation. If the size of the logfile is greater than the value set in the maxFileSize (in kilobytes) property, a rotation is performed, which renames the current logfile by suffixing the filename with '1'. All existing logfiles are moved backwards one place, that is, '.2' to '.3', '.1' to '.2'. The property maxLogFiles can be used to specify how many files are to be kept.

Handling errors

Properly handling the errors that invariably occur in software applications is of the utmost importance. This, again, is a topic that arguably should have been covered prior to coding our application, rather than at this late stage. Luckily, though, as we have been leaning on tools within the Yii Framework to autogenerate much of our core application skeleton, our application is already taking advantage of some of Yii's error handling features.

Yii provides a complete error handling framework based on PHP 5 exceptions, a built-in mechanism for handling program failures through centralized points. When the main Yii application component is created to handle an incoming user request, it registers its `CApplication::handleError()` method to handle PHP warnings and notices. It registers its `CApplication::handleException()` method to handle uncaught PHP exceptions. Consequently, if a PHP warning/notice or an uncaught exception occurs during the application execution, one of the error handlers will take over the control and start the necessary error handling procedure.

> The registration of error handlers is done in the application's constructor by calling the PHP functions `set_exception_handler` and `set_error_handler`. If you prefer to not have Yii handle these types of errors and exceptions, you may override this default behavior by defining a global constant `YII_ENABLE_ERROR_HANDLER` and `YII_ENABLE_EXCEPTION_HANDLER` to be false in the main `index.php` entry script.

By default, the application will use the framework class `CErrorHandler` as the application component tasked with handling PHP errors and uncaught exceptions. Part of the task of this built-in application component is displaying these errors using appropriate view files based on whether or not the application is running in debug mode or in production mode. This allows you to customize your error messages for these different environments. It makes sense to display much more verbose error information in a development environment, to help troubleshoot problems. But allowing users of a production application to view this same information could compromise security. Also, if you have implemented your site in multiple languages, `CErrorHandler` also chooses the most preferred language for displaying the error.

You raise exceptions in Yii the same way you would normally raise a PHP exception. One uses the following general syntax to raise an exception when needed:

```
throw new ExceptionClass('ExceptionMessage');
```

The two exception classes the Yii provides are:

- `CException`
- `CHttpException`

`CException` is a generic exception class. `CHttpException` represents an exception that is intended to be displayed to the end user. `CHttpException` also carries a `statusCode` property to represent an HTTP status code. Errors are displayed differently in the browser, depending on the exception class that is thrown.

Displaying errors

As was previously mentioned, when an error is forwarded to the `CErrorHandler` application component, it makes a decision as to which `view` file to use when displaying the error. If the error is meant to be displayed to end users, such as is the case when using `CHttpException`, the default behavior is to use a view named *errorXXX*, where *XXX* represents the HTTP status code (for example, 400, 404, 500). If the error is an internal one and should only be displayed to developers, it will use a view named *exception*. When the application is in debug mode, a complete call stack as well as the error line in the source file will be displayed.

However, this is not the full story. When the application is running in production mode, all errors will be displayed using the *errorXXX* view files. This is because the call stack of an error may contain sensitive information that should not be displayed to just any end user.

When the application is in production mode, developers should rely on the error logs to provide more information about an error. A message of level **error** will always be logged when an error occurs. If the error is caused by a PHP warning or notice, the message will be logged with category `php`. If the error is caused by an uncaught exception, the category will be `exception.ExceptionClassName`, where the exception class name is one of, or child class of, either `CHttpException` or `CException`. One can thus take advantage of the logging features, discussed in the previous section, to monitor errors that occur within a production application.

By default, `CErrorHandler` searches for the location of the corresponding view file in the following order:

1. `WebRoot/themes/ThemeName/views/system`: The system view file under the currently active theme.

2. `WebRoot/protected/views/system`: The default system view file for an application.

3. `YiiRoot/framework/views`: The standard system view folder provided by the Yii Framework.

So, you can customize the error display by creating custom error view files under the system view folder of the application or theme.

Yii also allows you to define a specific controller action method to handle the display of the error. This is actually how our application is configured. We'll see this as we go through a couple of examples.

Let's look at a couple examples of this in action. Some of the code that was generated for us as a by-product of using the Gii CRUD generator tool to create our CRUD scaffolding is taking advantage of Yii's error handling. One such example is the `ProjectController::loadModel()` method. That method is defined as follows:

```
public function loadModel()
{
    if($this->_model===null)
    {
        if(isset($_GET['id']))
            $this->_model=Project::model()->findbyPk($_GET['id']);
        if($this->_model===null)
         throw new CHttpException(404,'The requested page does not
exist.');
    }
    return $this->_model;
}
```

We see that it is attempting to load the appropriate Project model AR instance based on the input *id* querystring parameter. If it is unable to locate the requested project, it throws a CHttpException as a way to let the user know that the page they are requesting, in this case the project details page, does not exist. We can test this in our browser by explicitly requesting a project that we know does not exist. As we know our application does not have a project associated with an ID of 99, a request for `http://localhost/trackstar/project/view/id/99` will result in the following page being returned:

This is nice, because the page looks like any other page in our application, with the same theme, header, footer, and so on. This is actually not the default behavior for rendering this type of error page. Our initial application was configured to use a specific controller action for the handling of such errors. We mentioned this was another option for how to handle errors in an application. If we take a peek into this configuration file, we see the following code snippet:

```
'errorHandler'=>array(
    // use 'site/error' action to display errors
    'errorAction'=>'site/error',
),
```

This configures our error handler application component to use the `SiteController::actionError()` method to handle all of the exceptions intended to be displayed to users. If we take a look at that action method, we notice that it is rendering the `protected/views/site/error.php` view file. This is just a normal controller view file, so it will also render any relevant application layout files and will apply the appropriate theme. This way, we are able to provide the user with a very friendly experience when certain errors happen.

To see what the default behavior is, without this added configuration, let's temporarily comment out the above lines of configuration code (in `protected/config/main.php`) and request the non-existent project again. Now we see the following page:

Page Not Found

The requested page does not exist.

The requested URL was not found on this server. If you entered the URL manually please check your spelling and try again. If you think this is a server error, please contact the webmaster.

As we have not explicitly defined any custom error pages following the convention outlined earlier, this is the `error404.php` file in the Yii Framework itself.

Go ahead and revert these changes to the configuration file to have the error handling use the `SiteController::actionError()` method.

Now let's see how this compares to throwing a `CException`, rather than the HTTP exception class. Let's comment out the current line of code throwing the HTTP exception and add a new line to throw this other exception class, as follows:

```
public function loadModel()
{
    if($this->_model===null)
    {
```

```
        if(isset($_GET['id']))
            $this->_model=Project::model()->findbyPk($_GET['id']);
        if($this->_model===null)
            //throw new CHttpException(404,'The requested page does
not exist.');
             throw new CException('The is an example of throwing a
CException');
        }
    return $this->_model;
}
```

Now if we make our request for a non-existent project, we see a very different result. This time we see a system generated error page with a full stack trace error info dump along with the specific source file where the error occurred. The results were a little too long to capture in a screenshot, but it will display the fact that a CException was thrown along with the description The is an example of throwing a CException, the source file and then the full stack trace.

So throwing this different exception class, along with the fact the application is in **debug** mode, has a different result. This is the type of information we would like to display to help us troubleshoot the problem, but only as long as our application is running in a secure development environment. Let's temporarily comment out the debug setting in the root index.php file, in order to see what would be displayed when in production mode:

```
// remove the following line when in production mode
//defined('YII_DEBUG') or define('YII_DEBUG',true);
```

With this commented out, if we refresh our request for our non-existent project, we see that the exception is displayed as an end-user friendly HTTP 500 error, as depicted in the following screenshot:

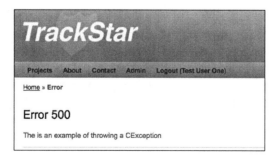

So we see that none of our sensitive code or stack trace information is displayed when in **production** mode.

Caching

Caching data is a great method for helping to improve the performance of a production web application. If there is specific content that is not expected to change upon every request, using the cache to store and serve this content can save the time it takes to retrieve and process that data.

Yii provides for some nice features when it comes to caching. The tour of Yii's caching features will begin with configuring a cache application component. Such a component is one of several child classes extending CCache, the base class for cache classes with different cache storage implementations.

Yii provides many different specific cache component class implementations that store the data utilizing different approaches. The following is a list of the current cache implementations that Yii provides as of version 1.1.2:

- CMemCache: Uses the PHP memcache extension.
- CApcCache: Uses the PHP APC extension.
- CXCache: Uses PHP XCache extension
- CEAcceleratorCache: Uses the PHP EAccelerator extension.
- CDbCache: Uses a database table to store cached data. By default, it will create and use a SQLite3 database under the runtime folder. You can explicitly specify a database for it to use by setting its connectionID property.
- CZendDataCache: Uses Zend Data Cache as the underlying caching medium.
- CFileCache: Uses files to store cached data. This is particular suitable to cache large chunk of data (such as pages).
- CDummyCache: This presents the consistent cache interface, but does not actually perform any caching. The reason for this implementation is to that if you are faced with situation where your development environment does not have cache support, you can still execute and test your code that will need to use cache once available. This allows you to continue to code to a consistent interface, and when the time comes to actually implement a real caching component. You will not need to change the code written to write to or retrieve data from cache.

All of these components extend from the same base class, CCache and expose a consistent API. This means that you can change the implementation of the application component in order to use a different caching strategy without having to change any of the code that is using the cache.

Configuring for cache

As was mentioned, using cache in Yii typically involves choosing one of these implementations, and then configuring the application component for use in the / protected/config/main.php file. The specifics of the configuration will, of course, depend on the specific cache implementation. For example, if one were to use the memcached implementation, that is, CMemCache, which is a distributed memory object caching system that allows you to specify multiple host servers as your cache servers, configuring it to use two servers might look similar to:

```
array(
    ......
    'components'=>array(
        ......
        'cache'=>array(
            'class'=>'system.caching.CMemCache',
            'servers'=>array(
                array('host'=>'server1', 'port'=>12345,
'weight'=>60),
                array('host'=>'server2', 'port'=>12345,
'weight'=>40),
            ),
        ),
    ),
);
```

To keep things relatively simple for the reader following along with the TrackStar development, we'll use the filesystem implementation, CFileCache, as we go through some examples. This should be readily available on any development environment that allows access to reading and writing files from the filesystem.

 If for some reason this is not an option for you, but you still want to follow along with the code examples, simply use the CDummyCache option. As mentioned, it won't actually store any data in the cache, but the code will execute against it just fine.

CFileCache provides a file-based caching mechanism. When using this implementation, each data value being cached is stored in a separate file. By default, these files are stored under the protected/runtime/cache/ folder, but one can easily change this by setting the cachePath property when configuring the component. For our purposes, this default is fine, so we simply need to add the following to the *components* array in our /protected/config/main.php configuration file as such:

```
// application components
    'components'=>array(
        ...
    'cache'=>array(
        'class'=>'system.caching.CFileCache',
    ),
        ...
),
```

With this in place, we can access this new application component anywhere in our running application via Yii::app()->cache.

Using a file-based cache

Let's try out this new component. Remember that system message we added as part of our administrative functionality in the previous iteration? Rather than get it from the database upon every request, let's store the value initially returned from the database in our cache for a limited amount of time, so that not every subsequent request has to retrieve the data from the database.

Let's add a new public method to our SysMessage AR model class to handle the retrieval of the latest system messages. Let's make this new method both public and static so that other parts of the application can easily use this method to access the latest system message without having to explicitly create an instance of SysMessage. This also will help in writing our test.

Test? You'd probably thought we forgot all about our test-first approach to development at this point. Well, we haven't, so let's get back to it.

Create a new test file, protected/tests/unit/SysMessgeTest.php, and add to it the following a fixture definition and single test method:

```
<?php
class SysMessageTest extends CDbTestCase
{
    public function testGetLatest()
    {
```

```
        $message = SysMessage::getLatest();
        $this->assertTrue($message instanceof SysMessage);

    }

}
```

Running this test from the command line will immediately fail due to the fact that we have not yet added this new method. Let's add this method to the SysMessage class as follows:

```
/**
    * Retrieves the most recent system message.
    * @return SysMessage the AR instance representing the latest
system message.
    */

public static function getLatest()
{

    //see if it is in the cache, if so, just return it
    if( ($cache=Yii::app()->cache)!==null)
    {
        $key='TrackStar.ProjectListing.SystemMessage';
        if(($sysMessage=$cache->get($key))!==false)
            return $sysMessage;
    }

        //The system message was either not found in the cache, or
//there is no cache component defined for the application
//retrieve the system message        from the database
    $sysMessage = SysMessage::model()->find(array(
        'order'=>'t.update_time DESC',
    ));
        if($sysMessage != null)
    {
        //a valid message was found. Store it in cache for future
retrievals
        if(isset($key))
            $cache->set($key,$sysMessage,300);
        return $sysMessage;
    }
    else
        return null;
    }
```

We'll cover the details in just a minute. First, let's get our test to pass. With this in place, if we run our test again, we still get a failure. But this time, the failure is because our method is returning null, and we are testing for a non-null return value. The reason that it is returning null is that there are no system messages in our test database. Remember, our tests are run against the `trackstar_test` database. Okay, no problem, fixtures to the rescue. Add a new fixture file `protected/tests/fixtures/tbl_sys_message.php` which is similar to look this:

```php
<?php
return array(
    'message1'=>array(
        'message' => 'This is a test message',
        'create_time' => new CDbExpression('NOW()'),
        'create_user_id' => 1,
        'update_time' => new CDbExpression('NOW()'),
        'update_user_id' => 1,
    ),
);
```

Also, ensure that the test case class is configured to be using the fixture by verifying the following code is at the top of the `SysMessageTest` test class:

```php
public $fixtures=array(
        'messages'=>'SysMessage',
    );
```

Okay, now we can fire off our test again, and this time it succeeds. The method should have tried to retrieve the message from the cache. But, as this was the first time for the request in our test environment, it would not yet be there. So, it proceeded to retrieve it from the database and then store the result into cache for subsequent requests.

If we do a folder listing for the default location being used for file caching, `protected/runtime/cache/`, we do indeed see one strangely named file (yours may be slightly different):

`8b22da6eaf1bf772dae212cd28d2f4bc.bin`

Which if we open in a text editor, reveals the following:

```
a:2:{i:0;O:10:"SysMessage":11:{s:18:"CActiveRecord_md";N;s:19:"18
CActiveRecord_new";b:0;s:26:"CActiveRecord_attributes";a:6:{s:2
:"id";s:1:"1";s:7:"message";s:22:"This is a test
message";s:11:"create_time";s:19:"2010-07-08
21:42:00";s:14:"create_user_id";s:1:"1";s:11:"update_time";s:19:"2010-
07-08
21:42:00";s:14:"update_user_id";s:1:"1";}s:23:"18CActiveRecord18_rela
```

ted";a:0:{}s:17:"CActiveRecord_c";N;s:18:"CActiveRecord_pk";s
:1:"1";s:15:"CModel_errors";a:0:{}s:19:"CModel_validators";N;
s:17:"CModel_scenario";s:6:"update";s:14:"CComponent_e";N;s:1
4:"CComponent_m";N;}i:1;N;}

This is the serialized, cached value of our most recently updated SysMessage AR class instance, which is exactly what we would expect to be there. So, we see that the caching is actually working.

> When running tests, executing the application in the test environment, against the test database, we might want to configure a different location to cache our test data. In this case, we might want to add to our test application configuration, protected/config/test.php, a cache component that is configured slightly differently. For example, if we wanted to specify a different folder to place the test cache data, we could add the following to our application components in this test config file:
>
> 'cache'=>array(
>
>   'class'=>'system.caching.CFileCache',
>
>   'cachePath'=> '/Webroot/trackstar/protected/runtime/cache/test',
>
>),
>
> This way, we won't alter our test results by reading that was cached from normal use of the main development application.

Let's revisit the above code for our new SysMessage::getLatest() method in a bit more detail. The first thing the code is doing is checking to see if the requested data is already in the cache, and if so, returns that value:

```
//see if it is in the cache, if so, just return it

if( ($cache=Yii::app()->cache)!==null)

{

    $key='TrackStar.ProjectListing.SystemMessage';

    if(($sysMessage=$cache->get($key))!==false)

        return $sysMessage;

}
```

As we mentioned, we configured the cache application component to be available anywhere in the application via `Yii::app()->cache`. So, it first checks to see if there even is such a component defined. If so, it attempts to look up the data in the cache via the `$cache->get($key)` method. This does more or less what you would expect. It attempts to retrieve a value from cache based on the specified key. The key is a unique string identifier that is used to map to each piece of data stored in the cache. In our system message example, we only need to display one message at a time, and therefore can have a fairly simple key identify the single system message to display. The key can be any string value, as long as it remains unique for each piece of data we want to cache. In this case we have chosen the descriptive string `TrackStar`. `ProjectListing.SystemMessage` as the key used when storing and retrieving our cached system message.

When this code is executed for the very first time, there will not yet be any data associated with this key value in the cache. Therefore, a call to `$cache->get()` for this key will return false. So, our method will continue to the next bit of code, which simply attempts to retrieve the appropriate system message from the database, using the AR class:

```
$sysMessage = SysMessage::model()->find(array(
    'order'=>'t.update_time DESC',
));
```

We then proceed with the following code that first checks if we did get anything back from the database. If we did, then it stores it in the cache before returning the value, otherwise, null is returned:

```
if($sysMessage != null)
{
    if(isset($key))
        $cache->set($key,$sysMessage->message,300);
    return $sysMessage->message;
}
else
    return null;
```

If a valid system message was returned, we use the `$cache->set()` method to store the data into cache. This method has the following general form:

```
set($key,$value,$duration=0,$dependency=null)
```

When placing a piece of data into cache, one must specify a unique key, as well as the data to be stored. The key is a unique string value, as discussed above, and the value is whatever data desired to be cached. This can be in any format, as long as it can be serialized. The duration parameter specifies an optional **time-to-live** (TTL) requirement. This can be used to ensure that the cached value is refreshed after a period of time. The default is 0, which means it will never expire, that is, it will live forever in the cache. (Actually, internally, Yii translates a value of `<=0` for the duration to mean that it should expire in one year. So, not exactly forever, but definitely a long time).

We are calling the `set()` method in the following manner:

```
$cache->set($key,$sysMessage->message,300);
```

We set the key to be what we had it defined as before, `TrackStar.ProjectListing.SystemMessage`, the data being stored is the message attribute of our returned `SystemMessage` AR class, that is, the message column of our `tbl_sys_message` table, and then we set the duration to be 300 seconds. This way, the data in the cache will expire every five minutes, at which time the database is queried again for the most recent system message. We did not specify a dependency when we set the data. We'll discuss this optional parameter next.

Cache dependencies

The dependency parameter allows for an alternative and much more sophisticated approach to deciding whether or not the stored data in the cache should be refreshed. Rather than declaring a simple time period for the expiration of cached data, your caching strategy may require that the data become invalid based on things like the specific user making the request, or the general mode or state of the application, or whether a file on the filesystem has been recently updated. This parameter allows you to specify such cache validation rules.

The dependency is an instance of `CCacheDependency` or its child class. Yii makes available the following specific cache dependencies:

- `CFileCacheDependency`: The data in the cache will be invalid if the specified file's last modification time has changed since the previous cache lookup.

- `CDirectoryCacheDependency`: Similar to the above for the file cache dependency, but this checks all the files and subdirectories within a given specified folder.

- `CDbCacheDependency`: The data in the cache will be invalid if the query result of a specified SQL statement is changed since the previous cache lookup.

- `CGlobalStateCacheDependency`: The data in the cache will be invalid if the value of the specified global state is changed. A global state is a variable that is persistent across multiple requests and multiple sessions in an application. It is defined via `CApplication::setGlobalState()`.

- `CChainedCacheDependency`: This allows you to chain together multiple dependencies. The data in the cache will become invalid if any of the dependencies on the chain is changed.

- `CExpressionDependency`: The data in the cache will be invalid if the result of the specified PHP expression is changed.

To provide a concrete example, let's use a dependency to expire the data in the cache whenever a change to the `tbl_sys_message` database table is made. Rather than arbitrarily expire our cached system message after five minutes, we'll expire it exactly when we need to, that is, when there has been a change to the `update_time` column for one of the system messages in the table. We'll use the `CDbCacheDependency` implementation to achieve this, since it is designed to invalidate cached data based on a change in the results of a SQL query.

We alter our call to the `set()` method to set the duration time to `0`, so that it won't expire based on time, but pass in a new dependency instance with our specified SQL statement as such:

```
$cache->set($key, $sysMessage->message, 0, new
CDbCacheDependency('select id from tbl_sys_message order by update_
time desc'));
```

> Changing the duration TTL time to `0` is not at all a prerequisite of using a dependency. We could have just as easily left the duration in as 300 seconds. This would just stipulate another rule to render the data in the cache invalid. The data would only be valid in the cache for a maximum of five minutes, but would also be regenerated prior to this time limit if there as a change to the `update_time` column occurred on one or more records in the table.

With this in place, the cache will expire only when the results of the query statement are changed. This example is a little contrived, since we were originally caching the data to avoid a database call altogether. Now we have configured it to execute a database query every time we attempt to retrieve data from cache. However, if the cached data was a much more complex data set, that involved much more overhead to retrieve and process, a simple SQL statement for cache validity could make a lot of sense. The specific caching implementation, the data stored, the expiration time as well as any other data validation in the form of these dependencies will all depend on the specific requirements of the application being built. It is good to know that Yii has many options available to help meet our varied requirements.

To complete the changes to our application to take advantage of the caching of data in our new method, we still need to refactor the `ProjectController::actionIn dex()` method to use this newly create method. This is easy. Just replace the code that was generating the system message from the database, with a call to this new method. That is, in `ProjectController::actionIndex()`, simply change this:

```
$sysMessage = SysMessage::model()->find(array('order'=>'t.update_time
DESC',));
```

to the following:

```
$sysMessage = SysMessage::getLatest();
```

Now the system message being displayed on the projects listing page is taking advantage of the file cache.

Fragment caching

The previous example demonstrates the use of data caching. This is where we take a single piece of data and store it in the cache. There are other approaches available in Yii to store fragments of pages generated by a portion of a view script, or even the entire page itself.

Fragment caching refers to caching a fragment of a page. We can take advantage of fragment caching inside of view scripts. To do so, we use the `CController::beginCache()` and `CController::endCache()` methods. These two methods are used to mark the beginning and the end of the rendered page content that should be stored in cache. Just as is the case when using a data caching approach, we need a unique key to identify the content being cached. In general, the syntax for using fragment caching inside of a view script is as follows:

```
...some HTML content...
<?php if($this->beginCache($key)) { ?>
...content to be cached...
<?php $this->endCache(); } ?>
...other HTML content...
```

If the call to `beginCache()` returns false, the cached content will be automatically inserted at that place; otherwise, the content inside the `if` statement will be executed and will be cached when `endCache()` is invoked.

Declaring fragment caching options

When calling `beginCache()`, we can supply an array as the second parameter consisting of caching options to customize the fragment caching. As a matter of fact, the `beginCache()` and `endCache()` methods are a convenient wrapper of the `COutputCache` filter/widget. Therefore, the caching options can be initial values for any properties of `COutputCache`.

Arguably one of the most common options specified when caching data is the duration, which specifies how long the content can remain valid in the cache. It is similar to the duration parameter we used when using the data caching approach for our system messages. You can specify the duration parameter when calling `beginCache()` as follows:

```
$this->beginCache($key, array('duration'=>3600))
```

The default setting for this fragment caching approach is different than that for the data caching. If we do not set the duration, it defaults to 60 seconds, meaning the cached content will be invalidated after 60 seconds. There a many other options you can set when using the fragment caching. For more information, refer to the API documentation for `COutputCache` as well as the fragment caching section of the definitive guide, available on the Yii Framework site: `http://www.yiiframework. com/doc/guide/caching.fragment`

Using fragment cache

Let's implement this in our TrackStar application. We'll again focus on the project listings page. As you recall, towards the bottom of this page, there is a list of the comments that users have left on the issues associated with each project. This list indicates who left a comment on which issue. Rather than re-generate this list upon each request, let's use fragment caching to cache this list for, say, two minutes. The application can tolerate this data being slightly stale, and two minutes is really not that long to have to wait for an updated comment list.

To do this, we make our changes to the listing view file, `protected/views/ project/index.php`. We'll wrap the call to our entire recent comments portlet inside this fragment caching approach, as such:

```php
<?php
$key = "TrackStar.ProjectListing.RecentComments";
if($this->beginCache($key, array('duration'=>120))) {
    $this->beginWidget('zii.widgets.CPortlet', array(
        'title'=>'Recent Comments',
    ));
    $this->widget('RecentComments');
    $this->endWidget();
    $this->endCache();
}
?>
```

With this in place, if we visit the project listings page for the first time, our comments list will be stored in the cache. If we then quickly (by quickly, we mean before two minutes have elapsed) add a new comment to one of the issues within a project, and then toggle back to the project listings page, we won't immediately see the newly added comment. But if we keep refreshing the page, once the content in the cache expires (a maximum of two min in this case), the data will be refreshed, and our new comment will be displayed in the listing.

> You could also simply add an `echo time();` PHP statement to the above cached content to see if it is working as expected. If the content is properly caching, the time display will not update until the cache is refreshed. When using the file cache, remember to ensure that your `/protected/runtime/` folder is writable by the web server process, as this is where the cache content is stored by default.

Page caching

In addition to fragment caching, Yii offers options to cache the results of the entire page request. Page caching is similar to that of fragment caching. However, because the content of an entire page is often generated by applying additional layouts to a view, we can't simply call `beginCache()` and `endCache()` in the layout file. The reason is because the layout is applied within the call to the `CController::render()` method after the content view is evaluated. So, we would always miss the opportunity to retrieve the content from the cache.

Therefore, to cache a whole page, we should entirely skip the execution of the action generating the page content. To accomplish this, we can use `COutputCache` class as an action filter in our controller class.

Let's provide an example. Let's use the page caching approach to cache the page results for every project detail page. The project detail pages in TrackStar are rendered by requesting URLs of the format, `http://localhost/trackstar/project/view/id/[id]`, where `[id]` is the specific project ID we are requesting the details of. What we want to do is set up a page caching filter that will cache the entire contents of this page, separately for every ID requested. We need to incorporate the project ID into the key value when we cache the content. That is, we don't want to make a request for the details of project #1, and have the application return a cached result for project #2. Luckily, the `COutputCache` filter anticipated this need.

Open `protected/controllers/ProjectController.php` and alter the existing `filters()` method as such:

```
public function filters()
{
    return array(
        'accessControl', // perform access control for CRUD
operations
        array(
            'COutputCache + view',  //cache the entire output from
the actionView() method for 2 minutes
            'duration'=>120,
            'varyByParam'=>array('id'),
        ),
    );
}
```

This filter configuration utilizes the `COutputCache` filter to cache the entire output generated by the application from a call to `ProjectController::actionView()`. The `+ view` added just after the `COutputCache` declaration, as you may recall, is the standard way we include specific action methods to which a filter should apply. The duration parameter specifies a TTL of 120 seconds (2 min), after which the page content will be regenerated.

The `varyByParam` configuration is a really great option that we alluded to before. Rather than putting the responsibility on you, the developer, to come up with a unique key strategy for the content being cached, this feature allows the variation to be handled automatically. In this case, by specifying a list of names that correspond to GET parameters in the input request. Since we are caching the page content of requests for projects by `project_id`, it makes perfect sense to use this id as part of the unique key generation for caching the content. By specifying `'varyByParam'=>array('id')`, `COutputCache` does this for us, based on the input querystring parameter, `id`. There are more options available to achieve this type of auto content variation strategy when using `COutputCache` to cache our data. As of this writing, the following variation features are available to use:

- `varyByRoute`: By setting this option to true, the specific request route will be incorporated into the unique identifier for the cached data. Therefore, you can use the combination of the requested controller and action to distinguish cached content.

- `varyBySession`: By setting this option to true, the unique session id is used distinguish the content in the cache. Each user session may see different content but all of this content can still be served from the cache.

- `varyByParam`: As discussed previously, this uses the input GET querystring parameters to distinguish the content in the cache.

- `varyByExpression`: By setting this option to a PHP expression, we can use the result of this expression to distinguish the content in the cache.

So, with the above filter configured in our `ProjectController` class, each request for a specific project details page is stored in the cache for up to two minutes before being regenerated and again stored in the cache. You can test this out by first viewing a specific project, then updating that project in some way. Your updates will not immediately display if done within the TTL of two minutes.

Caching entire page results is a great way to improve site performance, however it certainly does not make sense for every page in every application. A combination of the above three approaches: data, fragment and page caching, will probably need to be implemented in most real-world applications. We have really just scratched the surface of all caching options available within Yii. Hopefully this has whet your appetite to further investigate the full caching landscape available.

General performance tuning tips

Before we wrap up this final iteration, we'll briefly outline some other areas of consideration when working to tweak the performance of a Yii-based web application.

These more or less come straight from the *Performance Tuning* section of the Yii definitive guide, `http://www.yiiframework.com/doc/guide/topics.performance`. But it is good to restate them here for completeness and general awareness.

Using APC

Enabling the PHP APC extension is perhaps the easiest way to improve the overall performance of an application. The extension caches and optimizes PHP intermediate code and avoids the time spent in parsing PHP scripts for every incoming request.

Disabling debug mode

We discussed this earlier in the chapter, but it won't hurt to hear it again. Disabling debug mode is another easy way to improve performance and security. A Yii application runs in debug mode if the constant `YII_DEBUG` is defined as true in the main `index.php` entry script. Many components, including those down in the framework itself, incur extra overhead when running in debug mode.

Using yiilite.php

When the PHP APC extension is enabled, one can replace `yii.php` with a different Yii bootstrap file named `yiilite.php`. This can help to further boost the performance of a Yii-powered application. The file `yiilite.php` comes with every Yii release. It is the result of merging some commonly used Yii class files. Both comments and trace statements are stripped from the merged file. Therefore, using `yiilite.php` would reduce the number of files being included and avoid execution of trace statements.

> Note, using `yiilite.php` without APC may actually reduce performance, because `yiilite.php` contains some classes that are not necessarily used in every request and would take extra parsing time. It is also observed that using `yiilite.php` is slower with some server configurations, even when APC is turned on. The best way to judge whether to use `yiilite.php` or not is to run a benchmark using the included hello world demo.

Using caching techniques

As we described and demonstrated in this chapter, Yii provides many caching solutions that may improve the performance of a web application significantly. The available caching systems are as follows:

- If the generation of some data takes long time, we can use the data caching approach to reduce the data generation frequency
- If a portion of page remains relatively static, we can use the fragment caching approach to reduce its rendering frequency
- If a whole page remains relative static, we can use the page caching approach to save the rendering cost for the whole page

Enabling schema caching

If the application is using Active Record, one can turn on the schema caching in a production environment to save the time of parsing database schema. This can be done by configuring the `CDbConnection::schemaCachingDuration` property to be a value greater than `0`.

Besides these application-level caching techniques, we can also use server-side caching solutions to boost the application performance. The enabling of APC caching that we described above belongs to this category. There are other server-side techniques, such as Zend Optimizer, eAccelerator and Squid, just to name a few.

These, for the most part, just provide some good-practice guidelines as you work to prepare your Yii application for production, or as you troubleshoot an existing application for bottlenecks. General application performance tuning is much more art than science, and there are many, many factors outside of the Yii Framework that play into the overall performance. Yii has been built with performance in mind since its inception and continues to out-perform many other PHP-based application development frameworks by a long shot (see `http://www.yiiframework.com/performance/` for more details). Of course, every single web application will need to be tweaked to enhance its performance, but making Yii the development framework of choice certainly puts your application on a great performance footing from the onset.

Summary

In this final iteration, we turned our attention to making changes to our application to help improve its maintainability and performance in a production environment. We first covered application logging strategies available in Yii, and how to log and route messages based on varying severity levels and categories. We then turned focus to error handling and how Yii exploits the underlying exception implementation in PHP 5 to provide a flexible and robust error handling framework. We then learned about some different caching strategies available in Yii. We learned about the caching of application data and content at varying levels of granularity. Data caching for specific variables or individual pieces of data, fragment caching for content areas within pages, and full page caching to cache the entire rendered output of a page request. Finally, we provided a list of "good practices" to follow when working to improve the performance of a Yii-powered Web application.

Unfortunately, our TrackStar application is actually quite far from a complete, full featured task management system, and even many of the concepts covered were left to the reader to fully implement. However, a nice foundation on which to build has been laid, and now that you have the power of Yii on your side, you could very quickly turn this into a much more useable and feature-rich application. Also a great many of the examples covered will translate well to other types of Web applications you may be building. Good luck with your future projects, and happy developing!

Index

Symbols

About Packt Publishing

Packt, pronounced 'packed', published its first book "*Mastering phpMyAdmin for Effective MySQL Management*" in April 2004 and subsequently continued to specialize in publishing highly focused books on specific technologies and solutions.

Our books and publications share the experiences of your fellow IT professionals in adapting and customizing today's systems, applications, and frameworks. Our solution based books give you the knowledge and power to customize the software and technologies you're using to get the job done. Packt books are more specific and less general than the IT books you have seen in the past. Our unique business model allows us to bring you more focused information, giving you more of what you need to know, and less of what you don't.

Packt is a modern, yet unique publishing company, which focuses on producing quality, cutting-edge books for communities of developers, administrators, and newbies alike. For more information, please visit our website: www.packtpub.com.

About Packt Open Source

In 2010, Packt launched two new brands, Packt Open Source and Packt Enterprise, in order to continue its focus on specialization. This book is part of the Packt Open Source brand, home to books published on software built around Open Source licences, and offering information to anybody from advanced developers to budding web designers. The Open Source brand also runs Packt's Open Source Royalty Scheme, by which Packt gives a royalty to each Open Source project about whose software a book is sold.

Writing for Packt

We welcome all inquiries from people who are interested in authoring. Book proposals should be sent to author@packtpub.com. If your book idea is still at an early stage and you would like to discuss it first before writing a formal book proposal, contact us; one of our commissioning editors will get in touch with you.

We're not just looking for published authors; if you have strong technical skills but no writing experience, our experienced editors can help you develop a writing career, or simply get some additional reward for your expertise.

AJAX and PHP: Building Modern Web Applications 2nd Edition

ISBN: 978-1-847197-72-6   Paperback: 308 pages

Build user friendly Web 2.0 Applications with JavaScript and PHP

1. The ultimate AJAX tutorial for building modern Web 2.0 Applications

2. Create faster, lighter, better web applications by using the AJAX technologies to their full potential

3. Leverage the power of PHP and MySQL to create powerful back-end functionality and make it work in harmony with a responsive AJAX clientWrite better JavaScript code to enable powerful web features

Zend Framework 1.8 Web Application Development

ISBN: 978-1-847194-22-0   Paperback: 380 pages

Design, develop, and deploy feature-rich PHP web applications with this MVC framework

1. Create powerful web applications by leveraging the power of this Model-View-Controller-based framework

2. Learn by doing – create a "real-life" storefront application

3. Covers access control, performance optimization, and testing

4. Best practices, as well as debugging and designing discussion

Please check **www.PacktPub.com** for information on our titles

[PACKT] open source
PUBLISHING   community experience distilled

Building Websites with PHP-Nuke

ISBN: 978-1-904811-05-3   Paperback: 320 pages

A practical guide to creating and maintaining your own community website with PHP-Nuke

1. Step through creating your own web portal with PHP-Nuke

2. Simple and practical guidance to mastering PHP-Nuke

3. For people with basic knowledge of web development

PHP and script.aculo.us Web 2.0 Application Interfaces

ISBN: 978-1-847194-04-6   Paperback: 264 pages

Build powerful interactive AJAX applications with script.aculo.us and PHP

1. Get started quickly with script.aculo.us library with as little as one line of code

2. Explore Prototype library features, tutorials, code, and examples

3. Learn script.aculo.us' In-place Editing, Auto Completion, Sliders, Drag-and-Drop, Effects, and Multimedia

4. A book with less jargon, and more code explanation for building real-world examples —Tadalist clone, Digg and Delicious clones, 43 things.com clone

Please check **www.PacktPub.com** for information on our titles

[PACKT] open source ✤
community experience distilled

PUBLISHING

Magento 1.3: PHP
Developer's Guide

Design, develop, and deploy feature-rich Magento online stores
with PHP coding

Jamie Huskisson   PACKT

Magento 1.3: PHP Developer's Guide

ISBN: 978-1-847197-42-9   Paperback: 260 pages

Design, develop, and deploy feature-rich Magento
online stores with PHP coding

1. Extend and customize the Magento e-commerce
   system using PHP code

2. Set up your own data profile to import or
   export data in Magento

3. # Build applications that interface with the
   customer, product, and order data using
   Magento's Core API

jQuery UI 1.7

The User Interface Library for jQuery

Build highly interactive web applications with ready-to-use
widgets from the jQuery User Interface library

Dan Wellman   PACKT

jQuery UI 1.7: The User Interface Library for jQuery

ISBN: 978-1-847199-72-0   Paperback: 392 pages

Build highly interactive web applications with ready-
to-use widgets from the jQuery User Interface library

1. Organize your interfaces with reusable widgets:
   accordions, date pickers, dialogs, sliders, tabs,
   and more

2. Enhance the interactivity of your pages by
   making elements drag-and-droppable, sortable,
   selectable, and resizable

3. Packed with examples and clear explanations
   of how to easily design elegant and powerful
   front-end interfaces for your web applications

4. Revised and targeted at jQuery UI 1.7

Please check **www.PacktPub.com** for information on our titles

LaVergne, TN USA
16 August 2010
193443LV00003B/17/P